Connecting Inquiry and Professional Learning in Education

How might inquiry enhance the professional practice of student and practising teachers, teacher educators and other practitioners? What effect might this have on the learning of young people in and outside of the classroom?

Based on the findings of an international colloquium and drawing upon a range of practices from UK, USA, Canada, Europe and Australia, this book is designed to make explicit the connections between practitioner inquiry and teacher professional learning in initial teacher education and ongoing teacher professional development.

The contributors consider issues such as:

- the relationship between practitioner inquiry and pedagogical content knowledge;
- whether it is possible to scale up from small local and intensive innovations to more broadly based inquiry;
- inquiry's role in professional identity, both individual and communal;
- prevailing socio-political contexts and consequences for social policy formation.

Connecting Inquiry and Professional Learning in Education brings together writers who work in designing teacher education courses, and those who are practice-based researchers and policy makers. Crucially, many of these writers inhabit both spheres, and their accounts of how they successfully combine their multiple roles will prove vital reading for all those involved in examining and improving practice leading to enhanced teacher professional learning.

Anne Campbell is Professor of Professional Learning in the Carnegie Faculty of Sport and Education at Leeds Metropolitan University, UK.

Susan Groundwater-Smith is an Honorary Professor of Education in the Faculty of Education and Social Work at the University of Sydney, Australia, and leads the Coalition of Knowledge Building School.

Connecting Inquiry and Professional Learning in Education

International perspectives and practical solutions

Edited by
Anne Campbell and
Susan Groundwater-Smith

 Routledge
Taylor & Francis Group

LONDON AND NEW YORK

First published 2010
by Routledge
2 Park Square, Milton Park, Abingdon, Oxon, OX14 4RN

Simultaneously published in the USA and Canada
by Routledge
270 Madison Avenue, New York, NY 10016

Routledge is an imprint of the Taylor & Francis Group, an informa business

Typeset in Garamond Three and Gill Sans by
Florence Production Ltd, Stoodleigh, Devon
Printed and bound in Great Britain by
TJ International Ltd, Padstow, Cornwall

British Library Cataloguing in Publication Data
A catalogue record for this book is available from the British Library

Library of Congress Cataloging in Publication Data
Campbell, Anne, 1947–.
    Connecting inquiry and professional learning in education:
    international perspectives and practical solutions/Anne Campbell and
    Susan Groundwater-Smith.
        p. cm.
    Includes bibliographical references and index.
    1. Teachers – Training of.   2. Inquiry-based learning.
    I. Groundwater-Smith, Susan.   II. Title.
    LB1707.C35 2009
    370.71'1 – dc22   2009003490

ISBN10: 0–415–47812–X (hbk)
ISBN10: 0–415–47813–8 (pbk)

ISBN13: 978–0–415–47812–0 (hbk)
ISBN13: 978–0–415–47813–7 (pbk)

Contents

Contributors

Pat Broadhead was appointed to Leeds Metropolitan University, UK in February 2006 as Professor in the Carnegie Faculty of Sport and Education. She has extensive research and publications around integrated service development and in professionalism in early years education and care. She has evaluated Early Excellence Centres, Sure Start Local Programmes and was co-evaluator of a ground-breaking local partnership initiative in the City of York. She has chaired the Early Years Development and Childcare Partnership for three years when first established. She is currently chair of a national, membership-based early years organisation, TACTYC, concerned with training and professional development and is co-opted to UCET (University Council for the Education of Teachers) Executive to represent early years issues for whom she recently co-authored a well-received Occasional Paper on Every Child Matters and Teacher Education. She is on the Editorial Boards of *Early Years* and the *International Journal of Early Years Education*, and is a regularly invited keynote speaker in relation to early years issues and has advised Parliamentary Select Committees. She was also a member of the UCET 2020 vision group on futures thinking in ITT. She is lead author of a forthcoming book on developing and sustaining integrated services.

Anne Campbell was appointed as Professor of Professional Learning at Leeds Metropolitan University in 2007 and previously was Professor of Education at Liverpool Hope University, UK. She is currently a member of the British Educational Research Association Executive Council with a brief for supporting and developing practitioner research. She has been on the editorial boards of *Teacher Development* and *Educational Action Research* and has been consultant and researcher to various government bodies.

Her main area of research is professional learning, in particular inquiry and research-based learning, mentoring and the development of research partnerships with schools. She has published widely in the field of practitioners' professional learning and has an interest in ethical issues in practitioner research and in narrative and storytelling as research approaches, which illustrate practice and increase practitioners' access to using and doing research. Recent books include *An Ethical Approach to Practitioner Research: Dealing with Issues and Dilemmas in Action Research* (co-edited with S. Groundwater-Smith, Routledge, 2007) and *Practitioner Research and Professional Development in Education* (co-authored with O. McNamara and P. Gilroy, Paul Chapman, 2004).

Philippa Cordingly is Chief Executive of the Centre for the Use of Evidence in Education (CUREE).

David Cracknell is Professor of Education at the University of Chester.

Anne Davies is a Lecturer in the School of Education at Victoria University in Melbourne, Australia. She has a wide range of experience working as a teacher and researcher in primary, secondary and tertiary education settings as well as for federal and state governments, Aboriginal organisations and teacher unions.

Her current position as a Quality Portfolio Coordinator (Courses) connects her with a range of undergraduate and postgraduate programs which take a praxis inquiry learning approach to teacher education and continuing professional development.

Her research interests include collaborative research methodologies, school-university partnerships, praxis inquiry learning and authentic assessment with a particular interest in portfolios. She has a broad interest in the place of both learning and research in 'finding' the future. This was the subject of her Ph.D. research, which focused on the democratic quality of learning when practitioner research, innovation and continuing professional development are connected. This study pointed to the significance of interconnected layers of democracy including contextual, dialogic and collaborative action and their place in the practice of inquiry.

Susan Groundwater-Smith is an Honorary Professor of Education in the Faculty of Education and Social Work at the University of Sydney, Australia; as well as Visiting Professor at Leeds Metropolitan University, UK. She has co-authored a number of books that have been taken up in initial teacher education including: *Teaching: Challenges and Dilemmas* (Harcourt Brace, 1997); *Learning the Middle Years: More than a Transition* (Cengage Learning Australia, 2007); and *Secondary Schooling in a Changing World* (Harcourt, 2001). She has also written extensively on issues in relation to practitioner inquiry, quality and ethics. She has co-edited *An Ethical Approach to Practitioner Research: Dealing with Issues and Dilemmas in Action Research* (co-edited with A. Campbell, Routledge, 2007). Due also to be released is the co-authored title *Teacher Professional Learning in an Age of Compliance: Mind the Gap* (co-authored with N. Mockler, Chaos, 2009).

Moira Hulme is a Research Fellow at the Faculty of Education, University of Glasgow, UK, where she is involved in a number of projects relating to teacher education and teachers' work. In addition to coordination of the school–university collaboration, *Schools of Ambition*, recent research projects include *Pupil Participation in Scottish Schools* for Learning and Teaching Scotland and *Professional Culture Among Recent Entrants to the Teaching Profession* for the General Teaching Council for Scotland. Her previous experience includes teacher education for secondary and post-compulsory education.

Rob Hulme is Professor of Education in the Faculty of Education and Children's Services at the University of Chester, UK. He leads the Research Unit for

Trans-professionalism in the Public Services and is currently working on research development in teacher education. He also continues to work on international and global policy development in education.

Lynda Kelly is Head of the Australian Museum Eureka Prize, Web and Audience Research Unit. She has an international reputation with respect to her innovative methods for exploring the ways in which various audiences engage with Museum exhibitions. She works hard to be inclusive of the many groups who visit the Australian Museum with investigations into the needs of older visitors and people with disabilities. In particular she has worked in partnership with the Coalition of Knowledge Building Schools in New South Wales to explore the perspectives of young people, not only in terms of their responses to current exhibitions, but also in relation to the ways in which they might react to prospective exhibitions. Her Ph.D. study focused on learning in the Museum.

Bob Lingard is a Professorial Research Fellow in the School of Education at the University of Queensland, Australia. He has also been Professor at the Universities of Sheffield and Edinburgh. He researches education policy, school reform and critical pedagogies. He has been President of the Australian Association for Research in Education and is editor of the journal, *Discourse: Studies in the Cultural Politics of Education*. His most recent edited books include *Transforming Learning in Schools and Communities* (co-edited with J. Nixon and S. Ranson, Continuum, 2008) and the *RoutledgeFalmer Reader in Education Policy and Politics* (co-edited with J. Ozga, Routledge, 2007). He has a forthcoming book entitled *Globalizing Education Policy* (co-authored with F. Rizvi, Routledge, forthcoming).

Kay Livingston is Professor of Educational Research, Policy and Practice at the University of Glasgow, UK, and is currently chairing the review of the B.Ed. programme. She is also Head of International Education, Innovation and Research Policy at Learning and Teaching Scotland. In both these roles she works closely with policy-makers and practitioners at international, national and local levels. She is Editor of the *European Journal of Teacher Education* and Co-Chair of the Association of Teacher Education in Europe's Research and Development Group 'Professional Development of Teachers'. Prior to taking up her post at the University of Glasgow, she held a Chair in Education at the University of Aberdeen and was the Director of Scottish Teachers for a New Era (STNE). Her research interests include: innovative learning and teaching strategies, particularly strategies to encourage learners to take an active role in the learning process; initial teacher education and continuing professional development; international and intercultural education; school-based evaluation processes and the use of technology in learning and teaching. She has had responsibility for leading policy-related research and evaluation projects at national and international levels in all of these areas.

Colleen McLaughlin is a Senior Lecturer and Deputy Head of Faculty at the University of Cambridge Faculty of Education, UK, where she teaches and researches. She has worked in the fields of practitioner research, with particular reference to schools-university partnerships for educational research, and the personal, social and emotional aspects of education, including counselling. Before working in the university she taught in secondary schools and worked as an advisor in a local education authority. She has researched inquiry within networked learning communities, care and counselling in schools, positive alternatives to school exclusion, bystander behaviour in bullying and how universities can work in partnership with schools to generate useful educational knowledge. She is currently researching adolescence, mental health and school experience as well as communities of enquiry within partnerships between schools and universities. She is also very interested in the social and emotional aspects of collaboration. Recent books include: *Networking Practitioner Research* (co-authored with K. Black-Hawkins and D. McIntyre, Routledge, 2007) and *Researching Schools: Stories from Schools – University Partnership for Educational Research* (co-authored with K. Black-Hawkins, S. Brindley, D. McIntyre and K. Taber, Routledge, 2006).

Olwen McNamara is a Professor of Teacher Education and Development at the University of Manchester, UK, where she is Director of the Primary Initial Training Programme and Executive Director of the Teach First Northwest Programme. Her research interests are professionally focused with a particular emphasis on professional learning and mathematics education. She publishes widely in these fields and her authored books include: *New Teacher Identity and Regulative Government* (co-authored with T. Brown, Springer, 2005) and *Practitioner Research and Professional Development in Education* (co-authored with A. Campbell and P. Gilroy, Sage, 2004). She is editor of *Becoming an Evidence-based Practitioner* (RoutledgeFalmer, 2002).

Ian Menter is Professor of Teacher Education and Deputy Dean of the Faculty of Education, University of Glasgow, UK. He has been President of the Scottish Educational Research Association and an elected member of the Executive Council of the British Educational Research Association.

His main research interests are in teacher education and development, teachers' work, teacher enquiry and education policy. He has a particular interest in 'home international studies', which is comparative education research within the UK. He recently led a project for the Teaching and Learning Research Programme, entitled 'Learning to Teach in Post-devolution UK', and is currently leading major projects commissioned by the Scottish Government and by Learning and Teaching Scotland. One of these is the three-year project 'Research to support Schools of Ambition', an innovative scheme to support teachers in 52 secondary schools to research the implementation of their school improvement plans.

Publications include co-authorship of *Work and Identity in the Primary School* (Open University Press, 1997) and co-editorship of *The Crisis in Teacher Supply* (Trentham Books, 2002). He is lead author of *Convergence or Divergence?: Initial Teacher Education in Scotland and England* (Dunedin Academic Press, 2007).

Alexandra Miletta is an Assistant Professor at the City College of New York, City University of New York, USA. She is the co-author and editor of *Classroom Conversations: A Collection of Classics for Parents and Teachers* (The New Press, 2008).

Nicole Mockler is a Lecturer in the School of Education at the University of Newcastle, Australia, and an Honorary Associate of the Faculty of Education and Social Work at the University of Sydney. She completed her PhD thesis on the formation of teacher professional identity, and is co-author of *Learning in the Middle Years: More than a Transition* (with S. Groundwater-Smith and J. Mitchell, Cengage Learning Australia, 2007) and *Teacher Professional Learning in an Age of Compliance: Mind the Gap* (with S. Groundwater-Smith, Chaos, 2009). She is a Book Reviews

Editor of the *Educational Action Research Journal*, and her recent work is in the areas of teacher professional learning and identity, curriculum design and pedagogy, and education for sustainability.

Jean Murray is Professor of Education at the University of East London, UK, where she teaches on doctoral courses. Building on her background in schooling and teacher education, her research interests focus on exploring the academic and professional identities of teacher educators and their induction and career development within the higher education sector. She is also involved in various national and international research capacity building initiatives.

Kris Needham works for the Professional Learning and Leadership Development Directorate of the Department of Education and Training, New South Wales, Australia.

Petra Ponte has a background in Pedagogiek (as science of the child's upbringing) and Educational Studies. She has published in the fields of special and inclusive education, pupil guidance in schools for primary and secondary education, cross-cultural collaboration, teachers' professionalism, action research by teachers and postgraduate programmes as platforms. She is a Professor at Utrecht University of Applied Sciences and combines this post with her senior research post at ICLON, Leiden University (Graduate School of Teaching), both in the Netherlands. In addition to these roles, she is Honorary Professor of Education in the Faculty of Education and Social Work at the University of Sydney in Australia. She is an active participant in international networks and Co-ordinating Book Editor of the *Educational Action Research Journal*.

Peter Renshaw is Professor and Head of the School of Education at the University of Queensland, Australia. He has research collaborations with scholars in Finland, the Netherlands and Sweden. His research is framed by a sociocultural theory of education that foregrounds the social and cultural construction of knowledge and identity, and the responsibility of educators to create challenging, inclusive and supportive learning contexts for diverse groups of students.

Lynne Shiach is a Senior Lecturer and the B.Ed. Primary Programme Director at the University of Aberdeen, UK. She took up this post in 2003 and from then to the present has worked with a strong collegiate team of tutors in continually evaluating and developing the four year undergraduate degree programme. In June 2004, the B.Ed. Programme became the focus for transformation through the Scottish Government and Hunter Foundation funded research and development initiative, Scottish Teachers for a New Era (STNE). Lynne began her career in primary teaching in a small two-teacher rural primary school in the Northeast of Scotland. With a particular interest in Early Years Education she went on to lead learning in nursery and primary classes in a range of schools in Aberdeen and Sydney, Australia. She gained school leadership experience first as deputy head teacher and then as a head teacher in the city of Aberdeen. The local authority/University partnership developing through STNE affords her the opportunity to draw on her many years of professional and academic experience striving to strengthen student teachers, class teacher mentors and university tutors co-construction of learning to teach.

Acknowledgements

The editors would like to thank the following for their invaluable support:

- Leeds Metropolitan University for funding the Colloquium on which this book is based;
- Karen Smith for help in preparing the manuscript;
- Ian Kane for his substantial help with the editing process.

Abbreviations

ACP	applied curriculum project
AERS	Applied Educational Research Scheme
ALS	action learning sets
AM	Australian Museum
AR	action research
BASRC	Bay Area Schools Reform Collaborative
B.Ed.	Bachelor of Education
BERA	British Education Research Council
BPRS	best practice research scholarships
CARN	Collaborative Action Research Network
CKBS	Coalition of Knowledge Building Schools
COL	Community of Learners
CPD	continuous professional development
CUREE	Centre for the Use of Research and Evidence in Education
DCSF	Department for Children, Schools and Families
DfES	The Department for Education and Skills
ECM	Every Child Matters
ESRC	Economic and Social Research Council
HE	higher education
HEA	Higher Education Academy
HEFCE	Higher Education Funding Council for England
HEI	higher education institute
ICT	information communication technology
KITE	Knowledge and Identity in Teacher Education
ITE	initial teacher education
ITT	initial teacher training
LA	local authority
LTSU	Learning and Teaching Support Unit
NCSL	National College of School Leadership
NFER	National Foundation for Educational Research

NLC	Networked Learning Communities
NSW DET	New South Wales Department of Education and Training
OECD	Organisation for Economic Cooperation and Development
Ofsted	The Office for Standards in Education
PGC	Postgraduate Certificate
PGC in HE	Postgraduate Certificate in Higher Education
PISA	Programme on International Student Assessment
PRSIG	Practitioner Research Special Interest Group
QUANGO	quasi-autonomous non-government organisation
QSRLS	The Queensland School Reform Longitudinal Study
RBSC	Research-based School Consortia
SFR	Standard for Full Registration
SITE	Standard for Initial Teacher Education
STNE	Scottish Teachers for a New Era
SUPER	Schools University Partnership for Research
TACTYC	Training, Advancement and Cooperation in Teaching Young Children
TDA	Training Development Agency
THF	Teachers Hunter Foundation
TTA	Teacher Training Agency
UCET	University Council for the Education of Teachers
UDE	University Department of Education

Chapter 1

Introduction

Anne Campbell and
Susan Groundwater-Smith

This book is based upon an international colloquium convened by the editors
and held at Leeds Metropolitan University, 7–10 October 2007. The participants at the colloquium discussed the nature of teacher professional learning
in initial and continuing teacher education and across the spectrum of the
international landscape and teacher inquiry. Chapters in the book were
presented in draft to the three-day colloquium and subjected to critique and
debate.

The book's scope is wide but coherence is sought through a focus on how
inquiry might enhance the professional practice of student teachers, teachers
and teacher educators and other practitioners. The focus is also on the effect
that such development might have on the learning of young people inside and
outside the classroom. This focus takes us into a variety of different contexts
and sites: school experience (practicum) and university-based elements of
pre-service teacher education where students are assessed and develop their
professional learning; classrooms and schools where experienced teachers
inquire and improve their practice; networks and collaborations where practitioners collaborate for improvement; the university classroom where teachers
undertake research-based study and teacher educators develop curricula,
research expertise and inquire into their own practice; and finally, into other
communities of practice such as the museum education service, which supports
teacher development and student learning, and into the wider community of
local and national government and agencies, and to parents and carers and other
people who live in local sites. We also argue that sites for learning are
increasingly global and hope this book may contribute to professional learning
across the world.

There is a renewed interest in practitioner research and inquiry in both
teacher education and other related professional fields which stimulated the
formation of this book. It includes a variety of case studies including initial
(pre-service) teacher professional learning in Scotland, Australia and the United
States, through to policy formation and continuing teacher professional

learning in the Netherlands, Scotland and England. This book is designed to make explicit the connections between practitioner inquiry and teacher professional learning in initial teacher education (ITE) and ongoing teacher professional development. It draws upon a range of practices from the UK, the USA, Continental Europe and Australia and addresses the following questions:

- What could practitioner inquiry look like in the initial education of teachers?
- Does it go beyond problem-based learning? What role does assessment play in inquiry?
- What kinds of scaffolds are necessary or sufficient for preparing teachers to engage in practitioner inquiry in the formation of their practice?
- What is the relationship between practitioner inquiry and pedagogical content knowledge, considering postgraduate and undergraduate concerns?
- Is it possible to scale up from small local and intensive innovations to more broadly-based inquiry informed courses in the context of current government policies?
- Are there new orthodoxies in inquiry in research informed teaching of which we need to be cautious? (e.g. Teacher's research being colonised for instrumental purposes, the marketing of continuing professional development and the appropriation of pupil voice)
- Are there matters of professional identity, both individual and communal, that need to be explored?
- What does communication 'at the borders' look like? Who translates and into what language?
- What are the prevailing socio-political contexts and what are the consequences for social policy formation at the micro/mesa/meta levels?

This book aims to explore new ground by bringing into a conversation with each other the voices of those who work in designing teacher education courses, in both university and school, and those who are principally practice-based researchers and policy-makers. In a number of instances, several of the writers inhabit more than one of these worlds. By bringing them together the book aims to enable teacher educators, researchers and policy-makers to examine and improve practice leading to enhanced teacher professional learning.

Chapters 2 to 5 discuss the wider aspects of connecting inquiry to professional learning and focus on global, international phenomena affecting the field and serve as overviews of the major issues.

Chapter 2 arose from Campbell and McNamara's discussion of the plethora of terms used to describe practitioner research and inquiry and related professional learning in educational contexts. They found that the abundance and variation in terminology presented a complex and messy picture. Seeking to clarify their ideas through mapping the area, they aimed not to 'tidy' it up but to get an analytical purchase on the field.

Campbell and McNamara organise their chapter around a number of key questions about the field of practice-based research, inquiry and their relationship with professional learning. In addressing these questions they tackle issues about the 'making public' of practitioner research and advocate a review and rethinking of what this could mean for the field. They quote Cochran-Smith and Lytle (2007: 24) who 'use "practitioner inquiry" as a conceptual and linguistic umbrella to refer to a wide array of educational research modes, forms, genres and purposes'. They conclude that research and inquiry in the contexts described are closely aligned, and may often be the same activity. A case study of a project is examined and the themes are: the political context of teacher research; issues of ownership and autonomy; the role of academic partners; issues to do with representation of outcomes and practitioners used to illustrate the tensions in collaborative research partnerships. Ethics, trust and quality issues are raised and discussed as important factors in the recognition of practitioner research. In conclusion the chapter identifies the crucial role of academic partners in collaborative ventures with schools as a crucial one.

In Chapter 3, Lingard and Renshaw address the conception of research- based teacher education but essentially they work with the concept of 'research-informed' rather than 'research-based'. They argue that the use of 'informed' rather than 'based' gives relevant consideration to teacher professional discretion and the need for systemic trust relationships with teachers. They work with Pasteur's quadrant of research for knowledge and understanding, as opposed to research for use or applied purposes, the old pure/applied binary. However, they argue to eschew this simple binary; and advocate more collaborative relationships between researchers and research-informed teachers.

They consider how educational research actually reaches teachers and draw on the work of McMeniman et al. (2000) and Figgis et al. (2000), which was research commissioned in Australia by the federal government to consider the impact of educational research on policy and practice. Lingard and Renshaw argue that teacher education and teacher professional development requirements are framed to a very large extent by policy. For example, moves to link teacher education more closely with schools and the practicum, possibly mean the reduction of the formal research component in teacher education.

They draw on The Queensland School Reform Longitudinal Study (QSRLS) (Lingard et al. 2001, 2003: Hayes et al. 2006) and develop the concept of productive pedagogies after mapping classroom pedagogies in about one thousand Queensland primary and secondary school classrooms in 24 schools over a three-year period in English, Maths, Science and Social Studies. They argue the importance of a pedagogical disposition in educational researchers. In their view, teaching as both a research-informed and research-informing profession is a necessary development towards better schools and educational systems.

In Chapter 4, Broadhead takes us to an early years' focus and explores how 'insiders' (teachers in a primary classroom and teachers and nursery nurses working in early years' classrooms) and an 'outsider' (an academic researcher who enters their classrooms, with permission, to engage in joint research) can, together, influence wider and deeper understandings of learning and teaching in classrooms. She examines how joint research and emerging understanding might subsequently come to re-shape policy and practice when learning takes place for children, educators and educational researchers in the classroom. She also addresses some ethical aspects relating to outsiders when entering others' daily spaces.

Two research projects are reported, spanning 20 years or so, and Broadhead discusses her research into teaching and learning and the extent to which it had always sought to reveal the perspectives of the workers at the heart of the process, the educators. Castells' work (2004) on a process of social mobilisation referring to urban movements resonated with the early years' research and the connections to return play, in a conceptual and more clearly understood way, to early years' classrooms. Broadhead talks about resistance to the policy-political denial of the value of playful learning. In both the primary and the early years' research she sought to bring the voice of the child and learner to centre stage within classroom life by trying to understand what the characteristics of such classrooms might be, an ambition that rests within a long tradition of research and publication, its voice largely unheard in policy circles for some time. She describes the greatest leap forward towards understanding ethical practice and towards the realisation that research can only shape policy and practice if ethical and political awareness go hand in hand in collaborative educational research.

Continuing to focus on wider issues in the field, Hulme and Cracknell explore the value of practitioner inquiry in the development of common language and shared understandings for a group of mid-career professionals from a variety of public service backgrounds, brought together in order to formulate and disseminate responses to the *Every Child Matters* (2003) agenda for integrating services for children. It draws upon data gathered from multi-professional action learning groups and focus groups within the *Learn Together Partnership*, a collaboration between a university in the northwest of England and six local authorities (LAs) in the region in response to this national agenda. This chapter complements others in the book by broadening the perspective from teacher education to the wider workforce in children's services and explores the current English agenda for the development of multi-agency working. The work presented resonates with the book's international themes since the challenge of workforce 'integration' is an agenda with global reach.

The chapter draws on theories of 'third space' and 'hybridity' in arguing that the realistic achievement of such an integrated knowledge requires the creation of 'undecided' or 'third' spaces, in which professionals from a variety of backgrounds can engage in critical reflection and from which dialogues about new ways of working can develop. They are in tune with many authors in this book on the value and the necessity of professional learning communities. Hulme and Cracknell claim that we are still a long way from developing a meaningful or systematic notion of trans-professional knowledge for integrated service provision. Policy-makers appear to be clear about the goals of policy to 'join up' service provision in the legislative framework and policy pronouncements but the authors state that far less in evidence are the necessary strategies to construct new forms of professional learning. The authors conclude by pondering whether this kind of collaborative work can be embedded in the day-to-day reality of practice in multi-professional settings.

The foci in Chapters 6–14 move to more specific examples of projects around the world, with the intention of digging more deeply into the range of questions identified earlier in this chapter.

In Chapter 6, Ponte uses Smith's idea of teacher education programmes as platforms (Smith 2000) and then links this up with the Dutch interpretation of the word 'platform': as a group of people (in this case, teacher educators and students) who have come together for a common social or moral purpose (in this case, for the benefit of a democratic and just education). The central idea behind a programme as a platform is that the participants consult each other to decide what they will learn and how, the goals of learning and how that learning can be facilitated.

She discusses the differing contexts of prospective and experienced teachers and promotes a liberal approach to equality and quality of student learning. She argues that the aim of learning on platforms is broader than just the professional development of the individual student. Close links between professional education and work, in this case between programmes, schools and others, should also be geared to the professional development of the profession in relation to the emancipation of vulnerable pupils. These platforms create a meeting place, where the worlds of researchers, teachers, teacher education staff and others can learn from each other and engage in debate.

In Livingston and Shiach's chapter on the Scottish Teachers for a New Era (STNE) project, funded by the Scottish Government and The Hunter Foundation (THF), they describe and discuss the changes being made as the universities of Glasgow and Aberdeen develop a new model for teacher education. The project has focused on generating dialogue with key stakeholders about what it is that teachers need to know, care about and be able to do to work in twenty-first-century schools and learning communities. The underpinning principle of the direction in teacher education is that models can only be developed effectively through collaboration between colleagues in universities, LAs and schools. The development requires new approaches to learning and teaching, new ways of working to enable critical inquiry, reflection and action and new relationships with student teachers and with colleagues within the universities, in the LAs and in the schools. The approach to teacher education described in this chapter focuses on ensuring that inquiry and thoughtful reflection become natural for every teacher. The courses in the first two years of the new model have been restructured with the specific aim of providing opportunities for students to develop confidence in their own thinking about learning and teaching where questioning and reflection become essential to their development as learners and teachers. The changes include student involvement in programme design and assessment, student-led tutorials and a new investigative approach to school experience.

There is some similarity with Davies's (Chapter 10) programme in teacher education in Victoria, Australia where the issue of the process of change has highlighted the importance of communicative practices, of clarification in seeking understanding and of making values and beliefs explicit.

In Chapter 8, Murray concentrates on teacher educators themselves and on how new, authentic research identities can be forged through practitioner inquiry. The chapter draws on an analysis of relevant research and an illustrative case study of one new teacher educator's induction to debate how practitioner-based research might provide solutions to current challenges for new teacher educators. One of the starting premises is that supporting the development of new teacher educators as researchers is vital for a number of reasons, not least to build general research capacity in education, to ensure thriving teacher education communities, to maintain research-informed teaching in pre- and in-service courses, and to support the intellectual development of teacher educators and the teachers they teach.

Returning to a Scottish focus in Chapter 9, Menter and Hulme critically reflect on the needs of teacher researchers at different career stages in Scotland: beginning teachers, early career teachers (0–5 years) and experienced colleagues. It draws on a current research project to illustrate some of the dilemmas and tensions for teacher researchers and their supporters or mentors in this shared enterprise. *Research to Support Schools of Ambition* (2006–09) is a collaborative project funded by the Scottish Government wherein university-based mentors support teacher researchers in a network of 52 secondary schools (pupils aged 11–16/18 years) distributed throughout Scotland (Menter and Hulme 2007).

While reporting positive effects on teachers' professional learning through inquiry, the authors found that there have been major constraints on the achievement of the full potential for learning, an original aspiration of the project.

In Chapter 10, Davies is further along the path than her Scottish colleagues, Livingston and Schiach, and is reflecting on the place of assessment in an inquiry-based teacher education programme in Australia. She argues that while the assessment tasks create possibilities for praxis inquiry learning, they also restrict what is possible. She presents a complex assessment geography in which multiple tasks connect process and content. It highlights conditions for praxis inquiry learning as:

- authentic practice realised in various settings;
- Praxis Inquiry Protocol evident in clusters of practice;
- individual and collaborative activities that are shaped by artefacts of practice and commentaries that express understanding.

Moving to the American context, in Chapter 11, Miletta examines the educative value of designing and implementing original practitioner research projects in the classrooms of graduate students. She illustrates, through the voices of her students, how teachers' beliefs are shaped and changed by learning to do qualitative research. She shows how sustained inquiry can be a transformative learning experience, when guided by supportive peers.

The stories of doing small-scale research in a climate of high stakes testing are resonant with teachers in other parts of the world, especially England. These narratives are particularly powerful in detailing the processes of doing research and provide evidence of how political intervention shapes teachers' lives and work and links with current legislation such as *No Child Left Behind* (USA), *Every Child Matters* (England) and *A Curriculum for Excellence* (Scotland) as detailed elsewhere in the book. This chapter also addresses explicit notions of developing teachers' resilience in challenging urban school settings, particularly when teachers' autonomy is thwarted.

In Chapter 12, McLaughlin uses her experience of working within networks to explore what lessons might be learned about teachers' professional learning, school development and the scale and nature of partnerships or networks, in which teacher research is a central feature. She explores several questions. For what purposes might networks of researching schools be formed and developed? How were these purposes pursued in the networks studied? What conditions sustain and develop these different purposes? She draws on the work of the National College of School Leadership's (NCSL) Networked Learning Communities initiative and theories of networking which build on the American experience as documented by Lieberman (1999) and Lieberman and McLaughlin (1992).

She outlines a bigger vision of research activity being scaled up so that schools collaborate on the agendas of research and share with each other and the outside world the knowledge and learning, but concludes that is not easily achieved. Radical shifts are needed in the policy context. There has to be a shift in cultures in schools and the allocation of resources to this as a suitable task to engage in. She calls for an expansion of the range of research carried out, and quotes studies such as McNess *et al.* (2003) as welcome in the current context. She argues that the current instrumental focus of policy-makers is too shallow a vision and that shifts in climate, policy and practice required would be welcomed. These would build on a promising and potentially healthy trend which would enable educators to work together on the complex and profound challenges they face in making schooling for young people today meaningful and engaging.

Chapters 13 and 14 are situated in Australia and bring us face to face with the issues arising in that context.

In Chapter 13, Mockler and Groundwater-Smith explore the richness and depth of professional learning for both academics and classroom practitioners when they work alongside each other in conditions of mutual trust and respect. Like Miletta in Chapter 11, they are not sanguine regarding the challenges and difficulties. Learning to engage in professional trust is increasingly difficult as different players with different degrees of agency and differing professional agenda interact. Exposing uncertainties and challenging practice are risky. A project based on concepts surrounding Lesson Study but which became transformed into what the authors term 'Learning Study', with a much broader agenda, was the stimulus for the chapter.

The authors argue that such a transformation not only requires challenges to orthodoxies surrounding the methodology, but also to the adoption of the methodology by employing authorities who see it as a means of developing and delivering 'best practice' – a phrase eschewed by the authors.

In Chapter 14, Groundwater-Smith and Kelly connect inquiry and professional learning in a very different context – that of Museum Education, based on a long-standing partnership that involves schools, a university and a natural history museum in Sydney. It portrays the evolution of a set of methods that have captured student understanding and experience as a means of informing the museum of approaches to educational practices and of stimulating museum educators to inquire into their practice. Young people have acted as consultants to the museum, informing not only design principles in both real and virtual contexts but also ways in which they can be engaged and active agents when visitors. The authors argue for communication that understands and is respectful of the different cultural contexts within which each partner operates.

Chapter 15 serves as an illustration of reporting, through a podcast made by Philippa Cordingley in cooperation with Kris Needham and Mark Carter, the ways in which school leaders can effectively use a range of research resources, and makes explicit the underlying necessity, if teachers are to be influenced by research in their practice, for them to have easy access to it. Cordingley's is a macro approach. Mark Carter provides a clear and encouraging illustration of what can be done at the micro-level.

In the final chapter, the editors bring together the major themes identified in order to connect the issues surrounding inquiry and the potential impacts upon professional learning. They address why attention has been given to the agency of educational practitioners who inquire into practice, often in constrained contexts. They argue that the potential beneficiaries are not only those teachers who engage in this work, but also their academic partners who assist them and often thereby substantially deepen their own professional knowledge. There is recognition that the varying contexts within which practitioner inquiry takes place are significant determining factors that will shape both policy and practice. The chapter explores the different spaces within which professional learning can occur, how those spaces are managed and even at times colonised. It concludes by recommending ways in which leaders in the education profession, be they in the classroom, in school management, in bureaucracies or in academia can work together to contribute to the ongoing improvement of practice to the benefit of the millions of students in our schools. Kincheloe (2003: 22), when calling for 'teachers, students and parents to participate in the research act in education . . . and help determine what is designated educational knowledge', aptly concludes what this book aims to do: to take matters into our own hands and increase our professional agency.

References

Castells, M. (2000) *The Rise of the Network Society*, 2nd edn. Malden: Blackwell Publishing.

Cochran-Smith, N. and Lytle, S.L. (2007) 'Everything's ethics: practitioner inquiry and university culture' in A. Campbell and S. Groundwater-Smith (eds) *An Ethical Approach to Practitioner Research: Dealing with Issues and Dilemmas in Action Research*. London: Routledge.

Department for Education and Skills (2003) *Every Child Matters*. London: Stationery Office.

Figgis, J., Zubrick, A., Butorac, A. and Alderson, A. (2000) 'Backtracking practice and policies to research' in Department of Education, Training and Youth Affairs, *The Impact of Educational Research*. Canberra, Commonwealth of Australia: pp. 279–373.

Hayes, D., Mills, M., Christie, P. and Lingard, B. (2006) *Teachers and Schooling Making a Difference: Productive Pedagogies, Assessment and Performance*. Sydney, Commonwealth of Australia: Allen & Unwin.

Kincheloe, J.L. (2003) *Teachers as Researchers: Qualitative Enquiry as a Path to Empowerment*, 2nd edn. London and New York: Routledge Falmer.

Lieberman, A. (1999) 'Networks', *Journal of Staff Development*, 20(3): 1.

Lieberman, A. and McLaughlin, M.W. (1992) 'Networks for educational change: powerful and problematic', *Phi Delta Kappan*, May, 673–7.

Lingard, B., Ladwig, J., Mills, M. *et al.* (2001) *The Queensland School Reform Longitudinal Study*. Brisbane: Education Queensland.

Lingard, B., Hayes, D., Mills, M. and Christie, P. (2003) *Leading Learning: Making Hope Practical in Schools*. Buckingham: Open University Press.

McMeniman, M., Cumming, J., Wilson, J., Stevenson, J. and Sim, C. (2000) 'Teacher knowledge in action' in Department of Education, Training and Youth Affairs, *The Impact of Educational Research*. Canberra, Commonwealth of Australia, pp. 375–549.

McNess, E., Broadfoot, P. and Osborn, M. (2003) 'Is the effective compromising the affective?' *British Educational Research Journal*, 29(2): 243–57.

Menter, I. and Hulme, M. (2007) 'Research to support schools of ambition', *Education in the North*, 15: 47–50.

Smith, R. (2000) 'The future of teacher education: principles and prospects', *Asia Pacific Journal of Teacher Education*, 28(1): 7–28.

Chapter 2

Mapping the field of practitioner research, inquiry and professional learning in educational contexts

A review

Anne Campbell and Olwen McNamara

Introduction

The stimulus for this chapter came from the authors' discussion of the plethora of terms used to describe practitioner research and inquiry and related professional learning in educational contexts. The abundance and variation in terminology presented a complex and messy picture. We began by listing all the terms we had encountered in our reading and discussions. We sought to clarify our ideas through mapping the area, not to 'tidy' it up but to get an analytical purchase on the field; what it might mean for practitioners to be researching their own practice, how this relates to activities like inquiry, reflective practice, professional learning and how they are accounted for in the educational research literature. We thought we might develop a typology but, in the event, for the purposes of this chapter, we attempted first to organise our list of terms under three headings: practitioner research; practitioner inquiry; and professional learning: see Figure 2.1.

This did not, however, result in the elucidation to which we aspired; there were too many overlaps and cross-cultural differences in usage. For example, it could be argued that reflective practice was the basis of some approaches of action research and that self evaluation shared many of its features, yet neither we deemed research. Campbell and Groundwater-Smith (2007: 4) applaud the difference in language and 'hope it enriches the reading process and reminds us of the need for understanding each other's cultures and contexts in a global research community.'

We then thought of conducting a literature review but that was clearly too weighty an undertaking for one chapter and the time we had available. So we decided to inspect the three umbrella terms we had identified and attempt to start developing some principles for inclusion in order to define the parameters of the sub groups. This too proved challenging so we settled on a Venn diagram in which we hoped we might locate some of the key components to instigate a discussion of the complexities of the field. We also hoped it might

---

Practitioner research
- Action research
- Collaborative/ participatory action research
- Critical action research
- Teacher research
- Research lesson study
- Action research
- Participatory research
- Pedagogical research
- Curriculum research
- Evaluation research

Practitioner inquiry/enquiry
- Evidence based practice
- Self study
- Teacher inquiry
- Action inquiry
- Narrative inquiry
- Pedagogical inquiry
- Inquiry as stance
- Inquiry for social justice
- Social inquiry

Professional learning
- Inquiry based professional learning
- Action learning
- Evidence-based learning
- Evidence informed teaching and learning
- Reflective practice
- Coaching
- Mentoring
- Collaborative learning and team teaching

Figure 2.1 Terms used in research enquiry and professional learning

serve as a tool to reflect upon and unpick the terminology and associated discourses surrounding practitioner research, inquiry and professional learning.

In the process of our deliberations, a number of common themes began to emerge, and these posed questions through which we hoped to develop our thinking and around which we will organise this chapter. These questions, for example, might be about ownership and autonomy, and about the relationships between academic partners and practitioners. First, however, we need to situate our domain: practice-based research.

What is the field of practice-based research?

Practice-based research in the education field, we would argue, covers all research about and into practice, whether by practitioners or researchers. This

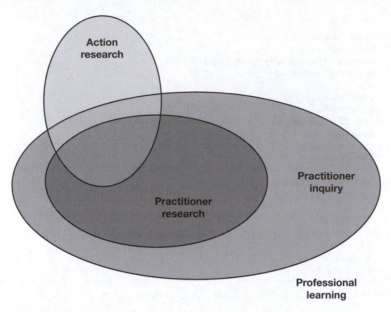

Figure 2.2 Some key components in the field of professional learning

would include research into contexts, pedagogy, curriculum and professional learning (Figure 2.2). We would also argue that much educational research is qualitative and applied, and has much engagement with, and relevance to, its participants, whether university or school teachers. Educational research also crosses the boundaries of theory and practice where it creates praxis, the synthesis of theory and practice. It is values driven with an emphasis upon doing what is regarded as equitable and honourable. Values and ethics should underpin research whether 'pure' or 'applied' and in educational research, knowledge creation is based on the inquirers' norms, values and interests. These should be articulated so that subjectivities are made conscious and shared. Furthermore, Gibbons *et al.* (1994) offer notions of mode 2 knowledge that emphasise reflexivity, and inquiry-contextualised results.

Furlong and Oancea (2005: 1) suggested practice-based research was 'an area situated between academia-led theoretical pursuits – such as historical research – and research-informed practice and consisting of a multitude of models of research explicitly conducted in, with and/or for practice.'

This huge field serves as a boundary within which to locate our knowledge and understanding of research. We attempt now to explore some characteristics of our three fields, not in order to develop a typology or hierarchy, because in practice these umbrella terms and the particular activities we have included within them are, and will continue to be, used variously/differentially in the literature in different cultures and settings. Instead, we hope to unpick the principles upon which we can begin to make distinctions between them to illuminate the discussion with some illustrations from a collaborative practitioner research project with which we have been involved.

What is practitioner research?

Practitioner research, located in the larger field of practice-based and applied research, is distinguished by its focus on research done by practitioners themselves, usually an investigation of practice with a view to evaluation or improvement. Practitioner research is often an umbrella term for many practice-based research activities undertaken by practitioners in the fields of education and social and health care.

This chapter focuses on teachers as practitioners, although much will be applicable to other professional groups, especially health and social care. We draw upon some of the literature from those fields to support ideas and aid clarification of terms. We turn to Stenhouse (1975), Elliott (1985, 1991), Cochran-Smith and Lytle (1993, 2007) and Zeichner and Noffke (2001) and their work which promoted curriculum reform and teachers as researchers of the curriculum and the practice of teaching. They foreground:

- teachers' work and teachers themselves as a basis for research;
- critical reflection and systematic study of practice;
- practitioner control and ownership of research.

Many of us in the field take these as key reference points for teacher research.

More recently, authors such as Dadds and Hart (2001), Campbell and Jacques (2003), Bartlett and Burton (2006) and McLaughlin *et al.* (2006) have described, discussed and evidenced a variety of initiatives where practitioners have undertaken research. Saunders (2004) was guest editor of a double edition of *Teacher Development*, which evidenced teachers' engagement with and in research and celebrated their success in a peer reviewed journal. These authors drew on teachers' research, which was supported through involvement in best practice research scholarships (BPRS), Networked Learning Communities (NLC), the National Foundation for Educational Research (NFER) and the Research Engaged Schools Project, and through award-bearing postgraduate courses that promoted practitioner research approaches.

Methodologically, practitioner research draws centrally on the methods of the 'family of action research' described by Kemmis and McTaggart (2005: 560) and other traditions and methodologies applicable to small-scale research such as case study and ethnography. Practitioners are often encouraged to be eclectic in their use of methods (Campbell *et al.* 2004: 80) and to address historical, sociological, cultural and philosophical influences in their research contexts, as well as more pragmatic concerns (Kinchloe 2003).

The relentless drive for raising standards in teaching and learning, partly through evidence-based practice, intense accountability pressures and emphasis on continuing professional development has contributed to a proliferation of practice-based and practitioner research and the search for evidence of improvement. Practitioner research has gained increasing recognition as a valued way of exploring and developing research-informed practice, not only in the UK but also in the North American and Australian contexts (Sachs 2003; Rowland 2005; Cochran-Smith and Lytle 2007). The Higher Education Academy (HEA) promotes pedagogical research by practitioners and for many new researchers in higher education (HE). This seems an attractive pathway, as demonstrated in Campbell and Norton (2007) in their efforts to build capacity at one institution. Developing reflective practice in a collaborative research community where practitioners undertake small action research projects is mirrored in many of the new universities (Burchell and Dyson 2005).

What of action research, a tradition almost exclusively associated with practice-based research and practitioner research? Elliott (1991: 69) describes action research as 'the study of a social situation with a view to improving the quality of the action within'. It was influenced by Lewin (1948) in America in the post-war 1940s as a research strategy for addressing social problems: analysis, fact finding, conceptualisation, planning, execution, more fact finding and evaluation. It was an iterative cycle: values driven, emancipatory and transformative. The fundamental aim of action research is to improve practice rather than produce knowledge, and this differs from most other research aims, but may be closer to Gibbons *et al.*'s (1994) mode 2 knowledge, which facilitates knowledge production via application. Perhaps it is time to revisit what constitutes teacher professional knowledge in relation to mode 2 knowledge and to research more about 'knowledge about practice'. Improvement of practice consists of realising those values that constitute its ends, for example 'justice' for legal practice, 'patient care' for medicine, 'preserving peace' for policing, 'education' for teaching. Such ends are not simply manifested in the outcomes but are intrinsic qualities of the practices themselves (Elliott 1991: 69).

Yet much of the work done in schools under the banner of school self-evaluation could be said to fall into this category. As can be seen in this annotated cycle, elements of performance management data gathering, analysis, evaluation and target setting fit perfectly with Elliott's action research (AR) cycle – yet would these be called research?

- It has a pedagogical aim (e.g. improving teaching of shape and space in year 6) which embodies an educational ideal (improving standards).
- It focuses on changing practice (curriculum development and/or teacher professional learning) and making it more consistent with the pedagogic aim.

- It gathers evidence about the extent to which practice is consistent or inconsistent with the aim (peer observation and monitoring, analysis of SATs results).
- In identifying inconsistencies between aspirations and practice, it problematises the assumptions and beliefs (theories) which tacitly underpin classroom practice (through performance management).
- It involves teachers in the process of generating and testing new forms of action for realising their aspirations and thereby new theories to guide their practice (target setting).
- It is a pedagogic process characterised by teacher reflexivity (what does the statistical and observational evidence say about me as a year 6 teacher?).

(Elliott 1995: 10–11)

Elliott claims that teaching is a form of action research and vice versa. Yet, would we wish to designate teaching 'practitioner research'? Clearly, practitioner research is not just about process, although those processes are intrinsic to it. But what else is involved? Lawrence Stenhouse (1975) seminally described research as 'systematic enquiry made public'. So, first, research must be 'systematic', and, second, it must be 'made public'. Comparing Elliott with Stenhouse, we see that the action research process may or may not be 'research' as, for example, it may fail on the 'made public' criterion, depending of course on how we conceptualise 'public'. The traditional interpretation is to present at conferences or to publish. Perhaps it is time to consider other interpretations such as networks, groups of practitioners working together on projects and internet resources. Some key issues arising from rethinking this area, to which we will return later, are ethics, trust and quality.

What is practitioner inquiry?

Examining the difference between practitioner research and practitioner inquiry causes us to consider some cultural and linguistic issues as well as epistemological and ontological ones. Carr and Kemmis (1986: 162) offer action research as a 'form of self-reflective inquiry'. Kember (2000: 35) sees action research as synonymous with action inquiry and as a methodological and rigorous form of action learning in which results are published and argues that, 'all action research (inquiry) projects are therefore action learning projects, but the converse is not true'. This implies that inquiry and research are of the same order and does seem to fit with work in the USA from Cochran-Smith and Lytle (2007) and Zeichner (2003), who talk about inquiry as research or inquiry as stance. Cochran-Smith and Lytle (2007: 24) address this point in a short review of working in the field:

We use 'practitioner inquiry' as a conceptual and linguistic umbrella to refer to a wide array of educational research modes, forms, genres and purposes. It is not our intention to suggest that the terms encompassed by the general phrase are synonymous nor do we want to blur the important ideological, epistemological, and historical differences that exist between and among them. Rather we hope to illuminate the differences across these forms of inquiry at the same time that we clarify some of their commonalities.

It seems sensible to accept that research and inquiry in the contexts described are closely aligned, and may often be the same activity.

A case study

What would we categorise under the field of practitioner research? What are the issues for us, as academics, entering into collaborations with practitioners undertaking research? Our case study is a project in which both authors were involved. Four consortia of schools, local authorities (LAs) and higher education institutes (HEIs) were funded for three years by the Teacher Training Agency (TTA), a quasi-autonomous non-government organisation (QUANGO) established in 1994 to manage teacher education. In this partnership we worked with the Manchester and Salford Schools' Consortium, and although located in a very particular time and context, it makes an interesting case study as it symbolizes, we think, the dawn of the era of colonisation of practitioner research by government. It is also interesting because of the significant questions it poses about collaborative practitioner research which we will explore through four familiar themes. We will illustrate these themes by drawing on the book that was written by the consortium project team (McNamara 2002).

Theme One: An illustration of the political context of teacher research

'The research-based consortia were born, in part, from a national debate about educational research instigated by the Teacher Training Agency (TTA, now the Training Development Agency, TDA) a self-styled 'catalyst for change' in this highly politicised arena. In their move to promote 'teaching as a researched-based profession' they sought to 'improve the accessibility of the existing stock of knowledge; improve the quality and relevance of research; help teachers play a more active role in conceiving implementing, evaluating and disseminating research'. This led to claims by some that the TTA wanted to 'get its hands on' government research funding. 'Allegations regarding the relevance, quality, and accessibility, of educational research to teachers were made by Hargreaves in the 1996 TTA Annual Lecture. Such was the battle-strewn landscape when the 'research-based consortia' entered the scene.

'Research-based' shifted into 'evidence-based' and was variously interpreted by protagonists as a formal and specialised evidence-base that would enhance professional autonomy and status; or, a technology of teaching that would deny 'craft' knowledge and reduce capacity for professional action. In the to-ing and fro-ing of academic debate, notions of 'recipe knowledge' and 'repertoire of skills' were tossed around and the teacher was positioned variously as kitchen orderly or master chef. Summer 1998 saw two further reports on the health of educational research funded by The Office for Standards in Education (Ofsted) and The Department for Education and Skills (DfES). Reynolds, launching the TTA Corporate Plan 1998–2001, denounced D-I-Y and pre-scribed a 'technology of teaching'. He invoked some interesting methodological metaphors, declaring teachers to have 'validity' but not 'reliability'. In the early days of the partnership, direct encounters between the protagonists in the debate included regular, but relatively minor, skirmishes in the boardroom of the TTA, where 'key contacts' of the consortia met with the National Steering Group, including representatives of all the major educational stakeholders. A further, and to us rather more distressing, assault came when we (two HE researchers) and two teacher colleagues offered a presentation of work in progress at the Collaborative Action Research Network (CARN) conference in October 1998. It was a hostile reception. How could this be called proper research? Was it supposed to be generalisable? Were we not traitors to the cause of educational research accepting funding, from the TTA? It was not exactly CARNage, but some did have to lick their wounds, while others were 'bloody but unbowed!' (McNamara 2002: 159).

Theme Two: Issues of ownership and autonomy

Issues of ownership and autonomy were apparent very early in the project. The TTA, assertive in their management of the projects, required consortia to develop a common pedagogic theme with a view to creating a coherent evidence base. Arguably this could be seen as commendable and worked well to facilitate collaborative learning in other consortia which were focused on the substantive areas of thinking skills, mathematics and disaffection. Our con-sortium, however, was focused on 'school improvement' and developing a 'common pedagogic theme' conflicted with one of our research design principles that required individual projects to be embedded in their school's development plan to support systemic change. We did eventually come to a mutually agreed accommodation with the TTA on a common theme. But even the notion of what constituted 'pedagogic' research was contested and when one of our projects, which focused on 'setting and streaming', was judged to have crossed that boundary, another heated debate ensued.

Theme Three: The role of academic partners

The eight research projects in the consortium were undertaken by a teacher researcher and an academic partner and these pairs operated discretely, and to a degree autonomously, a strength but also a weakness. This meant that relationships which were developed, positioned teachers very differently.

Most HEI and LA colleagues found it difficult to avoid paternalist relationships with individual teachers. The power differential was defined to include such terms as hierarchy, research experience, professional status, and attempts at empowerment of teachers, therefore, could easily fail. Again, a power dynamic inevitably operates between employers (the LA) and employees (the teachers). Gender dynamics added a further dimension to the developing picture. In the beginning all but two teachers were women; all but one of the HEI and LA men. In addition, the seven men of the HEI and LA were in positions of considerable power (inspectors, professors, principal lecturers); the eighth (a woman) breached convention in that she was at one and the same time the most powerful (as project coordinator) and (as Senior Research Fellow) the least. Apart from the teachers, that is!

A tempting conclusion would be that teachers end up at the bottom of the pile, whatever the talk about partnership, empowerment, critical friends, action research, co-researchers, and so on. This is not necessarily true. A judicious reading of the TTA might see it making all partners equal but some (the teachers) more equal than others. Teachers, it will be recalled, in the TTA grand plan, were to play a larger role in all phases of research – 'conceiving, evaluating, implementing and disseminating'. Again, a different power relationship between teachers and the HEI can be seen in the TTA 'teacher research grant scheme' (forerunner to the BPRS, a four-year project funding some 4,000 teacher researchers to the tune of £12 million) in which the grant holders (teachers) were required to use funds to buy support from HEI colleagues. In this requirement the TTA disrupted the unequal relation between teacher and academic and rebuilt instead a 'different-but-equal' model. We might speculate whether the equality spawned by such contracts, actually brought an increased subordination of all parties to the TTA. A question that arises is: 'Is this a UK problem or is it a global issue in research communities?'

In the event, all but one pair – of teacher researcher and academic partner – claimed to have engaged in a truly collaborative research venture, although within this the range of engagement of individuals in data collection, analysis, dissemination and writing up was vast. Of the one pair that did not represent themselves as engaged in a collaborative research, the HEI colleague wrote in the project report:

> Initially, the process of research was supposed to be teacher-led. It was, in the sense that the teacher decided on the focus of the research, while the researcher looked for practical and economical ways of addressing the teachers' concerns. The researcher concluded that the process, as opposed to the focus, was researcher-led: the teacher simply did not have the time to engage in research processes in a more active way. Her conclusion was

that such work was 'massive' and unrealistic to expect from the majority of teachers.

(Stronach 2002: 61)

Theme Four: Issues to do with representation of outcomes and practitioners

What of the visibility of practitioners that is often lost in the writing or authoring of the research outputs? In this case all but one was involved in the writing and all the projects reported in the chapters were authored or co-authored by practitioners. But this was not without debate.

The dynamics of the partnership can be usefully illustrated by exploring the unproblematic narrative genre adopted in the story of the project, which has involved the suppression of endless crises of identity. As the story evolved, and the envelopes fell though the letterbox, the characters were created, one by one. The 'we' who planned the consortium and agreed terms and conditions were the two HEI authors together with the head teachers of the schools and some of the teacher research coordinators. The 'we' who actually wrote the bid were largely the HEI staff. The 'we' who signed the contract was the Head of the Manchester School Improvement Service. The resulting consortium involved a cast too numerous to mention across, initially, two universities and two LAs. The attempt to reconcile these manifold identities at times involved the consortium in open and productive dissonance. Difference and ambiguity in the 'meshing subplots', not only between partners but also within institutions, became part of the lived experience. Where conflict occurred in the writing of the narrative accounts in the book, for example, the resolution involved not agreeing an 'authentic' reality, but agreeing what could not be said. Luckily, or unluckily, as the case may be, virtually all meetings, even from the early bidding phase, were either subject to a written record or taped, providing ample data for the authentication of 'accounts' and the interpretation of events. Autonomy, ownership of research focus, involvement in the process, representation of teacher researchers, writing up and dissemination are all illustrated there as infinitely problematic (McNamara 2002: 12).

These themes, hopefully, have helped to illustrate the issues arising from research partnership between schools, universities and local government. We can now move to our third area of concern, the relationship between research, inquiry and professional learning.

What is the relationship between research, inquiry and professional learning?

Arguably, engagement in teacher research and inquiry increases teacher ownership of the agenda for reform and improvement. In professional learning there has been a proliferation of terminology such as action learning, critical friendship groups, peer coaching, critical evaluation and analysis. The key discriminator we believe is that practitioner research and inquiry involves the teacher in systematic investigation and the gathering and synthesising of knowledge, whether theoretical or practical. Central to professional learning is the assimilation of knowledge rather than its gathering. Can inquiry and research-based professional learning involve the production of knowledge about practice in different ways than previously conceived?

The relationships between practitioner research and professional knowledge and learning are becoming clearer as teachers take ownership of their professional learning and manage change in their classrooms and schools through knowledge production in action research initiatives. The centrality of collaboration and networking was evident in the cases illuminated in Campbell and Macgarvey (2006), where teachers on an MA course in Practitioner Inquiry and Research were supported in leading their own learning through inquiry and research approaches (Campbell et al. 2004). Teachers spoke of 'cultural shifts' as a result of action research and described this as a movement away from the purely routine or superficial, to a situation in which pupil learning and teachers' strategic awareness and professional development were all subject to discussion and investigation. What also emerged was a complex web of skills, types of knowledge and professional dispositions and attitudes that are the anatomy of teaching and constitute professional knowledge. Taken alongside the work of Gibbons et al. (1994) and Day's (1999: 55) observations about good teaching, 'the application of wisdom, insight, experience, content knowledge and pedagogical and organisational strategies varies according to the context of the problem', we can see the impossibility of providing universal definitions and understanding of professional knowledge. The importance of context is paramount. We would argue that teachers doing research helps to contextualise professional knowledge and learning.

Ken Zeichner (2003: 319) identified several conditions under which school-based teacher research becomes a transformative professional development activity for teachers – and we would argue for those academic partners who support them, as the following:

- creating a culture of enquiry and respect for teacher knowledge;
- encouraging learner-centred instruction;
- developing and controlling their own foci for enquiries;
- engaging in collaborative work and study groups for intellectual challenge and stimulation.

We still need to know more about the relationship between teacher research and inquiry and teacher professional learning. We now turn to other key issues.

Ethics, trust and quality issues

Furlong and Oancea (2005, 2006), in their papers funded by the Economic and Social Research Council (ESRC), tackle the complex question of quality in applied and practice-based research. The paper was commissioned to inform the national Research Assessment Exercise and intended to support better understanding of the status and value of applied and practice-based research. Groundwater-Smith and Mockler (2006: 114) pose broad, over-riding 'ethical' guidelines for practitioner research, which require observation of ethical protocols, transparent processes, collaboration, justification to a community of practice and transformability in intent and action. The above help to form the criteria on which quality of research could be judged.

In the context of quality, the roles of critical friends and critical communities shape validity and authenticity. Some new networks of researchers emerged, such as BPRS (2000–2004), Schools University Partnership for Research (SUPER) (McLoughlin et al. 2006), the CARN and NLC supported by the National College of School Leadership (NCSL) (2002–2006). We believe the role of HE personnel in teacher research is vital in providing support for research through a wide range of partnerships. Collaboration, networking and critical appraisal are key to the research process and need to be nurtured systematically. Hargreaves (1994: 195) states:

> In their more robust (and somewhat rarer) forms, collaborative cultures can extend into joint work, mutual observation and focused, reflective inquiry in ways which extend practice critically, searching for better alternatives in the continuous search for improvement.

Trust, accountability, responsibility and ethics are key aspects of practitioner research. Campbell and Groundwater-Smith (2007), in their introduction to their edited collection on practitioner research and ethics, identify the major areas of concern for practitioner researchers as: whether anonymity for respondents and participants was always necessary; the sensitivities involved in working with young children or vulnerable young people or adults; the benefits and problems of collaborative research with participants; roles, relationships and power differentials, stakeholders, accountability and responsibility within research ventures and projects, especially within commissioned research projects; and the complex issues involved in informed consent. They also discuss the significance of the relationship between the field-based practitioner researcher and the academic researcher who may be acting as a research mentor and critical friend under the auspices of award-bearing courses or engagement in government initiated projects. Following moves to promote professional learning and development in the workplace, there is also an increase in the number of practitioners engaging in such action or inquiry-based learning supported by university staff or consultants, as identified above. Tensions are inherent in relationships between practitioners and academics in terms of the setting of the research agenda, the policy implications that may flow from it and the right to publish outcomes. Negotiating these relationships requires ethical probity where each party recognises, understands and respects mutual responsibilities. Moreover, each may be governed by research ethics standards institutionally determined. These may not always be compatible or serve the mutual interests. The boundaries may become more blurred when the academic researcher is engaged in investigating his or her academic practice either internally or in conjunction with the professional field, or where the academic researcher is formally engaged as a consultant in a practice-based research project. To achieve quality, ethics and trust are central.

Conclusion

Increasingly, classroom and school settings have become the sites of investigation of professional learning for educational practitioners. Inquiry-based learning has been employed in the UK by academia as a key device to develop knowledge and understanding since the early 1970s in curriculum development projects; initial education of teachers; and award-bearing courses at postgraduate levels. More recently, inquiry-based learning has been commandeered by the UK Government where it has been incorporated into performance management systems and used as a methodology to underpin professional development activities, for example best practice research scholarships (Furlong et al. 2003).

Crucially, teacher self appraisal and evaluation are very important to how current teacher research initiatives are viewed within the research community. A strategy to promote critical thinking and high quality of research might include:

- control of research questions and project design by the teacher researchers;
- high quality of support for research projects;
- robust processes of self monitoring, critical reflection and evaluation;
- transparent procedures for dissemination and promoting debate of research projects and findings;
- establishment of critical communities in which teachers' research is made public.

We have illustrated themes arising in practitioner research, inquiry and professional learning from the case study of the Research-based School Consortia (RBSC) which spawned the government funded NLC initiative in which HE partners were often notably absent with no requirement for a research mentor from HE. A review of NLCs and their links with HE reported only 30 per cent of NLCs actually engaged in collaborative activity with HEI (Campbell et al. 2005). The TTA Teacher Research Grants in which HE were required to be involved, were taken up by DfES under the £12 million BPRS programme, 2000–04, where HEI partners were again often absent. In the recent Continuing Professional Development awards tender (www.tda.gov.uk) for best practice in professional learning, yet again reference to HE is not visible.

More recently, the beleaguered circumstances of many English university education departments mean that they have not the capacity to support practitioners as a result of years of under funding of core activities, the loss of Quality Research funding and the impact of the Research Assessment Exercise on the research agenda, where the pressure for high status/quality outputs is seen in some quarters as antithetical to practitioner research.

We would argue that from the catalogue of government funded research initiatives in England in the last decade (the BPRS and TTA research grants and the RBSC described earlier) criteria have on the whole been tightly defined to ensure that teachers focused on the technical-rational level, researching the improvement of their pedagogical practice rather than directing their attention to matters of curriculum, strategy or policy. We would further argue that academic partners have gradually been either excluded, or have excluded themselves, from that learning climate. We would also argue that there is a critical role for academic partners in the plethora of practitioner research, inquiry and professional learning initiatives. If ethics, trust and quality are to be given the central place they deserve and governments are to recognise that an 'investment in the transformative agenda' (Groundwater-Smith and Mockler 2006) is necessary, then academic partners are not optional.

References

Bartlett, S. and Burton, D. (2006) 'Practitioner research or descriptions of classroom practice? A discussion of teachers investigating their classrooms', *Educational Action Research*, 14(3): 395–405.

Burchell, H. and Dyson, J. (2005) 'Action research in higher education: exploring ways of creating and holding space for reflection', *Educational Action Research*, 13(2): 291–300.

Campbell, A. and Jacques, K. (2003) 'Best practice researched: expectations of the impact of doing research in their classrooms and schools', *International Journal of Teacher Development*, 7(1): 75–90.

Campbell, A., McNamara, O. and Gilroy, P. (2004) *Practitioner Research and Professional Development in Education*. London: Paul Chapman.

Campbell, A., Keating, I., Kane, I. and Cockett, K. (2005) *Networked Learning Communities and Higher Education Links Project Report*. Nottingham: NCSL. (Available at www.ncsl.org.uk/research.)

Campbell, A. and Macgarvey, L. (2006) 'Producing and applying professional learning from recent initiatives promoting teachers as researchers: some illustrative and illuminative cases from the field', *British Educational Research Association Annual Conference*, 6–9 September 2006. Warwick, UK: Warwick University.

Campbell, A. and Norton, L. (2007) *Learning, Teaching and Assessing in Higher Education: Developing Reflective Practice*. Exeter: Learning Matters.

Campbell, A. and Groundwater-Smith, S. (2007) (eds) *An Ethical Approach to Practitioner Research: Dealing with Issues And Dilemmas in Action Research.* London: Routledge.

Carr, W. and Kemmis, S. (1986) *Becoming Critical: Education, Knowledge and Action Research.* Geelong: Deakin University Press.

Cochran-Smith, M. and Lytle, S. (1993) *Inside–Outside: Teacher Research and Knowledge.* New York: Teachers College Press.

Cochran-Smith, M. and Lytle, S.L. (2007) 'Everything's ethics: practitioner inquiry and university culture' in A. Campbell and S. Groundwater-Smith (eds) *An Ethical Approach to Practitioner Research: Dealing with Issues and Dilemmas in Action Research.* London: Routledge.

Dadds, M. and Hart, S. (2001) *Doing Practitioner Research Differently.* London: Routledge Falmer.

Day, C. (1999) *Developing Teachers: The Challenges of Lifelong Learning.* London: Falmer.

Elliott, J. (1985) 'Educational action research' in J. Nisbet and S. Nisbet (eds) *World Year Book of Research, Policy and Practice.* London: Kogan Page.

Elliott, J. (1991) *Action Research for Educational Change.* Buckingham: Open University Press.

Elliott, J. (1995) 'What is good action research? – some criteria', *Action Researcher*, 2: 10–11.

Furlong, J. and Oancea, A. (2005) *Assessing Quality in Applied and Practice-based Educational Research: a Framework for Discussion.* Oxford: Oxford University Department of Educational Studies.

Furlong, J. and Oancea, A. (2006) 'Assessing quality in applied and practice-based research in education: a framework for discussion' in *Counterpoints on the Quality and Impact of Educational Research, Special Edition of Review of Australian Research in Education*, 6.

Furlong, J., Salisbury, J. and Coombs, L. (2003) *Evaluation of BPRS.* London: DfES.

Gibbons, M., Limoges, C., Nowotny, H., Schwartzman, S., Scott, P. and Trow, M. (1994) *The New Production of Knowledge: The Dynamics of Science and Research in Contemporary Societies.* London: Sage.

Groundwater-Smith, S. and Mockler, N. (2006) 'Research that counts: practitioner research and the academy' in *Counterpoints on the Quality and Impact of Educational Research, Special Edition of Review of Australian Research in Education*, Number 6.

Hargreaves, A. (1994) *Changing Teachers, Changing Times: Teachers' Work and Culture in the Post Modern Age.* London: Continuum.

Kember, D. (2000) *Action Learning and Action Research: Improving the Quality of Teaching and Learning.* London: Kogan Page.

Kemmis, S. and McTaggart, R. (2005) 'Participatory action research: communicative action and the public sphere' in N.K. Denzin and Y.S. Lincoln (eds) *The Sage Handbook of Qualitative Research*, 3rd edn. London: Sage.

Kincheloe, J.L. (2003) *Teachers as Researchers: Qualitative Inquiry as a Path to Empowerment.* London: Routledge Falmer.

Lewin, K. (1948) *Resolving Social Conflicts: Selected Papers on Group Dynamics.* New York: Harper & Row.

McLaughlin, C., Black-Hawkins, K., Brindley, S., McIntyre, D. and Tabor, K. (2006) *Researching Schools: Stories from a Schools-University Partnership for Educational Research.* London: Routledge.

McNamara, O. (ed.) (2002) *Becoming an Evidence-based Practitioner.* London: Falmer.

Rowland, S. (2005) 'Intellectual love and the link between teaching and research' in R. Barton (ed.) *Reshaping University: new relationships between research, scholarship and teaching*. Buckingham: Open University Press.

Sachs, J. (2003) *The Activist Teaching Profession*. Buckingham: Open University Press.

Saunders, L. (2004) 'Editorial teacher development', *Special Double Issue*, 8(2 and 3): 117–26.

Stenhouse, L. (1975) *An Introduction to Curriculum Research and Development*. London: Heinemann.

Stronach, I. (2002) 'Happily ever after' in O. McNamara (ed.) *Becoming an Evidenced Based Practitioner*. London: Falmer.

Zeichner, K. and Noffke, S. (2001) 'Practitioner research' in V. Richardson (ed.) *Handbook of Research on Teaching* (4th edn). Washington, DC: AERA.

Zeichner, K. (2003) 'Teacher research and professional development', *Educational Action Research*, 11(2): 319.

Chapter 3

Teaching as a research-informed and research-informing profession

Bob Lingard and Peter Renshaw

Introduction

About a decade ago, the Teacher Training Agency (TTA) in England, now the Teacher Development Agency, argued that teaching ought to be a research-based profession. However, very quickly, as Anne Campbell and Olwen McNamara point out in their chapter in this book, this was changed to an evidence-based profession. It is the earlier conception which we see as more ideal and which we will consider in this chapter, even though we will work with the concept of research-informed rather than research-based. Our use of 'informed' rather than 'based' gives relevant consideration to teacher professional discretion and the need for systemic trust relationships with teachers. Evidence-based is a much more reductive conception and has been applied to contemporary policy development in England as well. The Rudd Labor government in Australia is also framing its policy actions generally and in relation to the professions as evidence-based. We reject evidence-based as it does not allow for any leeway in respect of professional practice, nor in relation to policy production. On the latter, we can see policy as the authoritative allocation of values (Easton 1953), thus meaning evidence (research derived) is only one of a host of factors, including professional knowledge, in addition to values, which ought to inform policy production (Head 2008). Values underpin both the production of policy and policy content. In our view, the same applies to professional practice, including the work of teachers in classrooms and heads/principals across schools. Research evidence is only one factor which does inform teacher classroom practices. Thus, we prefer evidence-informed, rather than evidence-based, as well as research-informed rather than research-based, to pick up on the need for professional discretion. Furthermore, there are different epistemologies which underpin research, usually with claims to the production of generalisable knowledge and understanding, and that of professional practice, which is located in the specificities of particular classrooms, even though practice-based or practitioner research has been, as traditionally conceived, more in line with a particular conception of 'use'.

It is these matters which we will traverse in this chapter, both descriptively and normatively. In doing so, we reject a model of teachers as simply translators or interpreters of educational research done elsewhere. We also reject a view of teachers as only the 'objects' of research they are, can and ought to be researchers too. However, we also reject a view which sees teachers' research option as only teacher inquiry or action-research. We argue for the necessity of a 'researchly' disposition for teachers, a disposition which ought to be instilled, we argue, through initial and continuing teacher education, all located within an ecumenical definition of education research, recognising that this needs to be a broad field and that such a definition needs to be defended (Lingard *et al.* 2001; Whitty 2006). Thus, in our view, teacher education is the place where the 'researchly disposition' ought to be encouraged, indeed developed and become an important part of teacher habitus.

We are concerned to understand what teaching as a research-informed profession might mean. Here we will be dealing with Pasteur's quadrant of research for knowledge and understanding, as opposed to research for use or applied purposes, the old pure/applied binary. As we will argue, however, we eschew this simple binary; we will argue for more collaborative relationships between researchers and research-informed teachers. Our stance here has implications for how we define educational research. Here we see multiple functions for educational research and epistemologies, stretching well beyond the instrumental ones of informing policy and practice in utilitarian ways. For instance, we agree with Willinsky (2001), who argues that educational research should also contribute to democratic discussions within the polity about the purposes and practices of schooling, critiquing current policies and practices. In this sense, Willinsky's stance is that educational research and researchers should take a public pedagogue role, contributing to broader public education. Leo Bartlett (1989), in his Presidential address to the Australian Association for Research in Education, argued that educational research (as opposed to the more descriptive 'education research') should engage teacher practices and education policy-makers 'educatively'. We would argue that just as the teacher habitus should include a 'researchly disposition', that *pace* Willinsky and Bartlett, educational researchers should have a 'pedagogical disposition'.

Within our eclectic definition of educational research, we stress the importance of quality (Yates 2004; Blackmore *et al.* 2006). The quality calculus applies, we argue, to practice-based research as well (Furlong and Oancea 2006), while also acknowledging as Campbell and McNamara note in their chapter, that the field of practitioner research is very diverse with many different descriptors used in the literature.

In what follows, we first consider how educational research actually reaches teachers. We are also concerned with more normative considerations of how research ought to reach teachers. We work with a couple of conceptualisations of this matter and develop them somewhat, drawing on McMeniman *et al.* (2000) and Figgis *et al.* (2000), research commissioned in Australia by the federal government to consider the impact of educational research on policy and practice. We then go on to consider what this might mean for defining and constructing the field of educational research and the quality considerations therein. Here we are concerned with design research. We also acknowledge at the outset that so-called 'pure' or 'blue skies' educational research, where the research problem to be researched and the methodological and theoretical frameworks adopted are determined by the researcher, has been under some pressure in many countries by governmental attempts to establish research priorities and methodological gold standards. In the USA, for instance, George W. Bush sought to constitute empirically randomised controlled trials as the standard against which claims for government research support would be evaluated (Anyon *et al.* 2009: 1). Indeed, in most countries around the world in recent times there have been attempts by governments to steer these research agendas in particular directions, to particular research problems, using particular research methodologies and eschewing high theory (Luke and Hogan 2006; Ozga *et al.* 2006; Anyon, *et al.* 2009).

Thus the second section of this chapter defines and defends a broad definition of educational research against attempts to narrow it through particular policy frames and attempts to restrict the research possibilities available to teachers. Implicit in the argument is an ideal construction of the teacher as research-informed with a 'researchly disposition', what we might see as reflexive habitus, and an ideal construction of a broad field of educational research. This is predicated on the assumption that teacher education should be grounded in research evidence, but recognising that it, as with both policy and practice, is also grounded in values and professional judgements. We also argue that the development of a researchly disposition should be a central feature of teacher education's purposes and a 'pedagogical disposition' a central element of research training for educational researchers. We also extend the concept of teaching as a research-informed profession to teaching as a research-informing profession as manifested in design research in education.

Research and teachers

In this section we will look at two attempts to conceptualise the relationships between teachers, their practices and educational research. These are descriptive accounts based on research which attempted to map backwards from teacher practices, teacher talk about their practice links to research and the ways in which teachers became aware of the research which was part of the melange of factors which informed their practice. These two pieces of research are McMeniman (2000, Figure 3.1) and Figgis *et al.* (2000, Figure 3.3), which were commissioned as part of a broader study of the impact of educational research by the Research Evaluation Programme of the Federal Department

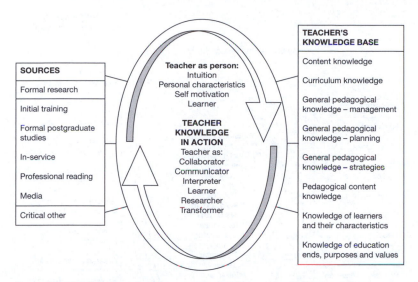

Figure 3.1 Teacher knowledge in action and the sources influencing their actions

Source: McMeniman *et al.* 2000: 384

of Education in Australia (at the time, the Department of Education, Training and Youth Affairs).

In Figure 3.1, McMeniman *et al.* attempt to encapsulate teacher knowledge in action, that is, the relationships between various types of knowledge and practice. The column on the left of the figure purports to adumbrate the ways in which research knowledge reaches teachers and thus become a part of the bricolage of knowledge which inform their practices, including pedagogical and assessment practices. Here we see formal research listed, presumably to refer to research conducted by educational researchers rather than teachers. The other media through which research reaches teachers include initial teacher education, formal postgraduate studies, professional development programmes, professional reading and the media. We would also see teacher union publications as a subset of media and professional reading, through which research is mediated to teachers. The final factor is critical others, for example, a highly respected colleague in the school who has research knowledge or a visiting celebrity academic who has run a seminar or given a public lecture.

We would make several comments about this useful, but incomplete, list. First, we believe that education policy must be added to the list of sources of teacher research knowledge. For the last 20 years or so, educational systems have been steered by policy, what has been called the 'policy phenomenon' (Taylor *et al.* 1997). In our view then, one of the most significant avenues through which research reaches (in multiple ways) teachers has been through policy (Hardy and Lingard 2008). The research underpinnings of policy have also been of a particular kind, reflecting the research for/of policy binary

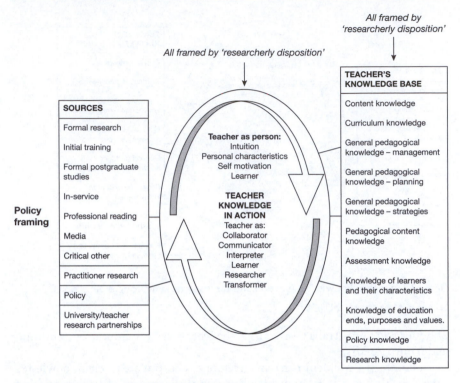

Figure 3.2 Research and teacher knowledge in action

Source: Developed from McMeniman *et al.* 2000: 384

within policy studies and the differing, yet complementary, engineering or enlightenment relationships between research and policy (Trowler 2003). Furthermore, in the context of globalization, policy and policy discourses now sometimes have their gestation from beyond the nation, for example in the national reviews and reports of the Organisation for Economic Cooperation and Development (OECD) (Henry *et al.* 2001). Global policy discourses and their research underpinnings have been mediated at the national level through policy, another contributing factor to the policy phenomenon. This policy phenomenon is manifest in England, for example in the development of policy sociology in educational research, almost as a replacement for sociology of education, an example of how broader policy frames and constrains research agendas and thus the research knowledge which affects teachers.

Over the last 20 years or so, globalisation in its neo-liberal market form has seen a transformation of schooling systems, as education policy has been rearticulated as the production of the requisite human capital for the economy, and as systems have been restructured according to new public management. This has witnessed a new steering at a distance and the construction of new forms of outcomes accountability, through which both the system and schools are managed. The archetypal example here is contemporary English schooling. This has been accompanied by an overwhelming focus on performativity and the collection of student outcome data of various kinds (Ball 2008), which have deeply affected curricula, classroom cultures and pedagogies. This policy as numbers approach (Rose 1999) has also pressured schools to 'research' this data, picking up on base-lines, trends and value-addedness, an approach which has also framed central policy development and research. Such data are now also collected globally, for example the OECD's Programme on International Student Assessment (PISA), another example of the new performative culture and another way in which research reaches teachers through policy, here policy gestating beyond the nation. This new policy reality also helps constitute the policy problems which frame educational research agendas.

To the left of McMeniman *et al.*'s sources of educational research, we would also add policy, because teacher education and teacher professional development requirements and so on are framed to a very large extent by policy. For example, moves to link teacher education more closely with schools and the practicum, possibly mean the reduction of the formal research component in teacher education. Think about teacher education 'reforms' in the UK from the mid-1980s and the removal of the educational foundations from teacher education curricula and the related move to enhance the school and practicum component. Broader policy also frames research agendas, as already noted.

In terms of such policies helping to frame research in education and how it reaches teachers and their practices, we can also think of policy attempts to create university/teacher partnerships around research and the related development of informed practice. The 'Innovative Links between Universities and Schools for Teacher Professional Development' is a very good policy example from Australia. This was funded by the federal government between 1994 and 1996 and sought to enable university academics and teachers to work together as co-researchers on practice and other professional issues. The Applied Educational Research Scheme (AERS) in Scotland, funded by the Scottish government, is another approach which has attempted to build networks of researchers, policy-makers and practitioners. There has also been a long tradition of site-based practitioner research, including teacher action-research. As Mitchell *et al.* (2008: 4) have recently commented, 'Site-based inquiry, reflection, and practitioner research within professional communities, have been widely recognised as means for exchanging ideas, building professional knowledge and taking action in classrooms'. We think here of the well-known work of Carr and Kemmis (1986) and Cochran-Smith and Lytle (1999) and more recent research work, which argues the need for the creation of collaborative teacher professional learning communities in schools and for a developmental role for research in relation to them (Louis *et al.* 1996). Thus we also need to add to the sources of teachers' research knowledge, 'practitioner research' and 'university academics/teachers as co-researchers', recognising that concepts such as 'action research' and 'practitioner research' provide a 'semantic and practical bridge', connecting teachers, research and university researchers (Mitchell *et al.* 2008: 4).

Thus our first major comment and addition to McMeniman *et al.*'s account is to add policy to the left of the sources and to add policy as a source of teacher research knowledge, as well as practitioner research and university academics/ teachers as co-researchers to the sources of teachers' research knowledge (see Figure 3.2 for the reworked model).

In respect of McMeniman *et al.*'s column adumbrating teachers' knowledge base, we would also make a number of necessary additions. We would add 'assessment knowledge' after pedagogical content knowledge in the list and recognise that there is a whole research literature about that. At the end of the list, we would also add policy knowledge and relevant research knowledge.

Central to our argument about teaching as a research-informed profession is the need for a researchly disposition amongst teachers. McMeniman *et al.* distinguish between teacher as person (including intuition, personal charac-teristics, self motivation and learner) and teacher as 'collaborator, communi-cator, interpreter, learner, researcher, transformer'. It is the interplay of these two sets of characteristics and practices that they describe as 'teacher know-ledge in action'. It is here that we would argue teacher knowledge in action should be framed by a researchly disposition, embodied in teacher habitus, becoming central to teachers' 'feel for the game' of teaching, to utilise concepts from Bourdieu's theoretical framing of the relationships between fields and practices. We will return to this concept of researchly disposition later in the chapter.

We turn now to a consideration of the Figgis *et al.* (2000) study, which backtracked or backward mapped from teacher practices to research, what they call a 'user-centric' approach to understanding education research impact. At the outset, we should say that Figgis *et al.* were concerned with how educational research conducted by education researchers (not by teachers) impacts on teachers and schools. They are not concerned with teacher or practitioner research in its multiple variations (see Campbell and McNamara's chapter). Figure 3.3 demonstrates the findings of the Figgis *et al.*'s research on impact.

As Figure 3.2 shows, they see the relationship between research/researchers and practitioners/policy-makers and professional problems as having some potentially direct relationships, but as largely being mediated by a 'connecting web'. They comment in a most useful way on researchers' and practitioners' different kinds of relationships to this mediating web. Regarding practitioners, they note:

> there is a real gap between practitioner/policy-maker and the connecting networks: something has to motivate educators to venture into the connecting web – some driver is required to energise them to seek new

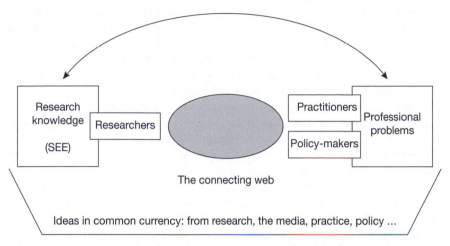

Figure 3.3 Relationships between policy, research and practitioners
Source: Figgis *et al.* 2000: 367

knowledge, to exert themselves beyond the demands of their daily work.

(Figgis *et al.* 2000: 366)

In respect of educational researchers, they make a similar point about the desultory segue between educational research and the connecting web. They note:

> there is a real gap between research knowledge and the connecting networks: research has to be propelled out of its abstract conceptual space and into arenas where educators can engage with it and decide if and how it will be useful to them.

(Figgis *et al.* 2000: 366)

Figgis and her colleagues also make the point that it is easier to discern the connecting web in relation to specific research projects rather than in a generalised way. They also make some further useful observations about practitioners/policymakers in relation to the connecting web and educational research. They suggest practitioners decide for themselves when and whether to engage with the connecting web; that they are 'constructivist learners', not 'passive receptacles', waiting for research answers to professional problems; and that their involvement relates to their motivation and appetite for research information. It is on this latter point, that we would stress the significance of what we have been calling the need for teachers to have a researchly disposition as central to teacher habitus.

On the connecting web itself, Figgis *et al*. suggest that it is a 'learning space', that both sides of the space or connecting web bring vast sources of knowledge to it: one-way messages have to be very powerful to connect to practitioners; and the most effective mode of connection is two-way enabling substantive conversations between researchers and practitioners (a feature as well of teacher professional learning communities in relation to research).

There are significant policy implications of the Figgis *et al*. research, particularly about research dissemination and impact. The model implies as well, arguably, the need for a pedagogical disposition amongst educational researchers. This disposition would entail a desire for multiple forms of dissemination. However, we would also point out that contemporary policy about research and a range of research assessment exercises valorise pure research with research questions established by researchers, and its dissemination in high status, internationally refereed, fully peer-reviewed research journals. These rarely form part of teachers' professional reading. Dissemination and impact of educational research in this sense are linked to the academic researcher community and its high status communication organs. In this realpolitik of contemporary educational research, there are real disincentives for academic researchers to even contemplate the connecting web. Here then, the policy frames need to be augmented and the pedagogical disposition developed in neophyte educational researchers.

We now draw on an example from personally involved research to illustrate how important a conceptualisation of the connecting web as a learning space is to ensuring effective research dissemination and impact on professional practices. The Queensland School Reform Longitudinal Study (QSRLS) (Lingard *et al*. 2001, 2003; Hayes *et al*. 2006) developed the concept of productive pedagogies after mapping classroom pedagogies in about one thousand Queensland primary and secondary school classrooms in twenty-four schools over a three-year period in English, Maths, Science and Social Studies. This research was mediated and disseminated to teachers through a short document especially prepared for teachers by the Department of Education (Education Queensland), who had commissioned the research and distributed to schools and teachers throughout Queensland. Productive pedagogies and a renewed focus on the significance of teacher practices to good and equitable student outcomes, were endorsed politically and by the Department and took on a powerful salience with the Department, which employed consultants to conduct professional development with teachers throughout the state about the productive pedagogies.

Some of the researchers, including both of us, were involved in such professional development with teachers, which could also be seen as research dissemination. However, in all of this work, the point was made about how the model of productive pedagogies had been constructed from the inter-weaving of a large dataset of pedagogical maps, cogeneric factor analyses and adjudication of potential multidimensional models of pedagogies through the lens of relevant theory and research. This is an abstracting process, seeking to develop a 'universalistic model' of pedagogies. However, the point was always made in teacher professional development meetings that this research-based model of productive pedagogies was not akin to an algebraic equation which could simply be factored into classroom practices. Rather, the stress was always on the need for teachers to mediate the model through their relevant professional knowledge and understandings of the specificities of their school, its student population, the school's communities and the specificities and contingencies of their classrooms. Here we were recognising the differing logics of practice of research of the QSRLS kind and teacher classroom practices. In a sense this helps us to see research dissemination in education as a process of learning across different communities (one of research, one practice). We also always attempted to do this professional development work in a respectful way with teachers.

This productive pedagogies research did have real impact in schools and in the research community. Its professional impact resulted because all the necessary features of Figgis *et al.*'s 'connecting web' were acknowledged and utilised. Professional development in relation to the research was constructed as a learning space; there was recognition of the knowledge on both sides of the connecting web; a powerful, officially endorsed research finding/model was placed on the connecting web; and there was recognition of the need for two-way, substantive conversations across the connecting web. This situation can be contrasted with policy about pedagogies in other educational jurisdictions, for example, England and New South Wales, where pedagogical policy derived from research has been imposed with little respect for teachers, where the policy has been done to teachers and there have been no substantive conversations within the learning space of the connecting web. We would also argue that a researchly disposition was very enabling in strengthening teachers' mediated take-up of the productive pedagogies research in Queensland. A pedagogical disposition amongst the researchers also contributed to the effective 'implementation'/'mediation' of productive pedagogies in many Queensland classrooms.

The field of educational research

We turn now to a consideration of teachers in relation to educational research and at the outset suggest that the field of educational research needs to be broad, including multiple theoretical and methodological approaches. Teachers as researchers or practitioner research can be seen as one important part of the field. However, teacher inquiry and practitioner research have been regarded almost as second-level research paradigms in educational research – relevant mainly to improving professional practices rather than to furthering the general field of education research and theory. In recent years, design research in education (The Design-based Research Collective 2003) has cut across established research paradigms in interesting and transformative ways. We argue that in relation to the teachers' contribution to research, the notion of design research elevates the importance of teachers as research collaborators, not just at a local level in relation to context-specific professional practices, but in terms of developing more general insight and transferable knowledge about teaching and learning processes. Design research blends applied and theoretical preoccupations and positions teachers as equal partners with academic and university-based researchers in the production of knowledge (The Design-based Research Collective 2003). Design research involves iterative cycles of theoretically-informed design, enactment, analysis and redesign in contexts of everyday practice. However, the purpose is not simply to improve practice locally, but to create a body of knowledge about learning and teaching that can inform theory and practice generally. Teachers collaborate with researchers as equal and complementary partners in the design process.

One of the celebrated examples of design research is the Community of Learners (COL) project that Ann Brown and Joe Campione orchestrated during the 1990s (Collins *et al.* 2004). The COL project was conducted in context – in Oakland schools in California during the 1990s – with teachers who were employed by the local school district, but the insights about learning and classrooms have been influential internationally in numerous educational systems. In terms of theory per se, the COL project drew upon language and communication theories consistent with a Vygotskian perspective. The design process revealed the importance of including a diversity of student voices, along with the teacher's voice, within the learning environment, so that multiple ways of representing ideas and experiences were made available to community members. Students came to see themselves as authors and co-authors of ideas within the community and this led to a greater appreciation of the importance of a diversity of identities, experiences and knowledge for effective learning to occur.

There are many such examples in the research literature where programmatic research on learning and teaching has progressed through partnerships between teachers and researchers (Logan and Sachs 1997). It is misleading to regard these projects simply as examples of teacher-inquiry, or teachers' practice being influenced by the uptake and transformation of research at a local level. Rather, the research itself is an outcome of a history of collaboration where the identities of teacher and researcher, of insider and outsider, of producer and consumer, are collapsed. For example, in reflecting on recent advances in understanding diverse cultures of learning, Renshaw (2007) noted that progress in this field had been achieved by partnerships between academics and outstanding teachers whose practices were articulated and documented in extended dialogues with the academics and the research community over many years. The intention of such research was not limited to improving professional practice; it had political, policy and pedagogical goals and it drew upon theory-informed design research to further these objectives. The research from these projects was published in high status international refereed journals whose audiences in the first instance were likely to be academics and graduate research students rather than professionals and teachers in schools. In this sense, teaching is not just a research-informed profession, but also a research-informing profession. Not every teacher will enter into design research projects, but on the other hand it is difficult to envisage the field of educational research progressing without academic researchers entering into design research partnerships with teachers. This is why a pedagogical disposition is so important in educational researchers.

Conclusion: teaching as a research-informed profession and research-informing profession

In the current policy contexts of governments seeking to 'manage' educational research, we stress the need to defend among the professional associations of educational researchers a very broad definition of educational research, with quality being an important factor in all theoretical and methodological approaches and for all educational researchers. We have documented the multiple ways that educational research reaches teachers with policy increasingly playing an important role. We have, following Figgis *et al.*, also shown the significance of the 'connecting web' to conversations among and between educational researchers and teacher practitioners and outlined certain features of the web which encourage such collaborative dialogue, including respectively pedagogical and researchly dispositions. We have stressed the significance of a pedagogical disposition among educational researchers as vital to their negotiation and engagement with the connecting web and practitioners (and policy-makers in education) and also central to the multiple modes of dissemination of their research. We have also stressed the necessity of a researchly disposition among teachers to engage fully with the connecting web and to being involved in research in multiple ways. Such a disposition, we argued, should be developed in initial and continuing teacher professional education. Beyond this, however, we have briefly outlined the significance of design research in education to the construction of teaching not only as a research-informed profession, but also as a research-informing profession. In our view, teaching as both a research-informed and research-informing profession is a necessary development towards better schools and educational systems and ought to be supported and thereby strengthened by all within the broad educational community, including researchers, practitioners and policy-makers.

References

Anyon, J., Dumas, M., Linville, D., Nolan, K., Perez, M., Tick, E. and Weiss, J. (2009) *Theory and Educational Research: Toward Critical Social Explanation.* New York: Routledge.

Ball, S.J. (2008) *The Education Debate*. Bristol: The Policy Press.

Bartlett, L. (1989) 'New and old testaments of alliance in educational research', *The Australian Educational Researcher*, 16(1): 17–38.

Blackmore, J., Wright, J. and Harwood, V. (eds) (2006) *Counterpoints on the Quality and Impact of Educational Research*. Lilydale, Victoria: AARE.

Carr, W. and Kemmis, S. (1986) *Becoming Critical: Education, Knowledge and Action Research*. Geelong: Deakin University Press.

Cochran-Smith, M. and Lytle, S.L. (1999) 'Teacher learning in professional communities: three knowledge-practice relationships' in P. Pearson and A. Iran-Nejad (eds) *Review of Research in Education*, pp. 251–307. Washington, DC: American Educational Research Association.

Collins, A., Joseph, D. and Bielaczyc, K. (2004) 'Design research: theoretical and methodological issues', *The Journal of the Learning Sciences*, 13(1): 15–42.

Easton, D. (1953) *The Political System*. New York: Knopf.

Figgis, J., Zubrick, A., Butorac, A. and Alderson, A. (2000) 'Backtracking practice and policies to research' in Department of Education, Training and Youth Affairs, *The Impact of Educational Research*, pp 279–373. Canberra, Commonwealth of Australia.

Furlong, J. and Oancea, A. (2006) 'Assessing quality in applied and practice-based research in education: a framework for discussion' in J. Blackmore, J. Wright and V. Harwood (eds) *Counterpoints on the Quality and Impact of Educational Research*. Lilydale, Victoria: AARE.

Hardy, I. and Lingard, B. (2008) 'Teacher professional development as an effect of policy and practice: a Bourdieuian analysis', *Journal of Education Policy*, 23(1): 63–80.

Hayes, D., Mills, M., Christie, P. and Lingard, B. (2006) *Teachers and Schooling Making a Difference: Productive Pedagogies, Assessment and Performance*. Sydney: Allen & Unwin.

Head, B. (2008) 'Evidence-based policy: three lenses', *Australian Journal of Public Administration*, 67(1): 1–11.

Henry, M., Lingard, B., Rizvi, F. and Taylor, S. (2001) *The OECD, Education Policy and Globalisation*. Oxford: Pergamon Press.

Lingard, B., Hayes, D., Mills, M. and Christie, P. (2003) *Leading Learning: Making Hope Practical in School*. Buckingham: Open University Press.

Lingard, B., Ladwig, J., Mills, M., Bahr, M. and Chant, D. (2001) *The Queensland School Reform Longitudinal Study*. Brisbane: Education Queensland.

Logan, L. and Sachs, J. (1997) *Meeting the Challenges of Primary Schooling*. London: Routledge.

Louis, K.S., Kruse, S.D. and Marks, H.M. (1996) 'Schoolwide professional community' in F. Newmann and associates (eds) *Authentic Achievement: Restructuring Schools for Intellectual Quality*. San Francisco: Jossey-Bass.

Luke, A. and Hogan, D. (2006) 'Redesigning what counts as evidence in educational policy: the Singapore model' in J. Ozga, T. Seddon and T.S. Popkewitz (eds) *Education Research and Policy: Steering the Knowledge-Based Economy*, pp. 170–84. London: Routledge.

McMeniman, M., Cumming, J., Wilson, J., Stevenson, J. and Sim, C. (2000) 'Teacher knowledge in action', in Department of Education, Training and Youth affairs, *The Impact of Educational Research*. Canberra, Commonwealth of Australia, 375–549.

Mitchell, J., Hayes, D. and Mills, M. (2008) *Crossing School and University Boundaries to Reshape Professional Learning and Research Practices*, unpublished paper, Charles Sturt University.

Ozga, J., Seddon, T. and Popkewitz, T. (2006) 'Introduction: Education research and policy – steering the knowledge-based economy' in J. Ozga, I. Seddon and T.S. Popkewitz (eds) *Education Research and Policy: Steering the Knowledge-Based Economy*, pp. 1–14. London, Routledge.

Renshaw, P. (2007) 'A commentary on the chronotopes of different "Cultures of Learning": transforming classrooms from trading-places into relational-places of learning', *International Journal of Educational Research*, 46: 109–15.

Rose, N. (1999) *Powers of Freedom: Reframing Political Thought*. Cambridge: Cambridge University Press.

Taylor, S., Rizvi, F., Lingard, B. and Henry, M. (1997) *Educational Policy and the Politics of Change*. London: Routledge.

The Design-based Research Collective (2003) 'Design-based research: an emerging paradigm for educational inquiry', *Educational Researcher, 32*(1): 5–8.

Trowler, P. (2003) *Education Policy*, 2nd edn. London: Routledge.

Whitty, G. (2006) 'Education(al) research and education policy-making: Is conflict inevitable?' *British Educational Research Journal*, 32(2): 157–76.

Willinsky, J. (2001) 'The strategic education research program and the public value of research', *Educational Researcher*, 30(1): 5–14.

Yates, L. (2004) *What Does Good Education Research Look Like?* Maidenhead: Open University Press.

Chapter 4

'Insiders' and 'outsiders' researching together to create new understandings and to shape policy and practice

Is it all possible?

Pat Broadhead

Introduction

This chapter explores how 'insiders' (teachers in a primary classroom and teachers and nursery nurses working in early years' classrooms) and an 'outsider' (an academic researcher who enters their classrooms, with permission, to engage in joint research) can, together, influence wider and deeper understanding of learning and teaching. The chapter examines how this joint research and emerging understanding might subsequently re-shape policy and practice when the research emerges from the place where learning takes place – for children, educators and educational researchers – the classroom.

With these explorations and examinations, the chapter also addresses ethical aspects relating to outsiders when they enter others' daily spaces – the spaces of children and adults – and the inherent dangers of exploitation and manipulation that might come into being if care is not taken. In entering classrooms, the researcher brings an authority and power inherent in being perceived as a skilled researcher by the educator. When teachers and nursery nurses are being asked to share their knowledge and insight, they may not perceive of themselves as experts in matters of teaching and learning. To feel 'expert' as an educator is rare and often transient as new classes of children, new curricula and new policy requirements shift the sands of certainty with unfailing regularity. In the two examples of insider–outsider research contributing to this chapter, in each case, the outsider has established the focus for the research and the insiders have, in different ways, participated in data production through reflection. In both cases, I have endeavoured to enter the classrooms as an outsider who sought to combine authentic enquiry with respect for professional knowledge.

When I began to engage in insider–outsider research, the early work was substantially influenced by Schon's (1983) premise that competent practitioners usually know more than they can say. Schon maintained that uncertainties, far from being external indicators of a need for professional progress, are the potential basis for enhanced effectiveness. These uncertainties constitute a positive and inevitable facet of classroom life wherein educators who can recognise them as such are able to accept the challenge of implementing new strategies while simultaneously acknowledging and assimilating revised pedagogies. For Schon, enhanced practice was founded on perceived wisdom and not on deficiencies (Broadhead 1989). Around this time, others were writing about the importance of, but the inherent challenges in exposing, the craft knowledge of teachers (McNamara 1980; Calderhead 1987; Zeichner et al. 1987; Brown and McIntyre 1993). With my early work on insider–outsider partnerships framed by these reference points, I was seeking to confront the challenge of creating equally weighted partnerships with educators; this is still the case in more recent work with educators, both of which are reported in this chapter.

The next section outlines the two research foci from previous and current research in classrooms. It is the more recent work that informs this discussion of influences on understanding, policy and practice in this chapter but some reference to the earlier work is needed to demonstrate that building a repertoire of ethical practice as an insider–outsider researcher is, in effect, a lifetime's work; the challenges should not be under-estimated. It is also in reflecting back on the earlier work that I began to see more clearly the political dimensions of this research as a form of resistance to a deeply, unsatisfactory status quo, particularly in relation to what has been happening to playful learning in early years' settings in England but also in terms of what has happened in primary classrooms.

Humphrey (2007) writes of 'activating the hyphen' between the insider and the outsider by confronting the challenges of inhabiting two different life-worlds at different times (for her, the worlds of the University and a Trade Union). This has resonance in that the outsider seeking insider status must learn to affirm the values of being both insider and outsider in relation to these real worlds. She writes (2007: 15):

> The perpetual crossing-over between life-worlds gave birth to a complex narrative which surpassed anything that I could have produced had I been simply an insider or an outsider.

This resonates because without the insights from the reflective engagements of the practitioners in my research, the research outcomes would have been only partially formed and the potential for impact on personal and wider pedagogical practice and on policy development would, similarly, have been substantially reduced. My claim here is that such partnerships can change perspectives and practice for the educators and the researcher, as well as creating a robust platform from which wider influences on policy and practice might spring.

Given the ethos of the last 20 years of educational 'reform' there is one more point to be made before moving on to look at the two examples of insider–outsider research on which this chapter is focusing. This relates to how understanding of learning in primary and early years' classrooms is created and disseminated; this, after all, has been the essence of my work during this period. In 1980, Michael Armstrong wrote: *Closely Observed Children: The Diary of a Primary Classroom*. It was based most substantially in the classroom of Stephen Rowland, a then primary teacher who went on to publish a similar text in *The Enquiring Classroom* (1984). In many ways, these books and others like them were the potential 'voices' of policy shaping. In the absence of any political interest in schools and classrooms at this time ('learning' is not included because I do not believe that any government policy reform since 1988 has had any interest in, nor sought any understanding of, learning in primary and early years' classrooms); it was texts such as these that sought to illuminate the relationships between teaching and learning and to inform practice development and enhancement. Each of these texts sought to illustrate what my own work would subsequently seek to illuminate also – what primary classrooms looked like when the act and art of teaching created the greatest potential for learning. These studies and others like them showed the complexities inherent in and the huge potential of creating spaces for teaching and learning where pupils had as much right and opportunity as teachers to shape the agenda for learning and where teachers took risks in order to enhance pedagogy, how they calculated those risks and how they overcame related uncertainties to move forward in the efficacy of their practice (Broadhead 1995). This chapter argues that these are the issues we need back on the educational policy agenda.

Primary teachers' perspectives on good practice

This research was undertaken for my Ph.D. in the period 1986–89. Those were interesting times. The Education Reform Act of 1988 was about to set teaching and learning in England on the cusp of some radical and far-reaching changes and the ethos of primary schools and classrooms was about to change substantially as a result of successively emerging educational policies. This would culminate around the turn of the century with the first prescriptions for *how* to teach (as opposed to *what* to teach enshrined in the National Curriculum and its subsequent amendments and revisions) entering the policy framework. These prescriptions were contained within the literacy and numeracy strategies which were never statutory but achieved almost complete saturation thanks to inspection requirements in this period. Foreshadowing these changes and around the time I was designing and beginning the Ph.D., also emerging were 'prescriptions' for good primary practice, as defined by those outside the classroom. As an ex-primary teacher myself, I began to wonder where the teachers'/educators' voices were in this emerging debate and this subsequently became the focus for my research (Broadhead 1987).

The first phase of the research involved twenty-two teachers in reflective, semi-structured interviews around three questions, which they received in advance of the interview:

- Can you recall four or five instances when things went well in your classroom?
- Can you recall occasions or periods when you felt that your practice changed?
- Can you recall any times when you were experiencing difficulties in your practice?

What emerged from these reflections was that, in some cases, individual primary teachers had gradually become curious as to why some children were not learning as efficiently as they had initially envisaged and they had gradually become bold enough to explore the possibility that a child's difficulties might be founded within their own teaching strategies rather than in any relative inability to learn that might come from within the child. It was only at this point that I, as a researcher, began fully to acknowledge the sensitive nature and ethical protocols relating to the terrain. Their recounted curiosity seemed to connect (for some teachers) with a perceived need to initiate pedagogical changes within their existing patterns of organisation and provision and as some of the interviews progressed these teachers were able to recount the changes they had made, why they had made them and what impact they had subsequently perceived the changes to have had on the children's learning processes.

From this point, the research moved to a more intensive phase of partnership with six of the original 22 teachers. Here, the researcher took the role of non-participant observer over several days of practice with the teachers continuing to reflect at lunchtime and days' end on what had gone well, where there had been difficulties, and plans for progression. It was at the point of first entry to one of these classrooms that I got a real wake-up call as an outside researcher entering the insider's space when Denise, a teacher of six- and seven-year-olds remarked: 'I know what you're doing, you're coming to see if what I say I do in the classroom is what I really do, aren't you?'

Denise was not familiar in practice with Schon's work on espoused theory and theory in action, but she intuitively understood and framed the potential underpinnings of my actions here and it was, I am sure, contributory to my own and the research's salvation that she had the confidence in herself and in me to frame these reservations in quite this way. Metaphorically speaking, her remark stopped me in my tracks; it made me question my intentions and expectations. Most importantly, it forced a rethink of my value system around our changing relationship (and my relationships with the five other participating teachers). That moment represented a substantial step-change in my work as researcher; it put me on the reflective path in understanding the nature and impact of insider–outsider relationships but it also 'hit me' in relation to dissemination. I entered the domain of 'teacher voice' in its early phases of conceptualisation (Nias 1989; Goodson 1991) and I began to see for the first time that this thesis was not 'my' work but was 'our' work. The understandings I would bring to bear on conceptualising 'good primary practice' were not 'mine' but were 'ours'. Anything I wrote, said or thought about this issue would be as spokesperson for all participants and I sought to make explicit both for them and with them how our roles complemented each other in determining the attributes that we each brought to the research. In Broadhead (1989: 136) I explored in some detail each of the attributes, as summarised in this following paragraph:

> The researcher brings the focus for the research, the reserves to sustain the focus, her skills as a non-participant observer and the professional knowledge being elicited from other practitioner participants. The teacher brings a willingness to be involved in joint research in addition to their ongoing teaching responsibilities, a capacity to reflect on actions in promoting learning through teaching, a cumulative store of professional knowledge (none of which, each of the teachers remarked, had ever been tapped into before in such an intensive way) and they also brought a personal understanding of the teaching/learning experiences ongoing in the classroom; they knew the children and their lives in ways the outsider could only guess at and with this knowledge small events in the daily life of the classroom could take on quite different perspectives in terms of breakthroughs in learning for individual children.

Although not conceived of as action-research, the research for the Ph.D. was beginning to conceptually engage with notions around communities of learners and of their potential for collective impact on policy and practice. Barazangi (2006) explores similar perspectives in seeking to change pedagogical experiences within the taught social science based on action-research approaches that are advocated by action researchers who can only intuit, rather than theorise their experiences. Barazangi talks of the need to resist becoming an authoritarian expert and of the need to ethically engage with principles and understandings that allow all individuals to act on their own behalf (Young 1990). In reflecting on these and related ideas I have gradually come to understand how positioning oneself in this way is a journey of discovery in that it is not only the application of principles but is also a social process of trying to achieve a balance among many different elements; we seek to act and reflect on our own behalf while also keeping the needs and interests of community members in mind. This then was the beginning of my journey in a world where teachers' perspectives were soon to diminish in their capacity to impact on policy and practice and where politicians and policy-makers' voices were growing stronger by the year.

The teacher is:	Learners are:
Noting the noise level	Not exceeding a working noise level
Scanning the area	Sustaining a regular working pace
Listening to conversations	Occasionally off task returning to task
Observing body language	Enthusiastic
Minimally concerned with control	Talking and listening
Assessing extent of off-task behaviour and deciding whether to intervene	Acting as a learning resource for peers
Noting the levels of interest during on-task behaviour	Using initiative, being self-directed and self-determining
Relaxed and engrossed	Extending activity beyond initial teacher requirement
Seldom approached by learner	Seldom approaching the teacher with low level requests
Witnessing problem solving	Absorbed and problem solving; testing hypotheses
Interacting with a wide range of children individually or in groups	Identifying and asking relevant questions of peers and teacher
Challenging individuals and groups with appropriate task related questions	Engaging in peripheral learning – peripheral to the teacher's orientation – not the child's

Figure 4.1 The characteristics of optimum times for facilitating learning – feeling good in action

From the doctoral research and sharing the emerging analysis and findings with the six teachers, the research identified the characteristics of optimum times for facilitating learning in primary classrooms as determined by teachers through reflection on action with me during phase two of the research. This is briefly demonstrated in Figure 4.1 above, characterising what teachers and learners were doing during the times when teachers felt good about their teaching and when they believed the potential for effective learning was evident (Broadhead 1995: 323).

In these classrooms, and at the 'best' times, the teacher is released to observe, monitor, interact and assess the level of match between task and learner and any subsequent learning difficulties. These teachers had come to recognise that, and could communicate the ways in which, much valuable learning occurs in the classroom when children are not in direct contact with the teacher and sometimes, when they are not actually engaged in the task that has been set. I had come to realise these aspects also as I had observed these teachers and children at work and discussed the day's events with the teachers. These teachers shaped my pedagogical understanding even as they framed and articulated their own. These understandings shaped my broader philosophical perspectives and ideology of good practice that for me re-affirmed and made more explicit my own political (small 'p') perspectives on teaching and learning. They would subsequently also reaffirm my own resistance to the Political (large 'P') ethos emerging from the 1988 Reform Act onwards where increasingly directive and authoritarian stances on teaching and its manifestation would be taken by subsequent governments and inevitably also by schools and teachers.

Play and learning in early years' settings

My interest in playful learning in young children pre-dates the above research. It began as the dissertation for a Bachelor Degree as a mature student and followed on into a full-time M.Phil and was subsequently revisited, having secured a first post in higher education and after completing the Ph.D. Three questions had also driven this research (Broadhead 1997, 2001, 2004):

- What potential do traditional activities have for supporting cooperative endeavour across the 3–7 age range?
- What range of sociable and cooperative behaviours are children exhibiting and utilising across the age range?
- How do these interface in facilitating intellectual commitment?

Briefly, the research has sought over many years to illustrate how cooperative play facilitates intellectual development for young learners through their complex use of language and action. It has sought to illustrate and detail these complexities in new and theoretically underpinned ways and in relation to the practitioner's pedagogical repertoire – to link learning with teaching in play endeavour in educational settings. The majority of this research has been undertaken jointly with educators utilising an observational tool which has been devised within the research and also working with educators who have made substantial contributions to its evolution and application. This tool, *The Social Play Continuum* (Broadhead 2004, 2006) supports both observation of and post-observation discussion around playful learning. In this insider–outsider partnership, as with the above research in primary classrooms, the educator brings a detailed knowledge of the individual children and their learning, development and progression to the understanding of playful learning, while the outside researcher brings a broader knowledge of the theoretical underpinnings to these discussions along with her opportunities to observe and work with many others across a range of early years' classrooms. With hindsight, I now realise the extent to which this research also had a political dimension – both 'large Ps' and 'small ps', being both a resistance to a prevailing educational ethos (large 'P') and being rooted in a philosophy about how learning occurs for children and adults alike – through the personal ownership of ideas and knowledge gained within communities of learners (including adults) rather than through the imposition of knowledge and understanding. In both areas of research I had been striving to both understand and share this personal philosophy but as time moved on, I also began to perceive it as essential to understand and share it as a means of resistance to a prevailing ethos.

The joint play research has been most substantially ongoing from the early 1990s onwards at a time when the impact of educational reform, testing and league tables were working against the sustaining of a playful learning agenda in educational settings (Moss and Penn 1996; Anning 1997; Broadhead 2004). When one of the larger projects began, in the mid-1990s working across five schools in one local authority, the reception class teachers were interviewed (the reception year is for four- and five-year-olds, not yet formally subject to the requirements of a National Curriculum and at this time, just being embraced within curriculum development for the three- to five-age range). The comments of this teacher, Marie, were replicated in similar form in every interview. She is talking about the perceived constraints of an early years' curriculum which is evolving in an era of formality wherein the classroom ethos has become predominantly determined by the teacher. This conflicts with her personal theoretical frameworks of how young children learn and the freedom they need to playfully engage in the learning process:

> I feel I am being pushed in many ways by target setting, of getting the children to a certain standard, ready to access national curriculum at level 1. I feel I am being pushed by the government in one way – you must get children doing this – but feel that little children shouldn't be doing this until they are ready. I do feel that we push children into formal work far too early and I hope that a review of the learning goals will bring more flexibility for reception teachers to interpret the curriculum in a way that suits the needs of children.
>
> (Broadhead 2004: 13)

Marie was asking for the chance to do something that those primary teachers I had researched with in the earlier period had had the opportunity to do, and in the case of the ones I had researched with most substantially in phase two, had accepted the challenge to do, to work out how best to support learning in their classrooms. In sharp contrast to those earlier teachers, Marie had felt she had lost the right to choose the best way of supporting learning. This was an important impetus for her participation in the research. Another impetus was that she felt that her participation in the research gave her a justification for bringing playful learning back into the classroom, something she and others felt they needed a justification for, in the then current climate. This chapter would argue that these are political acts, albeit borne of personal convictions, but nevertheless using the research to find voice in the public sector and seeking for ways to contradict the prevailing broader political-educational climate. These teachers were agreeing to re-introduce activities and resources into their reception classrooms that had been there once (in another era) and which had subsequently disappeared in the moves towards teacher-directed learning that had accompanied testing, in their view. The educational ethos had changed and playful learning opportunities had all but disappeared in many reception classrooms; in seeking to bring them back, we were collaborating in what they saw as an act of resistance to an inappropriate prevailing educational ethos. In inviting them into and working with them during this research, I had drawn them into this act of resistance to a dominant and unsatisfactory ethos and there were clearly ethical implications in this.

From this period of research came one of the most exciting outcomes of the research into playful learning so far. Again, with hindsight and perhaps most clearly as part of the process of writing this I came to understand how this emergence was an integral part of the political resistance to prevailing and unacceptable norms, both on my part and the part of the educators I worked with in this particular project and in subsequent projects once this new concept had emerged.

Using The Social Play Continuum as an observational tool, myself and each of the teachers had independently judged instances of observed play to be in one of four domains – associative, social, highly social and cooperative – the latter representing the most intellectually challenging play. This assisted in triangulating our decisions regarding our independent judgements and served to validate the Continuum as a useful tool. In looking at the instances of play in the Cooperative Domain, we noted the extent to which the play experiences were especially open-ended; the children had access to resources that allowed them to determine their play themes and to change and develop these themes without any input from adults. The play opportunities that most substantially led to play in the Cooperative Domain were in sand, water and large construction. Collectively, at a project meeting, we resolved to build on this and each teacher designed an open-ended role-play area in their classroom using cardboard boxes, wooden clothes horses, fabric and a wide range of other open-ended resource materials. Our joint observations, again using The Social Play Continuum, revealed that 12 out of 12 of the observations of these new, open-ended role play areas, were in the Cooperative Domain and 'going off the scale'. The levels of engagement via reciprocal language, action and inter-action, by the children were revealing new ways of interacting that we had not previously captured. In discussions about the area with her class one day, the teacher said to the children: 'I'm tired of calling it the open-ended role-play area, it's such a mouthful; what shall we call it'? One five-year-old had remarked: 'It's the whatever you want it to be place because it can be whatever you want.' She was conceptualising this space in the classroom as her own; she understood that once she entered it, different rules of engagement applied than for other parts of the classroom or for activities within the wider classroom. She had abstracted its meaning from her own extensive engagements within it; meta-cognitively she understood herself and her peers and the adults to be different in relation to this space. It was perhaps a place of resistance to the prevailing norms she had come to understand as 'school'. Understanding and naming the area and its associated opportunities in this way may have been this five-year-old's first political action. The name and the concept have since received wide coverage in articles and presentations that both I and some of the insider researchers have given.

Ethical and political perspectives on insider–outsider research

Eikeland (2006: 37) is highly critical of conventional research ethics which he refers to as 'condescending ethics' in the way in which they create and sustain the 'othering' of 'subjects', although he also acknowledges that 'we all are "others" to each other' (2006: 45). He deems it unsuitable for action research while also acknowledging the ambiguity of all approaches that deem themselves to be ethical. As stated earlier in this chapter, the research reported here has never been conceived of as 'action research' other than my own attempts, probably most substantially articulated as recently as this chapter and with considerable hindsight, in reflecting on my actions as an insider researcher, as contiguous with the main research foci which, in both elements of my research have been a focus on learning and teaching. Denise, with her astute comment alerted me to the dangers of 'othering' long before I ever heard the term, and in so doing she simultaneously engaged me with an ethics of action and interaction that had not previously been explicit in my thinking nor in my research. She helped me begin the shift from the place and space of 'my research which I am doing with teachers' to one of 'joint research'. In the early days of researching primary classrooms, I am not sure it was ever 'joint research' in the way it subsequently became with the play research. By the time Marie made her comments on the frustrations and restrictions of her work as a reception teacher, I understood the dangers of 'othering' more clearly and introduced the research as reliant on joint and equally weighted endeavour between insider and outsider. I set the research up as a community endeavour where I and the 'insiders' (along with their head teachers) came together on a regular basis to make explicit and discuss our findings and insights. I believe I was better placed by this time to achieve what Eikeland (2006: 45) describes as follows:

By distinguishing the practice and community of enquiry from the concrete practices of how, for example, individual teachers teach in their classrooms, or more generally from how specific groups of workers solve their tasks, and how work is organised, it becomes possible to introduce and establish communities of inquiry while being more relaxed – less 'ideological' – about specific ways of organising and doing things, and let an open inquiry and collaborative experimentation reveal what works and what doesn't. Hence, when the common and uniting element of community is inquiry and learning rather than specific ways of doing anything concrete – pre-determined by tradition, habit, ideology or decree – 'community' can become non-repressive and cultivate diversity'.

Our unifying 'open enquiry' related to the three research questions which framed our study of sociability and cooperation in relation to play and learning in the early years, a study albeit instigated by an outsider but deemed for personal, professional and political reasons to be timely for the practitioners also. We focused on traditional forms of provision (these were the play activities that were re-introduced to classrooms for the research) and used a common tool – The Social Play Continuum – to unify joint research across the classrooms. The questions, the focus and the observation schedule were sufficient to bring coherence to the research without requiring common approaches to classroom organisation and pedagogy. Yet the collective impact of the joint reflections served to identify some substantially common ground in relation to understanding how play supported learning in early years' classrooms and what the pedagogical implications of this might be, as translated into practice in early years' classrooms. In addition, the joint framework resulted in a new and child-friendly political space of freedom and self-expression being introduced into these and subsequently other early years settings. I strongly query we would have arrived in this place and space without collaborative and longitudinal efforts within equally weighted research roles that drew from a combination of inner-outer perspectives.

The perspective on 'resistance' and the links with social movements is one I have immersed in only recently in relation to a publication I co-authored around a cooperative children's centre (Broadhead *et al.* 2008). We drew on the work of Calhoun (1994) and Castells (2000, 2004), who consider social influence, social change and the place of identity for groups attempting to influence change in society. In that book, we relate these concepts to the project identity that gradually emerged for the children's centre upon which the book focused. However, my readings and reflection generated links with my research into teaching and learning and the extent to which it had always sought to reveal the perspectives of the workers at the heart of the process – the educators. Castells' (2004) work in particular relates to social groupings that seek a communal cultural identity and argues that for this to happen a process of social mobilisation is needed. Castells is referring to urban movements here but this resonated with the early years' research where we were connected in our endeavours to return play, in a conceptual and more clearly understood way, to early years' classrooms. Collaboratively (if not quite collectively) we were resisting the policy-political denial of the value of playful learning. In both the primary and the early years' research, we also sought to bring the voice of the child and learner to centre stage within classroom life by trying to understand what the characteristics of such classrooms might be, an ambition that rests within a long tradition of research and publication, its voice largely unheard in policy circles for some time.

It is in better understanding the political aspects of these two research projects, albeit perhaps after a long journey of personal awareness raising that I doubt is yet finished, that I have made the greatest leap forward towards understanding ethical practice and towards the realisation that research can only shape policy and practice if ethical and political awareness go hand in hand in collaborative educational research.

References

Anning, A. (1997) *The First Years at School*. Buckingham: Open University Press.

Armstrong, M. (1980) *Closely Observed Children: The Diary of a Primary Classroom*. Oxford: Oxford University Press.

Baranzangi, N.H. (2006) 'An ethical theory of action research pedagogy', *Action Research*, 4(1): 97–116.

Broadhead, P. (1987) 'A blueprint for the good teacher? The HMI/DES model of good primary practice', *British Journal of Educational Studies*, 35(1): 57–71.

Broadhead, P. (1989) 'Working together towards a better understanding of the primary classroom' in P. Lomax (ed.) *The Management of Change*, BERA Dialogues 1. Clevedon: Multilingual Matters.

Broadhead, P. (1995) 'Changing practice, feeling good: primary professional development explored', *Cambridge Journal of Education*, 25(3): 315–26.

Broadhead, P. (1997) 'Promoting sociability and co-operation in nursery settings', *British Educational Research Journal*, 23(4): 513–1.

Broadhead, P. (2001) 'Investigating sociability and cooperation in four- and five-year-olds in reception class settings', *International Journal of Early Years Education*, 9(1): 23–35.

Broadhead, P. (2004) *Early Years Play and Learning: Developing Social Skills and Cooperation in Young Children*. London: Routledge-Falmer Education.

Broadhead, P. (2006) 'Developing an understanding of young children's learning through play: the place of observation, interaction and reflection', *British Educational Research Journal*, 32(2): 191–207.

Broadhead, P., Meleady, C. and Delgado, M.A. (2008) *Children, Families and Communities: Creating and Sustaining Integrated Services*. Berkshire: Open University Press.

Brown, S. and McIntyre, D. (1993) *Making Sense of Teaching*. Berkshire: Open University Press.

Calderhead J. (ed.) (1987) *Exploring Teachers' Thinking*. London: Cassell Educational.

Calhoun, C.I. (1994) 'Social theory and the politics of identity', in C.I. Calhoun (ed.) *Social Theory and the Politics of Identity*. Oxford: Blackwell Publishing.

Castells, M. (2000) *The Rise of the Network Society*, 2nd edn. Malden: Blackwell Publishing.

Castells, M. (2004) *The Power of identity*, 2nd edn. Malden: Blackwell Publishing.

Eikeland, O. (2006) 'Condescending ethics and action research: extended review article', *Action Research*, 4(1): 37–47.

Goodson, I.F. (1991) 'Sponsoring the teacher's voice: teachers' lives and teacher development', *Cambridge Journal of Education*, 21: 35–45.

Humphrey, C. (2007) 'Insider–outsider: activating the hyphen', *Action Research*, 5(1): 11–26.

McNamara, D. (1980) 'The outsider's arrogance: the failure of outside observers to understand classroom events', *British Educational Research Journal*, 6(2): 113–25.

Moss, P. and Penn, H. (1996) *Transforming Nursery Education*. London: Paul Chapman Publishing.

Nias, J. (1989) *Primary Teachers Talking*. London: Routledge.

Rowland, S. (1984) *The Enquiring Classroom*. Lewes: Falmer Press.

Schon, D. (1983) *The Reflective Practitioner*. London: Temple-Smith Ltd.

Young, I.M. (1990) *Justice and the Politics of Difference*. Princeton, NJ: Princeton University Press.

Zeichner, K. Tabachnik, B. and Densmore, K. (1987) 'Individual, institutional and cultural influences on the development of teachers' craft knowledge', in J. Calderhead (ed.) *Exploring Teachers' Thinking*. London: Cassell Educational.

Chapter 5

Learning across boundaries

Developing trans-professional understanding through practitioner inquiry

Rob Hulme and David Cracknell

Introduction

The chapter explores the value of practitioner inquiry[1] in the development of common language and shared understandings for a group of mid-career professionals from a variety of public service backgrounds, brought together in order to formulate and disseminate responses to the *Every Child Matters* (ECM) (2003) agenda for integrating services for children. It draws upon data gathered from multi-professional action learning groups and focus groups within the *Learn Together Partnership*, a collaboration between a university in the northwest of England and six local authorities (LAs) in the region. This chapter complements others by widening the lens from teacher education to the wider workforce in children's services and explores the current English agenda for multi-agency working. The work presented here resonates with the book's international themes since the challenge of workforce 'integration' is an agenda with global reach.

The most significant challenge presented by ECM is its requirement for inter-agency and multi-professional working. Practitioners are required to overcome professional boundaries in moving towards the goal of a more 'holistic' and ultimately, 'trans-professional' knowledge. There has been much recent work on the value of 'action research' or 'practitioner inquiry' in the promotion of collegial practices within areas of professional practice, (Cochran-Smith and Lytle 1993, 2001; Mason *et al.* 2002; Campbell *et al.* 2004, 2005), although there has been little attention to work across professional boundaries (Forbes 2006). There is evidence of tentative and limited acknowledgement within recent policy texts of the value of action research in 'building leadership capacity' among multi-professional team leaders (DCSF 2008: 16), yet nothing on how professionals might participate in inquiry to learn how to deal with the considerable agenda challenges to professional identities and organisational cultures.

The work presented here draws on theories of 'third space' and 'hybridity' in arguing that the realistic achievement of such an integrated knowledge requires the creation of 'undecided' or 'third' spaces, in which professionals from a variety of backgrounds can engage in critical reflection and from which dialogues about new ways of working can develop. It concludes that collaborative multi-professional practitioner inquiry offers a way forward in the development of the shared language and common understandings from which a 'trans-professional knowledge base' might grow. Our conclusions here reinforce those of McLaughlin *et al*. (2006) that practitioner research is instrumental in moving beyond established 'communities of practice' and towards the development of 'professional learning communities' A simple framework for reflection on 'action' around three key themes: reflections on one's own practice, reflection on the practice of others and reflection on policy is offered.

Policy context: towards 'trans-professionalism'

This is written in the context of an increasing international trend to integrate the provision of services for children and young people. This trajectory has its origins in the International Convention on the Rights of the Child (1989), and other international policy initiatives including 'Full Service Schooling', which translated into the English context as 'Extended Services' (Dryfoos 1994; Kronick 2002). It has influenced English policy response to this generic agenda emerging through ECM (2003).

The integration of services for young people in education, social work, health and the criminal justice system, with its attendant requirement for closer and more systematic inter-agency working and the development of a more holistic 'trans-professional' knowledge base, offers challenges for those seeking to understand the nature of professional learning across boundaries. Relating policy to practice in this area is problematic at each level – local, national and trans-national/global. The reform agenda encourages the integration of education, social work, health, and to some extent other service provision, with associated development of multi-professional and trans-professional collaboration.

Our study of the experience of practitioners working in multi-professional settings connected to ECM suggests that in assessing the challenges presented by extended services or integrated service provision, we should attempt to:

(a) assess the extent to which the professional knowledge of practitioners involved in the delivery of integrated children's services has influenced the objectives and manifestations of local policy; and

(b) to what extent their differing understandings of the issues involved in multi-professional working have been mediated through competing cultures, structures and policy directions in each local context.

At present, inter- or trans-professional work between professionals of this kind is embryonic. Attempts to encourage inter-agency working through the work of Children's Centres and *Sure Start* programmes have demonstrated that there is a need to overcome professional and disciplinary boundaries in arriving at a notion of an 'expanded professionalism'. Despite the prominence of this agenda in public policy across the services nationally and globally, it is riddled with definitional uncertainty and an absence of a conception of a meaningful notion of a 'holistic' trans-professional knowledge base.

Professionals working within integrated contexts now relate to an increasing number of partners which raises significant issues for professional learning and practice (Coleman 2006). The existence of multiple identities in complex teams presents a number of challenges: the generation of shared understandings and a shared language across the different knowledge bases informing pro-fessional practice (for example, medical, social, psychological and educational) and the diverse settings, communities and cultures. This new terrain requires new forms of collaborative working and a commitment to the co-construction of knowledge. One of the theoretical challenges is to consider how relationships between practitioners in Early Years and Extended Services and school settings are being remodelled in pursuit of 'joined up' service provision.

Our work suggests that while there are examples of appropriate new forms of multi-professional collaboration, we are a long way from developing a meaningful or systematic notion of trans-professional knowledge for integrated service provision. Policy-makers are clear about the goals of policy to 'join up' service provision – this is made very clear in the legislative framework and policy pronouncements but far less in evidence are the necessary strategies to construct new forms of professional learning. More democratic and 'devolved' notions of social pedagogy, developed in Northern Europe (Moss 2007) have not been referenced in the formulation of policy in the UK, where the political project of coordinating services has been centrally driven policy but not divorced from notions of individual programme 'responsibilisation'. Where there has been some progress among practitioners, as may have been the case in Scotland (Nixon *et al.* 2002; Christie and Menmuir 2005; Forbes 2006), or in other settings in England (Anning *et al.* 2006), it has developed where practitioners have been provided with the space in the context of practice to negotiate their own meanings with collaborative partners and to 'own' these emergent forms of 'trans-professional' knowledge.

The challenge for practitioners in adapting and moving into more integrated processes and practices for children's services, from within their separate originating professional backgrounds, is complex and multi-faceted (Nixon *et al.* 2002: 409). They need to come to terms individually and collectively with what might be described as the geology (historically grounded cultures of participating professionals) and the ecology (continuous emergent change in policy and organisational structures) of complex systems around children, young people and families (Cracknell 2007). The use of practitioner inquiry in professional development for inter- and multi-agency working is helpful in responding to the tensions and challenges arising from policy on integrated service provision (Campbell and Groundwater-Smith 2007; Cracknell and

Scanlon 2008; Hulme 2008). In particular, when practitioner inquiry is open and critical it can be very effective in stimulating inter-professional dialogue, opening up spaces and offering opportunities for professionals to theorise their own action and to relate this to the practice of others.

Theoretical context: practitioner inquiry in third spaces

Our approach was founded on an attempt to make a connection between the dislocated experiences of all those within the partnership, including our-selves. We found 'Third Space' theory and 'hybridity theory' (Bhabha 1994; Aoki 1999) to be useful in setting the context. The transgressive nature of the underpinning concepts, clearly resonated with our central purpose of exploring the development of common language and shared understanding. It offered a theoretical basis for exploring professional cultural exchange and the develop-ment of trans-professional knowledge.

We set out to explore the idea of practitioner inquiry through ALS and small-scale practice – based inquiry as 'Third Spaces' that play a significant role in the process of reflection and change. We came to see these structured experiences as 'sites' where practitioners could think and develop, individually and collectively, and where the process of change could be nurtured, drawing on but not constrained and dominated by, the influence of current practice or the requirements of policy to initiate 'solutions' to 'problems'. Bhabha[2] develops a notion of inter-disciplinarity through the 'liminal' or 'interstitial' category that occupies a space 'between' competing cultural traditions and critical methodologies, an 'innovative site of collaboration, and contestation' where 'border discourse' takes place (Mitchell 1995: 82; Perloff 1998). Bhabha goes on to develop a 'hybridity' paradigm, arguing that this third space is a 'hybrid' site that witnesses the production, rather than just the reflection of cultural meaning Bhabha (1994: 1):

> It is that Third Space, though unrepresentable in itself which constitutes the discursive condition of enunciation that ensure that the meaning and symbols of culture have no primordial unity or fixity; that even the same signs can be appropriated, translated, re-historicized and read anew.
>
> (Bhabha 1994: 37)

Bhabha argues that 'The time of liberation is . . . a time of cultural uncertainty' (ibid.: 35), when everything is called into question. It forms part of his project to develop a theory of the 'translation' of social difference in which people are 'free to negotiate and translate their cultural identities' (ibid.: 38) without being bound in antagonistic binarisms. This can be a very uncomfortable process. Bhaba recognises that this notion of 'liberation' is arrived at only after social and individual identities have been partially surrendered or altered.

The notion of 'hybridity' then, examines the condition of being 'in-between' several different sources of knowledge. Within this construct, discourse can be both productive and constraining in terms of social and cultural practice and the development of identity. Hybridity applies to the integration of competing knowledge and discourses; to the reading and writing of texts and to individual and social spaces, contexts and relationships. However, it does not always imply the successful production of 'new' knowledge or the production of harmonious, uncontested relationships.

Third Space theory presented three applications for our work:

(a) as a way of *building bridges* between professional knowledge and discourses;
(b) as a *navigational space*, a way of moving across and functioning within differentdiscourse communities; and
(c) as a *conversational space* where cultural, social, and epistemological change takes place as competing knowledge and discourses are drawn together (Moje 2004: 43–44).

This work reinforces our approach to practitioner inquiry in emphasising the importance of space for dialogue between participants that is safe, secure and supportive, space that 'stands outside' the formal areas of practice.

The Learn Together Partnership

Methods of inquiry

Our work here draws on evidence from an action research project focused on developing the notions of 'trans-professional' working referred to above, through the *Learn Together Partnership*. The focus for this work is a partnership established between the university and six LAs and their partner agencies.

The project brings together practitioners and researchers in the broad fields of education, health, social care and other services – incorporating teachers, social workers, health service staff and those from within the criminal justice system. The research design arises from developmental work to establish networks of professional learning and across children's and community services. Practitioner inquiry was employed in three distinct ways to encourage inter- and intra-professional dialogue and debate. The purpose was to provide a 'third' space in which to stimulate a new kind of 'hybrid' professional learning founded on the development of shared understandings and a shared language across the different professional and organisational knowledge bases that inform practice and the diverse settings, communities and cultures. To this end, our methodological position was premised on the assumption that the significant challenges of multi-professional and inter-agency working are best met through a participative and inclusive deliberative process.

The primary source of data presented below was a series of focus groups organised for groups of professionals who have various responsibility levels for leading the development of multi-professional or interagency working. Participants explored and articulated ways in which the small-scale research projects they had been involved in had helped to change their approach to working with other professionals by reflecting upon their own practice. They were asked to consider what the major sticking points had been and to identify new ways of working which enabled collaborative work across boundaries.

Data on practitioners' perspectives was also collected through workshops where professionals from differing backgrounds were presented with common case study scenarios of children, young people and families and during which were invited to develop a group identity and response. Further data came from reflective reports on extended shadowing visits to professionals from contrasting backgrounds and structured workshop exchanges in which practitioners were able to share stories in a safe and supportive, reflective and stretching environment.

ALS provided a source of evidence and energy for our project. 'Action Learning' as an application of action research was appropriate for our purposes since in each application, action informs reflection and is informed by it (Dick 1997). Within this approach, learning and research are forms of understanding and in both change results. The participants in this research took part in a series of ALS sessions, which provided structured and facilitated opportunities to engage with problems involving working in multi-professional settings. Exchanges within the sessions were confidential and later group participants were asked to reflect. A number of participants highlighted the significance of this regular, structured opportunity for endorsing the principle of reflective inquiry for developing dialogues.

The data gathered from these three sources was analysed using thematic network analysis (Attride-Stirling 2001).[3] The global theme emerging from the reported views of the focus group participants was that engagement with collaborative practitioner inquiry opened up the spaces that facilitated new 'trans-professional' dialogues. We broke this theme down into three basic themes of: reflections on one's own practice, reflection on the practice of others and reflection on policy. Our analysis is divided into two parts. The first outlines the challenges involved in developing trans-professional understandings and the second studies responses to this challenge of hybrid/new ways of working. The three themes are identified within both parts A and B.

A. Challenges in developing shared language and common understandings: the sticking points

Reflection on individual action

The quest for shared understanding within situated contexts of practice has proved to be the greatest challenge for ECM, evoking clear tensions between competing conceptions of the professional knowledge base(s) informing practice in children's services. The literature outlines a significant issue with 'silo' thinking or 'practitioner resistance' on the part of professionals across the range. Our focus group participants perceived physical (place) and psychological (professional culture) separateness or distance as significant obstacles.

> You might feel safe when you go back to your own office but where does that safe zone go when you start sitting in a room together?
>
> (Focus group participant)

It may be that the major cultural issue here is not professional but organisational. Participants in our focus groups commented on how difficult it was for individual professionals to 'think outside the box', particularly where there was no institutional memory for integrated working. It is the act of common or collaborative reflection that provides the 'third space' in which to contextualize individual action and leads to a broader cross and cultural understanding:

> In India we had to be 'trans-professional' for generations, it's the only way we've been able to provide services! We need to learn here how people operate together in situations where there is nothing.
>
> (Workshop participant)

This theme reinforces work conducted in the United States by Hal Lawson, which suggested that initiatives designed to create collaborative interagency working in the United States were seen to work best when professionals were able to 'theorise their own action' in relation to other professionals (Lawson 2004; Lawson *et al.* 2008).

Reflection on the practice of others

There is evidence of an awareness that existing organisational and professional identities and cultures act as a countervailing force to integration. This is also reflected in sensitivities about differences of organisational structure, management, pay and conditions and comparative status:

> I think we all have a real struggle to achieve (integrated working) if hand on heart, I think if we were all asked to honestly say do you really see that child as a child or are you still thinking as a leader as a manager that that child is a client, patient or pupil.
>
> (Focus group participant)

In this latter sense, professional resistance to integration may be conceived as a form of 'principled infidelity'. There are, though, more conventional obstacles:

> Hierarchies get in the way . . . status has an incredible influence, (on multi-professional working), as some groups have more status than others.
>
> (Focus group participant)

> I think there is also a fear around some professional boundaries that they may be diluted if they share their skills with those of a lesser professional status.
>
> (Focus group participant)

Identity here is strongly associated with the 'value base' of individual professions:

> For me, some of it is to do with deep seated value systems that there are in service areas and one of the barriers is having a unified value system that is based centrally on the service user.
>
> (Focus group participant)

The tension between the requirements of policy for inter-professional dialogue and the enduring strength of unilateral cultures within multiple professional communities was regarded as the greatest sticking point.

Reflection on policy

Despite strong and broad-based political commitment to ECM, its requirement for inter-professional working runs counter to the evidence-based 'policy epidemic' that has impacted across the public services. There is a tension between the performative and managerial aspects of insular service-based policy regimes and the need to open up new dialogues:

> You have professionals in that their integrity and reputation as part of their job as a professional is to get the best academically out of the child, their professionalism is the most important thing to that individual and that's clearly a barrier to stopping everyone getting together and seeing things in the same light.
>
> (Focus group participant)

> At the end of the day we have got to deliver results and we don't do that by talking to other professionals.
>
> (High school teacher workshop participant)

It is difficult to 'manage' integration and probably impossible to steer the shared understanding required for trans-professional working through tightly implemented central policy objectives. There is an awareness of this among our multi-professional leaders:

One of the problems we have is that we have a lot of agencies in an area that are all falling over each other and everybody has to own whatever they do, they all have steering groups, etc., so if you try to do something integrated then it is always owned by somebody and that then immediately excludes somebody else.

(Focus group participant)

Providing sufficient time and space to shift, or allow adaptation of, the perceptions of leaders is an important feature of developing integrated and trans-professional approaches:

For some of the leaders it will be a generational change and if they don't give 'Every Child Matters' time to embed, they will put a sticking plaster over it and change it to something else but it is generational.

(Focus group participant)

B. Responses through practitioner inquiry

Reflection on individual action

A strong theme to emerge, when participants were asked what they have done differently as a result of their inquiry, is that embryonic trans-professional understanding develops through sustained and open contacts:

I think this has made us start with ourselves and our own value systems, it has made us challenge our own values and our own ways of working and particularly in respect to our leadership styles and how we support and encourage the people we work with and the teams we support.

(Focus group participant)

This reinforced our guiding principle on the programme that research as an elective activity offers the potential to open up new spaces for practitioners to assert their agency.

Reflection on the practice of others

Commonality of purpose and rapid development of common language, shared understanding and agreement on outcomes did emerge. This, of course, may reflect the particularity of the nature of events intended to stimulate reflection on shared purpose but it did reveal that space was provided to reflect outside of the 'managed' integration evident in the participants' workplaces:

The action learning stuff, where people have talked about their pressures and I think, god, I didn't even think that that would be an issue for somebody . . . you just see the variety and complexity of other issues for people here, it keeps you in touch with the real world, it keeps you in touch with some of the outside world instead of being insular . . . I think that has been valuable.

(Focus group participant)

There was evidence throughout our discussion of bridge-building potential. Engagement with research opened up new spaces for inter-professional 'conversations':

I think what it has helped me to do, it has given me somewhere to hang the confusion and the chaos at times so being part of the process but having somewhere to go to say that's ok, that's allowed, you should be feeling like that in the job that we are all trying to do, and I think that has been helping, but yeah the thinking and some more of the theoretical knowledge to underpin that.

(Focus group participant)

The 'problems' of organisational culture and 'resistance' may be overstated in some of the literature on interagency working. However, there are very considerable differences in the organisational cultures of social work departments, the National Health Service and schools. Participants in our project were aware of positive potential in this collaborative form of professional learning:

The collective inquiry we all invest in each other's solutions [through action learning sets (ALS)] has made us develop a greater respect for each other and have a greater understanding for each other's area of expertise because we have supported each other.

(Focus group participant)

There was some evidence of a new conception of integrated professional learning:

You have an understanding of the value that other people bring . . . having the understanding that if you work with other professionals to achieve something for a community, not just the individual then you will achieve your professional goals.

(Focus group participant)

Events such as this are great because we've all got together for the same purpose outside our Departments, there's no pressure on us from management to deliver or anything.

(Welfare Officer workshop participant)

Reflection on policy

It is possible to interpret some of our participants' responses as embryonic notions of 'hybridity'. Professional silos had been overcome and evidence emerged of the recognition of difference along with embryonic acknowledgement of the common purposes of practice, and even the collective power of common moral purposes:

> It has allowed us to take time out and start to centralise on the child and family, rather than being quite driven in our own agendas.
>
> (Focus group participant)

The application of theory and understating of the role of individual and collective action leads to the development of an understanding of how to manage, mediate or adapt policy in the workplace context:

> There is an African saying that 'it takes a village to raise a child' and its like the idea that the child is the focal point and you have the village or professionals each adding their own bit so they are all contributing then to the development of that child, focusing on the child instead of focusing on professional performance.
>
> (Focus group participant)

This 'adaptation' of policy objectives can involve the creative application of theoretical perspectives developed through practitioner inquiry:

> The theory has been great, there are occasions where I have been at meetings or talking with other agencies and you quote a bit (of it) and you get things done because people embrace it, you can use it as a useful tool.
>
> (Focus group participant)

> There are so many things that you have to compartmentalise or pull away before you can see that, and coming back to the reflective aspect of it, it allows you to do that, so its not just a case number; its ok, what does this child need, what professionals have we got that can give the appropriate support at the appropriate time.
>
> (Focus group participant)

That agency or sense of empowerment can be in the interpretation of the leadership role in developing interagency working:

> I think in terms of leadership, I think what people are looking at in the chaos of the multi-agency bit is someone to give it some direction so if you can bring some clarity, that is leadership in itself, it's just replenishing what you know and bringing it into that context.
>
> (Focus group participant)

It is possible to interpret this as a reflection of the 'legitimation' of action research and collaborative work for fulfilling the requirements of policy for interagency working. Practitioners are aware that despite the current consensus about the efficacy of this work, it is ultimately a political project and the partial approval of action research for leadership may be the most expedient way to temporarily bridge the gap between professional communities without stepping too far outside the individually performative and managerialist workplace cultures.

Conclusions: practitioner inquiry for 'trans-professional' learning?

The challenges of the promotion of integrated service delivery are considerable. ECM runs counter to the dominant trajectories of policy which provide a unilateral focus on 'performativity' and evidence of good practice within professional environments across the public sector. However, our evidence suggests that it is possible to develop more person-centred, integrated approaches if appropriate environments are created for professionals to participate in critical reflection.

Professionals can develop their own 'trans-professional' capacity through practitioner inquiry and action research but much more reflexive professional development is needed. One way of achieving this is through engaging with practitioners from different professional and organisational backgrounds in 'third spaces' or contexts conducive to practice-focused learning.

It is clear that in the English context, we are a long way from this position. However, there is evidence that the national policy context is changing. For the first time there is reference to 'action research' within the *National Professional Development Framework for Leaders and Managers of Children's Services* (DCSF 2008). This opens up the possibility for a more reflexive and critical approach to professional learning. However, as we note above, the potential for empowerment of professionals implicit in this development can be overstated. In this context, action research is not value-free. It is tied to the discourses of management often associated with leadership and their familiar emphasis on effectiveness, accountability and 'delivery'.

This latter point highlights the political nature of 'multi' professional leadership across the public services. Practitioners are required to work through the difficulties involved in overarching professional and organisational cultures. This process involves, for many, some uncomfortable compromises and the 'surrendering' of aspects of identity. At present, rising to the challenge of inter- or multi-professional work does not necessarily produce a more empowering sense of professionalism. The government's stated longer-term goal of achieving a 'trans'-professional knowledge for children's services is still beyond reach. European concepts of social pedagogy which would be helpful, run counter to the dominant trajectories of 'evidence-informed' policy in education and social welfare which effectively narrow spaces for professional creativity. Here lies the rub: for practitioners to open up the conversations and dialogues through engagement with action research which our participants found most rewarding, they must be provided with the spaces to define their own questions about their practice and others. This is challenging within individual professional environments, particularly schools. We can point to the success of our multi-professional ALS and focus groups but the particularity of these events must be acknowledged. Whether this kind of collaborative work can be embedded in the day-to-day reality of practice in multi-professional settings remains to be seen.

Notes

1   Following Cochran-Smith and Lytle, we have made use of 'practitioner inquiry' as a 'conceptual and linguistic umbrella' (Cochran-Smith and Lytle cited in Campbell and Groundwater-Smith 2007: 25) to refer to a variety of professional learning activities undertaken within the Learn Together Partnership. In the case of our multi-professional groups, it refers to inquiry-based learning undertaken by professionals from a variety of backgrounds, supported by ourselves and other university colleagues in a variety of workplaces, within the ALS, leadership focus groups and a Higher Education Funding Council for England (HEFCE) Escalate funded workshop.
2   We are grateful to Allan Owens of the University of Chester for his perspective on Bhabha.
3   We are grateful to Vanessa Watt for her transcription of the focus groups and her thoughts on qualitative data analysis.

References

Anning A., Cottrell, D., Frost, N., Green, J. and Robinson, M. (2006) *Developing Multi-professional Teamwork for Integrated Children's Services: Research, Policy and Practice*. Maidenhead: Open University Press.

Aoki, T. (1999) 'In the midst of doubled imaginaries: the Pacific Community as diversity and as difference', *Interchange*, 30(1): 27–38.

Attride-Stirling, J. (2001) 'Thematic networks: an analytic framework for qualitative research', *Qualitative Research*, 1(3): 385–404.

Bhabha, H. (1994) *The Location of Culture*. London and New York: Routledge.

Campbell, A. and Groundwater-Smith, S. (2007) *An Ethical Approach to Practitioner Research*. Oxford: Routledge.

Campbell, A. and Keating, I. (2005, 14–17 September 2005) *Shotgun Weddings, Arranged Marriages or Love Matches? An Investigation of Networked Learning Communities and Higher Education Partnerships in England*. Paper presented at the BERA annual conference, University of Glamorgan.

Campbell, A., McNamara, O. and Gilroy, P. (2004) *Practitioner Research and Professional Development*. London: Paul Chapman.

Christie, D. and Menmuir, J. (2005) 'Supporting interprofessional collaboration in Scotland through a common standards framework', *Policy Futures in Education*, 3(1): 62–74.

Convention on the Rights of the Child (1989) *United Nations. Treaty Series*, 1577: 3. (Available at www2.ohchr.org/english/law/crc.htm.)

Cochran-Smith, M. and Lytle, S.L. (1993) *Inside Out: Teacher Research and Knowledge*. New York: Teachers College.

Cochran-Smith, M. and Lytle, S.L. (2001) 'Beyond certainty: taking an inquiry stance on practice', in A. Lieberman and L. Miller (eds) *Teachers Caught in the Action: Professional Development that Matters*, pp. 45–60. New York: Teachers College Press.

Coleman, A. (2006) *Collaborative Leadership in Extended Schools: Leading in a Multi- Agency Environment*. Nottingham: NCSL.

Cracknell, D. (2007) 'Layered and linked learning', *Professional Development Today*, 10(1): 11–17.

Cracknell, D. and Scanlon, T. (2008) *Action Learning – Sustaining the Learning and Securing the Action*. Conference Paper presented to International Action Learning Conference, 'Practices, Problems and Prospects'. Henley Management College, 17–19 March 2008.

Department for Children, Schools and Families (2008) *Leading and Managing Children's Services in England: A National Professional Development Framework*. London: DCSF. (Available at www.teachernet.gov.uk/publications.)

Department for Education and Skills (2003) *Every Child Matters*. London: Stationery Office.

Dick, B. (1997) *Action Learning and Action Research. Action Research and Evaluation On-Line*. (Available at www.scu.edu.au/schools/gcm/ar/arp/actlearn.htm).

Dryfoos, J. (1994) *Full-Service Schools. A Revolution in Health and Social Services for Children, Youth and Families*. San Francisco: Jossey-Bass.

Forbes, J. (2006) 'Types of social capital: tools to explore service integration?', *International Journal of Inclusive Education*, 1–16.

Hulme, R. (2008) *Towards 'Trans-professionalism?' Inter-agency Working in the Provision of Children's Services in Policy and Practice in England*. Paper presented to the American Education Research Association Annual Conference, New York, 28 March 2008.

Kronick, R.F. (2002) *Full Service Schools: A Place for Our Children and Families to Learn and be Healthy*, Springfield, IL: C. C. Thomas.

Lawson, H. (2004) 'The logic of collaboration in education and the human services', *The Journal of Inter-professional Care*, 18: 225–37.

Lawson, H., Anderson-Butcher, D., Cahoon-Byrnes, E. and Lawson, M. (2008) *Getting Inside the Black Box of a Complex, Collaborative Initiative by Eliciting Staff Members' Theories of Action*, paper presented to the Annual Meeting of the American Education Research Association Conference, 9–11 March 2008, New York.

Mason, T., Williams, R. and Vivian-Byrne, S. (2002) 'Multi-disciplinary working in a forensic mental health setting', *Journal of Psychiatric and Mental Health Nursing*, 9: 563–72.

McLaughlin, C., Black-Hawkins, K., Brindley, S., McIntyre, D. and Tabor, K. (2006) *Researching Schools: Stories from a Schools-University Partnership for Educational Research*. London: Routledge.

Mitchell, W.J.T. (1995) *'Translator translated'*, interview with cultural theorist Homi Bhabha, *Artforum*, 3(7): 80–4. (Available at http://prelectur.stanford.edu/lecturers/bhabha/interview.html.)

Moje, E.B., McIntosh-Giechanowski, K., Kramer, K., Ellis, L., Carrillo, R. and Collazo, T. (2004) 'Working toward third space in content area literacy: an examination of every day funds of knowledge and discourse', *Reading Research Quarterly*, 39(1): 38–70.

Moss, P. (2007) *What is Education? Social Pedagogy as an Approach to Integrating Education and Social Care*. Paper presented to Society of Education Studies Conference, Social Pedagogy: Integrating Care and Education for the Children's Workforce, 27 November 2007. The Institute of Education, University of London.

Nixon, J., Walker, M. and Baron, S. (2002) 'The cultural mediation of state policy: the democratic potential of new community schooling in Scotland', *Journal of Education Policy*, 17(4): 407–21.

Perloff, M. (1998) 'Cultural liminality/aesthetic closure? The "interstitial perspective" of Homi Bhabha' in H.K. Bhabha (1994) *The Location of Culture*, pp. 139–70. London and New York: Routledge. (Available at http://wings.buffalo.edu/epc/authors/perloff/bhabha.html.)

Chapter 6

Postgraduate programmes as platforms

Coming together and doing research for a common moral purpose

Petra Ponte

Introduction

In discussions about the quality of teacher education over the last twenty years, authors seem to have agreed about one thing, namely that the traditional transfer model is inadequate, because academic knowledge cannot simply be transferred in the expectation that teachers can apply this knowledge. Empirical research shows that teachers rarely use knowledge acquired in their teacher education (Beijaard and Verloop 1996; Hawley and Valli 1999; Gore and Gitlin 2004). However, this gap is not the only point of criticism. In line with Goodlad (1994), the critique can be summarised under three themes.

First, transfer-type programmes may provide students with a fragmented image of the profession, due to the fact that the connection to questions of daily practice is insufficient or absent, and the 'status quo' is taken as a starting-point (Elliott 1993; Darling-Hammond and Bransford 2005). As an alternative, Goodlad (1994: 117) proposed relating teacher education programmes to centres of inquiry:

> where the art and science of teaching are brought to bear on the education of educators and where the whole is the subject of continuous inquiry. In doing so, they demonstrate to their students the very processes of reflective renewal desired in individual teachers and schools.

The second criticism is that teacher education reform has rarely connected to school reform arguably necessary, because research shows that novice teachers quickly adapt what they do to what they see in their school practice (Tickle 2001; Cochran-Smith and Fries 2002). According to Goodlad (1994: 18):

> their education 'often prepares them to view and accept the regularities of schools as givens' and 'it is unrealistic to expect teachers to create schools for inquiry when the settings in which they are prepared are rarely reflective, introspective or self critical'.

This problem can be solved by a continuous process of educational renewal in which colleges and universities, the traditional producers of teachers, join schools, the recipients in an equal reciprocal partnership (Le Cornu and Ewing 2008).

The third criticism refers to the absence of any moral grounding of teacher education (Ax and Ponte 2008). Related to this, Goodlad (1994: 117) asserted that education is wrongly perceived by many as vocational and technical, rather than fundamentally intellectual, driven by the moral responsibility to contribute to a just and democratic education. 'A moral-intellectual perception of teacher education requires a mission and a setting which provides a context for inquiry.'

I propose to elaborate on some issues concerning a 'context for inquiry', starting with Smith's idea of teacher education programmes as platforms (Smith 2000). I will link this up with the Dutch interpretation of the word 'platform': a group of people (in this case, teacher educators and students) coming together for a common social or moral purpose (that is, for the benefit of a democratic and just education). An explicit link will be made to the moral claims made in action research that it contributes in a similar way.

Smith developed his platform idea for ITE, while this chapter focuses on continuing professional learning through accredited programmes of study at postgraduate level. Accordingly, I will discuss the difference between the context of prospective teachers and that of other experienced teachers before exploring the following questions:

- How can 'platform' be understood?
- How can students learn on the platform?
- Who decides what the students will learn on the platform?
- How is the learning to be organised on the platform?
- What are the necessary conditions for the platform?

Different contexts of prospective and experienced teachers

Smith's focus on initial education reflects the main concentration in teacher education reform discussions on teacher preparation and induction. There has been little discussion of postgraduate programmes for experienced teachers. Nevertheless, there seems to be agreement about the need for research-led approaches in both graduate and postgraduate programmes. Professional development of teachers in such programmes is accomplished by linking students' knowledge and experiences to academic knowledge and research. If a research-led attitude on the part of students is considered essential, the programmes themselves should also be research-led. One also frequently hears a plea for inquiry-based strategies such as action research, which supposedly contribute to just and democratic education, and to the collaboration of educational institutions and schools on an equal basis to realise these aspirations (Day and Sachs 2004; Groundwater-Smith 2007). Obviously, there are important differences between the context of student teachers, and that of experienced teachers (Ax *et al*. 2008).

One crucial difference is postgraduate students who study their own practice, for which they are fully responsible. They are the most important link between the teacher education programme and the educational field, while in ITE programmes the link is established through collaboration for teaching placements and through professional development schools. Postgraduate students are the 'field'. Experienced teachers participate in broader contexts such as trade unions, professional associations and diverse forms of collaboration. Therefore, the 'field' is not limited to schools, and other stakeholders are also part of it. Consequently, experienced teachers will raise a more varied range of questions, problems and moral dilemmas stemming from complex contexts and will be based on the urge to act for the sake of the children, making decisions which might have far-reaching moral consequences, even more so than in initial teacher education (Ax and Ponte 2008).

Post-initial programmes face the challenge of creating a setting which facilitates a flexible response to educational developments while enabling these developments to be related to underlying philosophical debates. Such flexibility is difficult to create. Partly this seems caused by the institutional context of semesters, modules, schedules and classes. These apparently neutral terms are often used in education casually without realising how such language is saturated with traditional notions. People often fail to realise how much thinking 'outside the box' can be stimulated, if these terms are discarded.

How can platform be understood?

A challenging solution might be offered by the term used by Smith (2000). He argued that a new infrastructure, a new model for teacher education, would be necessary, which he referred to as 'the platform of teacher education'. Such a platform should be a flexible, task-oriented infrastructure, where design and delivery of the programmes are integrated, and negotiated before and during the programme by all participants free of bureaucratic rules, university systems, strangleholds of semesters and years. It should be one that is the best for the students, reacting creatively to what has to be done, where knowledge is constantly refreshed, and where teacher education services are placed at the point of delivery.

The Longman Dictionary defines the term platform in its literal English sense as:

> a place where people can express their views publicly; a raised flat surface built along the side of the track at a railway station for travellers getting on or off the train, and a raised floor or stage for speakers, performers, etc.

Of course, Smith (2000) was not using the term literally but in a figurative sense. Therefore, I interpret his use of platform as a consistent body of goals, content, methods and organisational measures, which create a meeting place, where the worlds of researchers, teachers, teacher education staff and others can learn from each other and engage in debate. The central idea is that the participants consult each other to decide what they will learn and how. Consultation takes place at the start of the progamme and during the programme, which is characterised, according to Smith (2000: 21), by the integration of 'design and delivery of programmes: the platform is in a sense the programme' (Davis and Mayer 1998). Smith's off-centre thinking and his atypical language challenged me to explore important aspects of an educational setting in the development of a research-led approach in postgraduate programmes as platforms.

At first sight, the English term 'platform' as used by Smith seems to correspond with its widespread usage in the Netherlands for a group of people who define their aims and methods together on the job. However, in the Dutch meaning of the word, a platform is less neutral. It is a group who come together for a common, moral purpose, usually inspired by a feeling of having to stand up for particular interests. They usually do that by exchanging experiences and combining political or other forces to reach a shared moral goal.

A quick surf on the internet brought up numerous examples, such as: the European Platform for Dutch Education, to strengthen the European dimension in education; the Light Pollution Platform, to preserve the darkness as an aspect of the quality of the environment in which we live; and the Platform for Work, Health and Insurance, to collate and publicise information in these areas to help the unemployed. The founders of such platforms usually get involved on the basis of having equal status and from that position of equality they draw up or support shared goals and activities. They have a mission, exchange experiences and act together to gather factual information. They create a 'narrative' together, that often cannot be judged first in terms of whether it is right or wrong but mainly in terms of a shared sense of justice. The European Platform assumes that the European dimension in education is a worthwhile goal; the Light Pollution Platform takes the view that people have a right to darkness, and the third Platform aims to implement the ideal of giving people access to information about our social security system.

If we now draw a parallel with postgraduate programmes as platforms, we could define these platforms as a group of people – students, teachers educators and others – who come together for a common moral purpose, or a mission in the words of Goodlad (1994), that is a just and democratic education. They aim to achieve that through joint knowledge-construction in the interests of vulnerable children.

How can students learn on the platform?

Following the definition above, the platform should not only function for the benefit of individual students (teachers), but at the same time contribute to the development of the teaching profession. The platform, therefore, assumes an activist approach (Sachs 2002) in which there is an inherent tension between intrinsically and extrinsically directed professionalism (Ponte 2007). Intrinsically directed professionalism is based on self-direction. Professionals have the scope to formulate their goals and to determine how they want to achieve them. A classic example would be freelance artists. Extrinsically directed professionalism is based on self-regulation, meaning that professionals are expected to adapt to fit in with procedures laid down by others, to achieve objectives laid down by others. Their authority is limited to applying the procedures to achieving the objectives effectively. Professionals always have to find a balance between self-direction and self-regulation and the platform could offer students a setting in which to work with others to find that balance. The platform should enable them to develop insights into and experiment with alternatives; to cooperate with students, parents, colleagues; to share knowledge and insights; and to participate in the debate on the position of vulnerable pupils.

The implications of this approach will now be explored with the aid of the three visions of learning described by Laurillard (1993), the three worlds distinguished by Popper (1972) and five criteria of action research on the platform (Ponte 2007).

Three visions of learning, according to Laurillard (1993)

A postgraduate curriculum should lead to academic learning and can be based on the idea that the knowledge of professionals needs to be general and theoretical. Students are not expected to learn programatically but from abstract theories and concepts. Abstract knowledge is transferred, independent of contexts. Laurillard (1993: 15) called this 'academic learning as imparted knowledge'. As a reaction, more programmes started to offer practical, procedural knowledge in specific professional fields. Nevertheless, despite the focus on practice, this knowledge was still often taught formally. As stated already, teachers rarely use knowledge they have acquired outside the practice context in their work (Beijaard and Verloop 1996; Hawley and Valli 1999; Gore and Gitlin 2004), hence many writers have pleaded for an alternative vision of teacher education. In this alternative vision, 'learning must be situated in the sense that the learner must be located in a situation and what is known from that experience is known in relation to that particular context' (Laurillard 1993: 15). This is what she calls 'academic learning as situated cognition'. It is about learning from experience of what is immediately to hand. Such learning from experience only produces direct, context-based, practical knowledge, for direct application; knowledge geared to competent practice and not to describing and understanding reality from a distance.

Laurillard, therefore, had identified a theory-practice problem with both methods of learning: 'academic learning as imparted knowledge' appears not to lead to the application of theory in practice; 'academic learning as situated cognition' appears not to lead to abstract knowledge and so cannot, in fact, be said to be academic. Many authors (for an overview, see Merriam and Caffarella 1999) consider both approaches to be inadequate responses to a rapidly changing world. They point to the need for the kind of knowledge that enables people to keep responding to changing circumstances. They stress the need to link developments in practice to a certain distancing and the capacity to look differently at these developments. That requires abstractions (descriptions of reality) that can be compared with each other and are amenable to criticism. These abstractions help professionals, as Laurillard (1993: 26) put it: 'to go beyond their experience, to use it and reflect on it and thereby change their perspective on it, and therefore change the way they experience the world'.

Abstractions transcend immediate experience that a method of teaching maths works with one child and not another, or works in one situation but not another. They also transcend immediate attempts to do something different. An academic orientation requires that professionals explain why the method works or not and in whose interests. They have to be able to decontextualise such experiences and conceptualise them. For instance, they must explore and criticise the theoretical assumptions underlying the method of teaching maths, so that the method can be used differently, supplemented or modified. Consistent with the 'platform', teachers should be able to do this explicitly for the benefit of vulnerable pupils.

Laurillard (1993: 19) called this 'mediated learning' from 'articulated knowledge' and argued the importance of making a distinction between 'teaching abstractions' and 'enabling students to learn abstractions from multiple contexts'. The latter stands between the extreme of the purely situated knowledge, clearly not academic, and the purely abstract, which academic knowledge is often thought to be. 'Teaching abstractions' involves transferring general knowledge, which the students then have to apply, critical reflection and communication with peers.

The three worlds distinguished by Popper (1972)

'Mediated learning' from 'articulated knowledge', according to Laurillard, must apply to all academic learning and so should apply to both research and professional programmes. There is, however, a difference that can be clarified with using the 'three worlds' distinguished by Popper (Popper 1972; Bereiter and Scardamalia 1998).

A research-oriented curriculum mainly involves introducing students to the world of a specific scientific or academic discipline, what Popper relates to as 'world 3'. It is the world of concepts, theories and abstractions. The learner has to reconcile the knowledge from this world with his or her personal internal world of experience, what Popper calls 'world 2'. World 3 and world 2 are connected with the world of concrete actions in reality (world 1). The main problem for educators is to achieve a better fit between worlds 2 and 3, or between personal knowledge and academic knowledge available in a academic discipline. Professionally oriented programmes, on the other hand, are mainly geared to the actions that form part of a specific profession (world 1). The learner must not only reconcile actions in this world with his/her own experience (world 2), but also with the concepts, theories and abstractions of his/her profession (world 3). On professional programmes, making connections between worlds 2 and 3, is not chiefly in the service of world 3 (development of theories) but chiefly in the service of world 1 (concrete action in professional practice).

Criteria for action research on the platform

Students can link the three worlds through studying their own practice. Action research literature suggests a number of interactions could be necessary (Ponte 2007). They are:

1   the interaction between different areas of professional knowledge;
2   the interaction between the application of knowledge and knowledge-construction;
3   the interaction between knowledge at different levels;
4   the interaction between individual and collective knowledge; and
5   the interaction between academic and professional knowledge.

Interaction between different areas of professional knowledge

When defining the platform as a group together for a common moral purpose, learning cannot be solely instrumental knowledge: 'What strategies do I normally have at my disposal and how could I apply them?', but also ideological knowledge: 'What goals do I essentially want to achieve with my strategies and what are the moral-ethical pros and cons?'. Both these forms of knowledge are still, however, concerned with plans; either plans based on personal experience and knowledge (world 2) or plans based on existing theoretical abstractions (world 3). To identify the moral significance of this knowledge, it must be linked with empirical knowledge.

Interaction between the application of knowledge and knowledge-construction

Studying one's own practice means that learning should be characterised by the simultaneous construction and application of professional knowledge. By 'simultaneous' is meant the construction and the application of knowledge as part of the same cyclical process between worlds 1, 2 and 3; professionals apply knowledge, gather information, interpret that information and thereby construct new knowledge, which they then apply.

Interaction between different levels of professional knowledge

Finally, the ability to connect the three worlds by studying one's own practice requires knowledge on two levels. The first level concerns content knowledge (how to realise democratic and just education, how pupils from different backgrounds learn, what methods can be used). To construct this knowledge, students also have to develop methodological knowledge, about how to study their practice. It involves not only the instrumental procedures of, say, action research, but understanding the underlying conceptual assumptions. What is needed, according to Stringer (2007) is a theory of how to undertake a procedure as well as a theory of why and with what outcomes.

Interaction between individual and collective knowledge

Learning on the platform should not only be geared to the personal development of the individual, but also contribute to the development of the profession. Students can do that by constantly making connections between their own personal knowledge (world 2) and collective knowledge. Collective knowledge is primarily knowledge presented in such a way that it can be shared, for instance, by representing reality in the form of a model or by developing a particular classification of reality. Shared knowledge is, of necessity, abstracted knowledge, therefore, knowledge that people can debate. This abstracted knowledge can be used not only to improve actions in collective professional practice (world 1), but also to critically test and adapt the common academic knowledge base taken from world 3.

Interaction between academic and professional knowledge

The idea that theory (world 3) cannot prescribe how to act in practice (world 1) does not mean that learning through action research is atheoretical and that there is no general knowledge from world 3 that professionals can use. On the contrary, without theory, conceptions and abstractions, the knowledge of professionals get stuck at the level of uncritical experiences with everyday events (world 2) without consequences for future actions. Goodlad (1990) said that:

> practice alone is, of course, not enough; without some coordinating theory, some inter-connected ideas, purely practical subjects can ossify and degenerate into congeries of rules-of thumb and obsession with technique.

Practice without theory can become basely conservative; theory without practice can become arcane, unintelligible or simple trivial.

(Goodlad 1990: 54)

Who decides what the students will learn on the platform?

A programme can bring together the world of the necessary theoretical and conceptual knowledge, the student's personal internal experiential world and the world of concrete actions. This bringing together allows researchers, teacher educators and students to learn from each other with a view to improvement. Thus it is possible to speak of 'platform' as a professional community (Wenger *et al*. 2002) with two provisos. The first is a restrictive condition: the aims of a postgraduate programme cannot be determined only by teacher educators and students, as others (for example, government, professional associations, parents, researchers) also have a role. The second concerns an organisational consequence: programmes have to guarantee a level of schooling laid down by others but, at the same time, must ensure that students have sufficient scope to gear their work and schooling to each other. This is only possible when the guarantee of a particular level of education can be coupled with what Smith (2000: 21) called a 'flexible, task-orientated infrastructure, which is responsive to learner needs'.

In this sense, the concept of platform might be more complicated in education than in other domains. The idea that staff and students learn from each other and consult each other, does not mean that they are all contributing equally. Education is a managed process within qualification requirements. Both parties not only have different roles but different responsibilities. Arguably, this inequality can only be reconciled with the idea of platform, if the curriculum is seen as a co-production, resulting from the parties involved recognising each other's responsibilities and negotiating the respective relevances. It is important to make a distinction between teaching routes and learning routes. This distinction can be clarified as follows.

In the negotiation process, the programme is responsible for the quality of the infrastructure designed to give the students learning opportunities. Quality is defined in terms of a coherent body of goals, content, methods, organisational measures and assessment. The programme is required to provide adequate support and guidance to enable students to achieve a formally recognised level of competence, reflection and understanding. It is, therefore, also responsible for filling gaps in the students' knowledge and eradicating misconceptions and, in that sense, the jointly constructed 'narrative' is not only to be judged in terms of democracy and justice but also in terms of right or wrong, adequacy or inadequacy. If, for instance, a student wants to interpret a concrete interaction with a pupil from a psychoanalytical perspective, the educator has to judge this not only on the basis of the student's commitment to the pupil concerned, but also on the basis of whether the student has given a correct account of Freud's theories or accurately compared such theories with Piaget's. There could also be questions about psychoanalytical analysis compared, with a critical social analysis.

Thus the programme monitors the necessary level of knowledge to qualify and is bound by external requirements. However, this does not mean that the programme can speak up for the students. It should make a certain effort, but the students are ultimately responsible for their own learning: for how they wish to negotiate the infrastructure taking account of the interest of their profession and for the good of humankind (Ax and Ponte 2008; Kemmis and Smith 2008). The platform provides the opportunity to negotiate about what is relevant, about learning style and what support they want.

The outcome of this process of negotiation could eventually result in two-way learning: students learn from what the programme can contribute, but the teacher education staff also learn from what the students contribute (Le Cornu and Ewing 2008). A student's critical analysis of a concrete interaction with a pupil from a psychoanalytical perspective could, for instance, inspire the educator to look at his/her own view of Freud's theories in a different light and to start a debate on the issue with his/her peers. The student's interpretation could also prompt a joint exploration of the problem by the student and educator. Cochran-Smith called this the 'tradition of participatory democracy'. She said that:

> they [teacher educators] recognize that there are many people who have developed incisive and articulate critiques of teaching and schooling based on years of professional work inside schools. When it comes to reform-minded teaching, these emic perspectives are regarded as different from, but as important as, the etic critiques developed by people outside of schools. Programs based on collaborative resonance attempt to bring together people with inside and outside perspectives on teaching against the grain – not in order to homogenize ideas or create consensus in language and thought, but in order to intensify through collaboration the opportunities students have to learn against the grain.
>
> (Cochran-Smith 1994: 131)

How is the learning to be organised on the platform?

The negotiation between students and teacher educators about what is to be learned on the platform, and how, should result in the coordination of students' contributions and questions based on their research activities, together with general knowledge of content and methodologies provided by the programme and the general requirements regarding the level of necessary knowledge. However, accounts in the literature appear to indicate that learning to do action research is difficult and time-consuming (Ponte 2002). Developing a research-led method of working has to be conceived, therefore, as a process of socialisation. Action research cannot be treated as a discrete component of the programme to be introduced alongside, or even after, other components in a traditional curriculum, where a research project is a ritual that students do for the programme but will never use again (Ax *et al.* 2008).

This leads to the conclusion that studying issues from the students' own practice should be a constant theme running through the whole programme as a platform. This could involve a number of approaches. Students would always be given the opportunity to contribute and study their own issues, on their own, in pairs, in small groups, or even as a school team. Teacher educators and students could also work together on specific problems which can be used to introduce concepts and abstractions relevant to professional practice. Students could be asked to address relevant themes by carrying out a literature study, writing reviews or analysing cases. They could be asked to take certain programme modules that fit in with their own research, or to take part in weekly 'information markets', where staff, students and outside contributors provide workshops, lectures or seminars. Regular internal and external conferences could be organised, where staff, students and other stakeholders could present their work and debate it. Finally, students could be encouraged to make use of their own national and international networks outside the programme, with the aid of information communication technology (ICT). Supervision and guidance of students who are studying personally identified problems, and study activities arising from this process (which could differ between students) could be organised into networks or study groups, in which students would also support each other as critical friends. The programme would set standards for the scope, composition, quality and level of students' different study activities.

The aim would be a flexible, task-driven infrastructure geared to shared needs; an infrastructure in which, the design and delivery of programmes is partially integrated (Smith 2000). An important consequence is that the research carried out by students is a goal as well as a means. Educators are helping students to become agents; professionals with a research-oriented attitude and method of working, which enables them to continue to steer their own development and ultimately the profession as a whole. However, at the same time educators are educating students by developing a curriculum that allows them to work on their own practice in a research-led, reflective way from the outset. This does not mean that students have to be able to carry out fully-fledged action research from the beginning. Gradually this is achieved by allowing research-led activities to be a constant thread running through the programme from the beginning.

What are the necessary conditions for the platform?

The conditions for teachers' professional learning on the platform can be formulated in terms of internal conditions (within the programme) and external conditions (conditions in the environment of the programme).

Internal conditions

Action research would be the main strategy of the platform. It assumes that students will make their research findings public. This allows them to share and discuss their experiences. Similarly, researchers and teacher educators can also learn from students' research activities since action research also gives all participants the opportunity to 'learn abstractions from multiple contexts' (Laurillard 1993: 19) by getting feedback. In this way, as Somekh (1994) suggests, theory uses the critical insights of professionals to enable it to remain relevant to practice and to contribute to just democratic education.

Thus, one could argue that the construction of a research-led postgraduate curriculum should be based on reciprocity between the learning of the students and the learning of the teacher educators and researchers. It is based on the co-construction of knowledge, which makes specific demands on the expertise of the teacher education staff, not only their ability to teach but also their ability to do research. The research carried out as part of a professional programme demands a connection between Popper's three worlds, with the aim of improving the quality of world 1. That requires intensive professional interaction between the teaching and research tasks of the platform. It is also important in this context that teacher educators not only supervise and guide the students' research activities, but that they are given opportunity for their own research. Like the students, they should research their own teaching practice and be able to study the practice of education collaboratively.

Findings from earlier research (Ponte *et al.* 2005) have taught us, however, that this kind of research culture cannot always be assumed and although the development of such a culture can be encouraged and supported 'from above', it cannot be imposed and controlled bureaucratically. Moreover, it has to be achieved gradually, based initially on educators' small-scale experiences, first with their own case studies or action research and later with a research-led approach in their teaching.

External conditions

Clearly, the negotiation process between the education staff and the students does not take place in a vacuum. Education requires professionals constantly seeking a balance between self-direction and self-regulation. However, there is a third 'party' that decides whether the programme is relevant to the profession. That party is more diffuse, multi-layered and less visible than the students and the teacher education staff, but it is there. It consists, in the first place, of the situations where the students work, but it also includes national and local authorities, academia, the profession, parents, pupils and others. These parties do not only impose restrictions; they can also help in the critical debate about necessary qualifications for work in the education of vulnerable children and the approriate programme. Like the teachers, the teacher education staff should also, therefore, look for a balance between self-regulation and self-direction. The platform should function as an open community with a variety of external collaborations. The remaining question is how communication and collaboration could be organised, when it is known that the educational concept outlined in this chapter is not always supported as a matter of course by schools and others. It requires a thorough weighing up of priorities; above all, the programme as a platform is intended to facilitate the professional development of the students.

Conclusion

This is by no means the last word on this subject, but what is certain is that cooperation with external partners can only be successful when the parties involved know and acknowledge each other's specific responsibilities (Sachs 2002). It is reasonable to assume that the common focus shared by all parties is their commitment to improving education for all children. The quality of that education must be the ultimate criterion for the platform. Quality is a contested concept. In a management approach to curriculum construction, quality would equal effectiveness, as measured, for instance, by low drop-out rates. In a humanistic or liberal approach it equals quality of student learning (Marton and Morris 2002). The aim is broader than just the professional development of the individual student. Through close links between professional education and work, in this case between programmes, schools and others, it should also be geared to the professional development of the profession in relation to the emancipation of vulnerable pupils. This means that the programme also has a mission 'for the good of humankind' (Kemmis and Smith 2008). In that sense it can rightly be called a platform, in the widely used sense of the word in Dutch: that is a group of people from different contexts and with different responsibilities who cooperate with the aim of advocating a common moral purpose. It is a 'springboard' (Groundwater-Smith and Somekh 2007: 262) from which students, teacher educators and others commute to and from their personal and professional lives.

References

Ax, J. and Ponte, P. (eds) (2008) *Critiquing Praxis. Conceptual and Empirical Trends in the Teaching Profession*. Rotterdam: Sense Publishers.

Ax, J., Ponte, P. and Brouwer, N. (2008) 'Action research in the curricula of Dutch teacher education programmes', *Journal of Educational Action Research*, 16(1): 21–31.

Beijaard, D. and Verloop, N. (1996) 'Assessing teachers' practical knowledge', *Studies in Educational Evaluation*, 22(3): 275–86.

Bereiter, C. and Scardamalia, M. (1998) 'Rethinking learning' in D.R. Olson and N. Torrance (eds) *The handbook of education and human development*, pp. 485–514. Malden, MA: Blackwell Publishers.

Cochran-Smith, M. (1994) 'The power of teacher research in teacher education' in S. Hollingsworth and H. Sockett (eds) *Teacher research and educational reform*, pp. 22–51. Chicago: University of Chicago Press.

Cochran-Smith, M. and Fries, M.K. (2002) 'Sticks, stones and ideology: the discourse of reform in teacher education', *Educational Educator*, 30(8): 3–16.

Darling-Hammond, L. and Bransford, J. (2005) *Preparing Teachers for a Changing World*. San Francisco: Jossey-Bass.

Davis, S. and Meyer, C. (1998) *Blur: The Speed of Change in the Connected Economy*. Oxford: Caplove Publications.

Day, C. and Sachs, J. (eds) (2004) *International Handbook of the Continuing Professional Development of Teachers*. Buckingham: Open University Press.

Elliott, J. (1993) 'Three perspectives on coherence and continuity in teacher education' in J. Elliott (ed.) *Reconstructing Teacher Education: Teacher Development*, pp. 15–19. London: The Falmer Press.

Goodlad, J.I. (1990) *Teachers for our National Schools*. San Francisco: Jossey-Bass.

Goodlad, J.I. (1994) *Educational Renewal: Better Teachers, Better Schools*. San Francisco: Jossey-Bass.

Gore, J. and Gitlin, A. (2004) 'Re-visioning the academic-teacher divide', *Teachers and Teaching: Theory and Practice*, 10(1): 35–58.

Groundwater-Smith, S. (2007) 'Universities in the 21st century: the need for safe places for unsafe ideas. Questions of quality in practitioner research' in P. Ponte and B.H.J. Smit (eds) *The Quality of Practitioner Research: Reflections on the Position of the Researcher and the Researched*, pp. 57–65. Rotterdam: Sense Publishers.

Groundwater-Smith, S. and Somekh, B. (2007) 'Translating and transgressing the metaphor: developing an international understanding of "platform"' in J. Van Swet, P. Ponte, and B. Smit (eds) *Postgraduate Programs as Platform: A Research-led Approach*, pp. 259–271. Rotterdam: Sense Publishers.

Hawley, D.W. and Valli, L. (1999) 'The essentials of effective professional development: a new consensus' in L. Darling-Hammond and G. Sykes (eds) *Teaching as the Learning Profession*, pp. 127–151. San Francisco: Jossey Bass Publishers.

Kemmis, S. and Smith, T. J. (eds) (2008) *Enabling Praxis: Challenges for Education*. Rotterdam: Sense Publishers.

Kunneman, H. (1984) *Habermas' theorie van het communicatieve handelen. Een samenvatting. (Habermas' theory of communicative action. A summary.)* Meppel: Boom.

Laurillard, D. (1993) *Rethinking University Teaching: A Framework for the Effective Use of Educational Technology*. London: Routledge.

Le Cornu, R. and Ewing, R. (2008) 'Reconceptualising professional experiences in pre-service teacher education . . . reconstructing the past to embrace the future', *Teacher and Teacher Education*, 24(October), 1799–812.

Marton, F. and Morris, P. (2002) *What Matters: Discovering Critical Conditions of Classroom Learning*. Gothenburg: Acta Univeritatis Gothoburgenises.

Merriam, S.B. and Caffarella, R.S. (1999) *Learning in Adulthood. A Comprehensive Guide* (2nd edn). San Francisco: Jossey Bass.

Ponte, P. (2002) 'How teachers become action researchers and how teacher educators become their facilitators', *Journal for Educational Action Research*, 10(3): 399–423.

Ponte, P., Ax, J. and Beijaard, D. (2005) 'Don't wait till the cows come home: action research and initial teacher education in three different countries', *Teachers and Teaching: Theory and Practice*, 20: 517–588.

Ponte, P. (2007) 'Postgraduate education as platform: a conceptualisation' in J. Van Swet, P. Ponte and B. Smit (eds) *Postgraduate Programs as Platform: A Research-Led Approach*, pp 19–39. Rotterdam: Sense Publishers.

Popper, K.R. (1972) *Objective Knowledge: An Evolutionary Approach*. Oxford: Clarendon Press.

Sachs, J. (2002) *The Activist Teaching Profession*. Buckingham: Open University Press.

Smith, R. (2000) The future of teacher education: principles and prospects', *Asia Pacific Journal of Teacher Education*, 28(1): 7–28.

Somekh, B. (1994) 'Inhabiting each other's castles: towards knowledge and initial growth through collaboration', *Educational Action Research*, 2(3): 357–82.

Stringer, E. (2007) *Action Research*, 3rd edn. Los Angeles: Sage Publishers Ltd.

Tickle, L. (2001) *Teacher Induction: The Way Ahead*. Buckingham/Philadelphia: Open University Press.

Wenger, E., McDermott, R. and Snyder, W.M. (2002) *Cultivating Communities of Practice*. Boston: Harvard Business School Press.

Chapter 7

Co-constructing a new model of teacher education

Kay Livingston and Lynne Shiach

Introduction

The *Standard for Initial Teacher Education* (SITE) in Scotland (General Teaching Council Scotland 2006) says that teachers should be prepared not only to respond to changes in education but contribute to the process of change. The underlying message is that ITE should prepare teachers who are continuous learners themselves, able to engage actively with others in transforming the learning process. This active engagement in learning requires thinking, questioning and knowledge-creating teachers who recognise the need to work collaboratively, valuing diversity of perspectives, sharing learning and teaching problems and seeking solutions through ongoing inquiry.

This chapter looks at collaborative approaches to teacher education currently underway in Scotland. The aim is to design and implement a new teacher education programme working in collaboration with partner local authorities (LAs) and practitioners creating authentic connections between practitioner inquiry at the ITE stage and ongoing personal and professional learning. The challenges for colleagues at university, LA and school levels, working together to develop and support this new programme are many: new approaches to learning and teaching, new ways of working to enable critical inquiry, reflection and action and new relationships with student teachers and with colleagues. The challenges associated with changing, deep-rooted ways of working and thinking cannot be under-estimated nor the impact on personal and professional identity. However, collaboration offers opportunities for new learning, new shared perspectives, refreshed thinking and engagement in meaningful partnerships.

A collaborative model of teacher education

The development of a new model of teacher education in the Universities of Glasgow and Aberdeen has focused on generating dialogue with key stakeholders about what twenty-first-century teachers need to know, care about and be able to do in schools and learning communities (Livingston 2008). Underpinning the new direction in teacher education is the belief that new models can only be developed effectively through collaboration between colleagues in universities, LAs and schools. This is founded on the recognition that teacher education takes place within contexts that interact and are interdependent. The new models concern the preparation of teachers to work in schools that operate within specific local contexts as well as in an overarching education system. This emphasises the need for a collaborative approach in order to design and implement teacher education courses that prepare teachers for the micro-level classroom interaction within the school and its community and the macro-level education system, its policies and culture. As Leont'ev (1981) points out, an individual's activity is a system within a system of social relations. To make sense of the overlapping and interconnected layers of influence on teaching and learning for student teachers, a collaborative approach to teacher education is essential. The fundamental issue is not the new way of doing things versus the old way, rather it is a question of what is worthy of teacher education in today's society (Dewey 1981).

Teachers work in hugely varied and changing environments and the complexity of the teaching task is increasing, as is the range of ways that teachers need to be prepared. They must work with diverse populations of learners who have numerous and constantly changing influence. Moreover, knowledge about what and how people learn is continually developing. Interconnected learning communities mean teachers work with a wider range of professionals. Teachers need to be able to respond to individual learners and learning in and outside the school; in the family and community. This means there is a constant need for teachers to adapt and develop their knowledge, skills and values about learning and teaching, which in turn means that learning opportunities that start in initial teacher education need to continue throughout their career. The new model advocates a continuum of teacher development that begins with the B.Ed. (Primary) Initial Teacher Education Course, leads into an induction year that then links to a programme of ongoing professional development.

The emphasis on co-constructing the new model acknowledges that teacher education takes place in a number of settings and that the role of teacher educator is taken up by people working in the university and in the local community and school contexts. This necessitates universities and LAs acknowledging that the development of teachers is a joint responsibility. A collaborative, responsive ongoing inquiry approach is the only effective way for teacher education institutions and schools to recognise and develop a sense of co-responsibility for teacher preparation. Collaboration and inquiry not only connect people to each other but to new and diverse sources of knowledge and skills, and to different cultural settings with multiple impacts. The collaborative approach changes the nature of the activities, the processes and the people involved in teacher education through challenge and dialogue that extends and enhances learning (Livingston 2008). This sense of ongoing inquiry is what the new model of teacher education aims to achieve in order to assist the students in coming to know who they are and what they are capable of. However, not only do the students transform in this collaborative inquiry process, so do the tutors, the teachers involved and the LA personnel. Active participation in inquiry into teaching and learning is only possible through interaction and dialogue with others. The struggle for sense-making challenges everyone's thinking and puts the focus firmly on searching for understanding of the learning and teaching process in multiple contexts. This demands both personal and professional growth.

The involvement of schools in teacher education programmes and links between teacher education institutions, LAs and schools in delivering ITE is not new in the Scottish context (Livingston 2008). Brisard *et al.* (2005), in their review of models of partnership in programmes of ITE, identified two ways that the term 'partnership' is used. First, the partnership with LAs and schools concerning school experience, they describe as 'logistical arrangements' for the delivery of ITE. Second, they suggest the term 'partnership' refers to exploring and developing what learning to become a teacher means. The first is widely apparent, the second is not. There are, and there have been for many years, possibilities for teachers and LA personnel to participate in advisory groups and programme committees that are responsible for reviewing ITE programmes. However, this does not amount to significant agenda sharing or recognition of the roles that the teacher education institutions and schools play in teacher development nor does it offer wider opportunities for exploring how the two settings could build a continuum of teacher development. These linkages can only be termed 'loose-coupling'. It does not amount to continuous partnership in the development of teacher education programmes. The new models seek to develop 'deep' partnerships that involve ongoing co-responsibility and joint action.

In the development of the new model, a number of theories have informed our thinking about structure, organisation, content and processes. For example, we have drawn from the work of Vygotsky (1978), Dewey (1981), Bruner (1986) and Schön (1987) to inform our discussions. Our view is that social interaction helps us to make sense of the world: learning is viewed as a process that involves transmission and reproduction as well as creativity, reflection and transformation. We believe that through social interaction the relationship of people to the world changes as it extends their capacity to interpret and transform it for their own and other mutually beneficial purposes. Social interaction transforms individuals through involvement in collective activities that are culturally and historically situated. We suggest this collaborative approach will result in better outcomes than could be achieved through any one party working in isolation. By bringing together a range of differing perspectives and by explicitly sharing knowledge, those involved have the opportunity to develop mutual understanding that enables them to create new knowledge and meaning.

The importance of co-construction of teacher education by universities and schools has been highlighted by research that indicates a discontinuity between what student teachers said they learned in ITE and what they were able to do, were asked to do and what they wanted to do in school as teachers. McIntyre (2007), reviewing international evidence, suggested that student teachers found themselves unable to make much use in schools of what they had learned in higher education, and that what they had to learn *for* schools they believed they would have to learn *in* schools. He said that the evidence also showed that student teachers learned that what they *could* learn in higher education was what they *had* to learn *for* higher education; and they developed strategies to cope with the two different agendas of school and higher education. This is not only confusing but misses the opportunity to link theory and practice and develop an understanding of what the two different settings can offer to the learning to teach process. It suggests that they believe they have to conform to what was expected by the university tutors rather than developing their own understanding. This for many may mean a loss of creativity and personality in their development. Our premise is that a collaborative model, one where the teacher education programme is co-constructed by tutors from teacher education institutions, LAs, schools and the student teachers themselves, will provide opportunities for theory and practice to be linked in a meaningful way and enable everyone to benefit from and value the different kinds of knowledge and expertise available in university and in schools (Livingston and Shiach 2007). The model of collaboration proposed also makes explicit the inter-dependency of the settings in teacher development and that input from university, LA and school personnel is essential.

Implementation of the new model

A continuum of teacher development

In September 2005, student teachers at the University of Aberdeen embarked on a new programme entitled *Scottish Teachers for a New Era* (STNE) funded by the Scottish Government and the Hunter Foundation (THF). The six-year initiative is developing and implementing a continuum of teacher education in collaboration with partner LAs in the northeast of Scotland. The focus of years 1 and 2 of the programme is on the development of a deeper and broader conceptual knowledge and understanding of learners and the learning process. Years 3 and 4 have a pedagogical focus and are designed to link coherently with the induction year. Year 5 is the induction year when the new teachers begin their careers in schools. It builds on year 4 and the aim is that it will link to further mentoring in year 6. The plan is that year 6 will link to an ongoing programme of continuous professional development (CPD).

In September 2008, students at the University of Glasgow began their programme of teacher education in the central belt of Scotland. The two universities are developing approaches to teacher education unique to them but both based on the collaborative inquiry model. They share the same aims for teacher education: teachers who are enthusiastic continuous learners; who see themselves as leaders of active but challenging learning opportunities in and around the school community; who are able to draw from a deeper content knowledge and a broader understanding of the curriculum; have an inquiry approach to learning and teaching (including co-inquiry with pupils and other colleagues in school and in the wider community); understand and value the many influences on learning and learners, particularly the role of parents; are collegiate, value diversity and open to support and critique; and are flexible and confident exploring and adapting to new learning and teaching methodologies. The programmes emphasise active learner engagement through continuous inquiry. They challenge the view of a teacher as a technician who has to acquire a set of competences which are used to implement policy and deliver the curriculum. The inquiry approach applies to everyone involved in the teacher education programme – the student teacher, university tutor, LA officer, head teacher, teacher, community worker, and so on.

Understanding learners and the learning process

The approach challenges dominant views about learning to teach. The first year of the programme puts the emphasis on the learner and the learning process – student teachers understanding themselves as learners, understanding children's learning and educational values. This may not seem like a radical idea in teacher education yet it has required a shift in thinking from preparing teachers to teach to developing teachers as learners and practitioner inquirers. The students arrive at university with preconceived images of a teacher and teaching and with a set of expectations about the teacher education programme. Research suggests that the influence of student teachers' own schooling has a powerful impact on their development as teachers, acting as a filter during their teacher education programme and having an impact on what they are able to learn. These preconceived views about the role of a teacher and teaching create barriers which limit the ideas that the student teachers are able to embrace and engage with. Feiman-Nemser (2001) suggests that a typical pre-service programme is a weak intervention compared with the influence of teachers' own schooling. The difficulty is that the underlying values and beliefs about teaching and learning are often deeply embedded, which make it hard to encourage students towards new ideas and new approaches. Student teachers need opportunities and support to uncover and explore their assumptions and personal experiences which are usually based on a simplistic understanding of learning and teaching processes. This approach is challenging and uncomfortable but it is the start of the questioning and critical inquiry approach which is central to the new model. Teacher education programmes need to create opportunities for student teachers to engage in critical examination of their assumptions and beliefs in an explicit way during their first year. To offer support for the development of critical reflection, teacher educators need to understand more about the values and beliefs that create the perceptions about the role of the teacher in the learning process and the images of teaching that the students bring to their ITE programme. This requires teacher educators engaging with the student teachers in dialogue and inquiry about learning and teaching sharing, and negotiating, meaning in relation to both theory and practice. The active participation in learning and the heuristic approach embedded from the start of the programme is designed to develop teachers who take responsibility for progressing their own learning, adopt an investigative approach to all they observe and do, and constantly reappraise learning and teaching.

An inquiry approach

The development of students' capacity to reflect and develop a deeper under-standing of learning and teaching through investigation and dialogue has been evident in the rhetoric of course documentation for some time in Scotland, but student teachers who are able to engage actively in the learning process in a thoughtful way and who feel confident engaging in intellectual reasoning and critical reflection are less evident (Livingston 2008). There is a difference between students hearing about the theories of active engagement in learning, inquiry and reflective practice and adopting these approaches themselves. The new approach focuses on ensuring that inquiry and thoughtful reflection become a way of being for every teacher. The courses in the first two years of the new model have been restructured with the specific aim of providing opportunities for students to develop confidence in their own thinking about learning and teaching. Questioning and reflection are essential to their development as learners and teachers. The changes include student involvement in programme design and assessment, student-led tutorials and a new investigative approach to school experience.

New field experience

A collaborative approach is being taken in all aspects of the new model. However, in this chapter our focus is on the collaborative development and implementation of the new investigative field experience in the first year of the programme. We have chosen to analyse this aspect because it is very different from the previous type of school experience carried out by the students in their first year. Traditionally, the first experience of teaching in school took place early in the B.Ed. programme and thrust the students into the complex task of teaching a class of pupils. Lessons were prepared and delivered with only a superficial understanding of learners and learning processes. Now the students begin by investigating the many influences on children's learning in the community, the school as a whole and in classrooms. The inquiry approach aims to facilitate and deepen the students' connection of theory and practice through their adoption of the role of participant observer in school settings. This approach to field experience is new for everyone – teachers, head teachers, education tutors and students alike – and everyone is learning together.

The focus of inquiry is on the development of the students' understanding of the learning process – exploring the many and varied influences on children's learning in the family, community and school. The Bronfenbrenner (1979) *Ecological Framework* is used as a basis for analysis and discussion to raise awareness of the interconnectedness of these varied influences. The students undertake their field experience in pairs engaging in 'learning conversations' with the aim of developing a sense of collegiality, openness to critique and peer-mentoring from the outset. The students talk about their shared experience of observing and interacting with children and through joint reflection try to co-construct an understanding of the experience. The emphasis is on dialogue in order to uncover assumptions made during their investigations, to articulate their thinking, and to problematise knowledge through a questioning approach. The notion of students undertaking the field experience in pairs has been adopted to enable the students to build confidence through partnership in the classroom and to develop an understanding that teaching is not a task carried out in isolation. The peer-mentoring process offers the opportunity to understand the value of critical reflection carried out collaboratively.

The students are set tasks designed jointly by university tutors and teachers. In the classroom, the students engage in 'learning conversations' with pupils, teachers and others in school. They observe and interact with pupils in extra-classroom contexts in an effort to understand behaviour in different environments and the wide variety of influences on their learning. By shifting the focus of school experience from delivering a set of pre-planned lessons to an investigation of children's learning and the many influences on it, the aim is to help student teachers develop an understanding of learning with greater breadth and depth. The aim is also to develop the students' confidence in using the evidence gathered – questioning it, thinking about it and articulating how it could guide future learning and teaching.

The structure of the school experience has also been changed to try to over-come the difficulties student teachers often had connecting abstract theories met in the university to the specific context of the classroom and individual learners. A block of study in the university, followed by a block in school and back to the university without explicit opportunities to reflect, transfer and translate learning appeared to reinforce students' views that theory does little to inform practice, and vice versa. In the first and second years of the new B.Ed. programme, the field experience is organised in a series of single days embedded in a course of study in an effort to make a more coherent link between theory and practice and between learning in the university and school settings. The students explore theories of learning through reading, lectures and tutorials and then reflect on them through observation, interaction and investigation in authentic school settings. The practitioner inquiry approach means they use the evidence to reflect on the field experience generally and to engage in learning conversations about learning theories and child development theories. The skills to enable thoughtful reasoning, reflection and collaborative learning are challenging for many student teachers. We believe the development of these skills has to begin at the start of their programme and be integrated throughout ITE programmes if we are to realise the aim of developing flexible, adaptable, thinking teachers who feel confident continually questioning and re-appraising learning and teaching. This requires the development of a culture of continuous inquiry.

The process of change

Experience suggests that the complexity of bringing people together from teacher education institutions, LAs and schools needs to be made explicit in order to avoid misconceptions, misunderstandings and conflict. The notion of boundary crossing at any level is associated with overcoming barriers. Even analysis at a simplistic level shows that the universities, LAs and schools have different cultures and use different languages. A more in-depth analysis exposes differences in values and beliefs. We are not alone in recognising the difficulties of collaboration. Bringing people together from different contexts and the difficulties concerning modifying or changing deeply embedded views has been recognised in other studies. For example, Huberman (1999) identifies the gulf between the world of research and practice. He talks about two micro-worlds and explores what needs to happen to enable views to permeate the different worlds. He emphasises the challenge of making explicit the perceptual baggage that people from different worlds bring and the importance of finding opportunities for ongoing exchanges as catalysts for interaction. We believe that the various interconnections are possible by bringing people together and recognising the need to provide inter-subjective, negotiated space for communication. However, bringing people from the different worlds together is a first step but will not necessarily lead to meaningful interaction between them. Openness to inquiry, learning and seeking opportunities to learn from others is necessary. Added to this is an acceptance of the mutual benefit that can be derived.

The change to the new approach of teacher education in both the University of Glasgow and the University of Aberdeen has been both challenging and rewarding. The universities are at different stages in the development and implementation. However, already there are similarities in the challenges and successes identified. In considering the process of change, the following stages have been identified: familiarisation and clarification; implementation and interpretation; and embedding and sustaining interactions.

Familiarisation and clarification

The findings in relation to this stage of change are relevant to both universities. The collaborative approach brought people together. The approaches taken in this familiarisation and clarification stage were an attempt to move beyond loose-coupling towards greater interaction. At this stage the university and school personnel had to exchange information as a starting point for under-standing each other's views before being able to make connections. People from the different settings needed to 'tune-in' to what was happening in the other settings and to the values and beliefs that underpinned the 'other's thinking and actions. Spaces and opportunities had to be created for dialogue. It became clear that people from the different settings used different languages or used the same language but meant different things. At this stage clarification was not always sought, which often led to confusion and misunderstanding. This highlights the need to explicitly seek clarification. This process was generally not well used by people in either setting. However, it emerged as fundamental to developing a deep and shared understanding.

In the first stage of the process of change, misinterpretations interrupted the smooth flow of communication between the universities and schools. An intermediary or translator (a tutor who had recent experience of school) who interpreted meaning and facilitated understanding between the two settings was critical to the process of change. Translators who understand the language of both settings can help others to see and make sense of what are often hidden messages. They must move between the different settings, either to prepare the ground for interaction by identifying common themes of interest or by developing seeds of interaction that have emerged and need to be encouraged by translating their meaning. This role cannot be underestimated; it aided confidence-building. Through the work of the translator people became more accepting that they had a valuable contribution to make and that their views were genuinely being sought. Within the safe dialogic space, school personnel appeared to become more comfortable with their right and responsibility to contribute. More needed to be done at this stage to make explicit to those from the school setting that their knowledge, although different, was equally valuable and necessary. For example, the teachers' deep knowledge of school and community settings could not be provided by the university tutors. Gradually through the inquiry approach to teacher education, challenge was given and received in the spirit of mutual growth. Engaging in dialogue, people appeared stimulated by interest in the 'other's perspectives' which led to a process of mutual learning agreed as of benefit. Furthermore, collaboration development with the repeated use of norms enabled a shift towards valuing diversity and encouraging challenge. Thus trust was gradually established between people in each setting and signalled the development of greater interaction.

Implementation and interpretation

The collaborative approach moved into the second stage when the student groups embarked on their field investigations. As the implementation of field experience unfolded, it became clear that there were different views about the underpinning value of the new inquiry approach and the focus on the learning process rather than the craft of teaching. In addition, it was apparent there were different interpretations of the tasks the students were carrying out and of the levels and type of support that should be provided.

These differences indicated that the information flow in the first stage of the process of change was either not clear enough or not accessible enough to the teachers and tutors. The different interpretations could have been the result of differences in language understanding which were not apparent at the familiarisation and clarification stage. Assumptions appeared to be made about the new approach based on embedded beliefs developed from previous models of student placement in schools. This meant that in some cases both the teachers and the students had anxieties about things they thought they should be doing, yet often these were imagined expectations arising from previous experiences of school placements or hearsay. These assumptions had to be uncovered and made explicit in order to overcome potential barriers to the collaborative model of teacher education. In some cases, the realisation that the hidden needed to be made visible was not apparent until after the students had completed their field experience.

Some of the teachers, particularly those who had not been able to engage in prior dialogue were uncomfortable with the shift in focus from teaching to learning. Some teachers are apprehensive of the risk factors associated with the new approach. They view the implementation as too risky in an account-ability context. For example, they believe that students engaging in learning conversations with children would result in higher levels of uncertainty, unpredictability and ambiguity than the previous model of school experience. While some teachers feel able to cope, others feel uneasy. These feelings are not unusual in a process of change. Huberman (1999), referring to the feelings that arose in the participants in his study during the change process, said they used words and phrases such as, 'surprises', 'discrepancies', 'shocks', critical incidents' and 'a disorienting experience'. The results of our analysis indicate that it is necessary to improve the information flow and to understand more about the interactions that occur at the implementation stage and what conditions are required to sustain the feeling of a collaborative approach. We suggest that more intermediaries or translators from both settings are needed to reassure, talk through anxieties and expose assumptions and unrealistic expectations. In our view this would have helped to reassure the tutors, teachers and students and support the conceptual shift. We believe that this mediation and support system is necessary to build and sustain any feelings of trust that are developed in the familiarisation and clarification stage.

Some students were in a role in the classroom that did not meet their expectations of a programme that was teaching them how to teach. They expected to be 'teaching' according to the image of the teacher they had carried from their previous experience of being a pupil in school. The role of participant observer did not match their embedded image. This emphasises the values and beliefs that student teachers carry into their teacher education programme and the powerful way these views impact on what they do.

Our findings suggested that the change process is challenging for all. However, we believe that these insecurities and anxieties serve as a trigger for discussion which raises the potential for the development of deep level collaboration, reflection and re-appraisal of learning and teaching. Undoubtedly, the relationship between the universities and the schools has moved from a logistical one, placing the student in school, to discussion of the process of learning and teaching and the most appropriate models for the preparation of teachers. The evidence indicates that a shared agenda has begun to emerge between the different settings. However, more translators would have eased the process of change, facilitating the co-construction to be shared and understood earlier.

The function, the numbers and the importance to collaboration of translators requires further research. What was not clear during the implementation and interpretation stage was the conditions that are necessary to increase the likelihood of inter-subjectivity, the sharing of meaning. The findings indicate that the construction of relationships that enable the development of inter-subjectivity is crucial and that more support structures, to help everyone maintain confidence and assist them in their new roles, need to be in place. The translators in particular need to be 'sensitive to the feelings of people in the other world' and able to tune in to the identity of the other and the perceptions they hold in order to build trusting relationships. These trusting relationships, we believe, are a prerequisite for deep-level collaboration. Trust is particularly vital when the implementation stage pushes people beyond their 'zone of proximal development' (Vygotsky 1978). The messiness and the sense of risk may damage relationships and the earlier stage of familiarisation and clarification may need to be revisited. This underlines the fragility of collaborative processes and emphasises the need to pay attention to both cognitive and affective aspects in the development and implementation stages in the process of change. Interaction is required to build collaboration. However, interaction becomes difficult when people are anxious or lose trust: people may opt out of the changes proposed. It became clear that to move to the next stage in the process of change (embedding and sustaining the interaction between the university and schools), opportunities for multiple and continuous connections are needed.

Conclusion

The course development has necessitated a redefinition of current roles and practices, and a continuous learning approach, as new knowledge, skills, values, beliefs and structures are constructed jointly. This chapter has discussed some of the challenges for all the agents of change as new relationships are developed, different perspectives explored and a sense of co-responsibility embraced.

The implementation of the process of change has highlighted the import-ance of communicative practices, of seeking clarification to develop under-standing and of making values and beliefs explicit. Not everyone has felt comfortable with an approach that views knowledge as tentative and remains open to challenge and reconsideration. It has required people to learn new skills in observing, listening and negotiating, which in turn required new patterns of dialogue and learning through inquiry. This process has called for courage to take risks, particularly in putting forward points of view with people from settings perceived to be different. Power has had to be shared requiring both trust and respect. We believe this new way of working facilitates the develop-ment of deep-level collaboration, fosters inquiry approaches that challenge ideas, promotes meaningful reflection that enhances learning and offers a more effective approach to teacher education.

The new collaborative enquiry approach to learning has already provided evidence of more confident learning and readiness to question course content, assessment processes and ways of learning. Furthermore, students are willing to work with, mentor and critique peers to reflect on and challenge learning and where appropriate take individual or collective action. Most importantly, through the process of inquiry, the students are developing a personal stance concerning what it means to be a twenty-first-century teacher and recognising that they are on a career-long learning journey.

References

Brisard, E., Menter, I. and Smith, I. (2005) *Models of Partnership in Programmes of Initial Teacher Education*. Edinburgh: General Teaching Council.

Bronfenbrenner, U. (1979) *The Ecology of Human Development: Experiments by Nature and Design*. Cambridge, MA: Harvard University Press.

Bruner, J. (1986) *The Culture of Education*. Cambridge, MA: Harvard University Press.

Dewey, J. (1981) *The Later Works, 1925–1953*, J.A. Boydston (ed.). Carbondale, IL: Southern Illinois University Press.

Feiman-Nemser, S. (2001) 'From preparation to practice: designing a continuum to strengthen and sustain teaching in teachers college', Record 103, Number 6, December 2001, pp. 1013–55.

General Teaching Council for Scotland (2006) *The Standard for Initial Teacher Education*, December 2006, Edinburgh: General Teaching Council Scotland.

Huberman, M. (1999) 'The mind is its own place: the influence of sustained interactivity with practitioners on educational researchers', *Harvard Educational Review*, 69(3): 289–391.

Leont'ev, A.N. (1981) 'The problem of activity in psychology' in J. Wertsch (ed.) *The Concept of Activity in Soviet Psychology*. Armonk: NY Sharpe.

Livingston, K. (2008) 'New directions in teacher education' in T. Bryce and W. Humes (2008) *Scottish Education*. Edinburgh: Edinburgh University Press.

Livingston, K. and Shiach, L. (2007) 'Co-constructing a new model of teacher education', unpublished paper presented at *American Educational Research Association Annual Conference*, Chicago, 2007.

McIntyre, D. (2007) The proper role of universities in initial teacher education', unpublished paper presented at *Initial Teacher Education Seminar*, 27 February 2007, at Moray House School of Education, University of Edinburgh.

Schön, D.A. (1987) *Educating the Reflective Practitioner*. San Francisco, CA: Jossey Bass.

Vygotsky, L. (1978) *Mind in Society: The Development of Higher Psychological Processes*. Cambridge, MA: Harvard University Press.

Chapter 8

Academic induction for new teacher educators

Forging authentic research identities through practitioner inquiry

Jean Murray

Introduction

The starting points for this chapter are two current issues in the field of teacher education in England. First, recent changes suggest that a new generation of teacher educators faces increasing challenges in becoming research active and developing academic identities. Ironically, these challenges come at a time when the imperative for research capacity building initiatives in education has been identified (ESRC 2005). Second, research on the induction of new teacher educators (Boyd *et al.* 2007; Murray 2008) shows that provision can be uneven and sometimes inadequate. Other research on academic learning (Boud 2001; Trowler and Knight 2004) shows that the informal or non-formal knowledge (Eraut 2000), generated through workplace learning, is a key factor in effective academic induction. But for teacher educators, a number of factors inhibit the development of the full potential of this learning (Murray 2008). In particular, the fast pace of work in the sector and the need for individuals to make swift transitions from novice to expert may mean that there is little time or space for teacher educators to articulate the informal knowledge which occurs through workplace learning (ibid.). A powerful source of professional knowledge is therefore not developed to its full potential during induction.

This chapter draws on an analysis of relevant research and an illustrative case study of one new teacher educator's induction to debate how practitioner-based research might provide solutions to these issues. One of the starting premises for the writing is that supporting the development of new teacher educators as researchers is vital for a number of reasons, not least to build general research capacity in education, to ensure thriving teacher education communities, to maintain research-informed teaching in pre- and in-service courses (Dadds and Kynch 2003), and to support the intellectual development of teacher educators and the teachers they teach.

The chapter is structured in the following way. The first part provides the context for considering new teacher educators as researchers in university departments of education (UDE) in England. It analyses recent changes to teacher education, as well as providing an overview of research on teacher educators as neophyte researchers. A case study of Emily, a new researcher engaged in studying her own practices, indicates the power of well-framed practitioner research in forging new identities. The chapter then draws on an illustrative case study to explore further how university induction provision for new academics can support new teacher educators develop identities as both researchers and teachers of teachers. The case study discusses a model for induction, which aims to make authentic connections between informal work-based learning and practitioner inquiry within a formal learning structure (the Postgraduate Certificate in Higher Education (PGC in HE), a qualification taken by most new academics in the UK). This section of the chapter identifies that the model has a number of clear advantages in providing an introduction to research activities. In the conclusion a number of issues are raised about the long-term value and importance of this type of practitioner research in HE.

New teacher educators as researchers: contexts and issues

Tensions about the place of research activity in teacher education and teacher educators' work, particularly in departments where pre-service courses are the main area of enterprise, have persisted for decades (Maguire 1994; Goodson 1995). While the rhetoric of teacher education states that all teacher educators are actively involved in research (Fish 1995), other findings (Ducharme 1993; Maguire 2000; Murray 2007) indicate that there is a gap between this rhetoric and the 'reality' of research engagement for some individuals. The factors which restrict the time and opportunities available for teacher educators in some universities to participate in research are well known (Maguire 2000; Sikes 2006; Furlong 2007; Murray 2007). Within the research literature on teacher educators, it is also not uncommon to find this occupational group, particularly those new to higher education, positioned as 'uneasy residents in academe' (Ducharme and Agne 1989: 312), with their academic and professional identities seen as located across both HE and school sectors (Ducharme 1993; Maguire 1994, 2000; Murray 2002).

Recent changes in the field of education in England have made the maintenance of research bases within many teacher education departments increasingly tenuous (Bassey 2004). This shift in the field has in turn created new barriers for some teacher educators in becoming research active. One major change has been an alteration in the distribution patterns of the funding for educational research from the Higher Education Funding Council for England. This change means that the majority of universities providing teacher education no longer receive any core funding for research (Furlong 2007; Gilroy 2008). This situation has profound implications for the future quality of teacher education in England. Nationally there is now the very real prospect that education research may become dislocated from pre-service teacher education and from the work of teacher educators in many UDEs. As stated above, the irony is that these new barriers to teacher educators' engagement in research are arising at the same time as the need for research capacity building initiatives for education have been identified (ESRC 2005). They also coincide with government calls for school teaching in England to become a Masters-level profession. A full discussion of this situation is beyond the remit of this chapter; here my focus can only be on some aspects of the implications for teacher educators' engagement in research (but for broader analyses see, Dadds and Kynch 2003; Bassey 2004).

Evidence indicates that the Research Assessment Exercise of 2008 has had the effect of restricting definitions of what could be 'counted' as research activity in teacher education and who has been judged to be an 'active researcher' (Furlong 2007; Gilroy 2008). Other analyses show an increasing bifurcation between those who teach and those who research in teacher education, including greater use of 'teaching-only' contracts or hourly paid staff (Whitelaw et al. 2005). These changes have been compounded by instability in the pre-service sector due to demographic changes which have required both sharp increases and subsequent decreases in teacher supply within a five year period. Lastly, but by no means least, the impact of New Labour education policies on teacher education has been profound (Furlong 2005). In pre-service teacher education, for example, changing government requirements for pre-service courses have established a 'national framework of accountability' (Furlong, et al. 2000: 15) and a 'culture of compliance' (Menter et al. 2006: 50) for UDEs and the teacher educators working within them. Together these changes have generated multiple, and often contradictory, discourses and practices of teaching and research in the field. These are manifested in varying ways in different UDEs. In previous work (Murray 2008), I have argued that the teacher educators working in these contexts are a fragmented and uncertain professional group whose expertise and contribution to the epistemology and pedagogy of teacher education and schooling are often unarticulated.

New teacher educators: the findings of previous studies

Most teacher educators in England come into the university from previous careers in the school or Further Education sectors. This occupational shift has been identified as bringing about uncertainties and challenges, as well as changes in professional identities and the need for new professional learning (Boyd et al. 2005; Murray and Male 2005). Beyond the UK, other studies of new teacher educators (Ducharme 1993 in the USA; Acker 1996 in Canada) have also identified that individuals experience this change as challenging and sometimes stressful. Many teacher educators, for example, find some difficulties in adjusting to the academic expectations of HE-based teacher education work, particularly to requirements to become involved in research and publication (Ducharme 1993; Murray 2008). Others find challenges in the shift from teaching school-age pupils to teaching adults who are beginning or serving teachers.

There is limited evidence of how the recent changes to teacher education in England, outlined above, affect new teacher educators and the ways in which they engage in research. But the findings of the Knowledge and Identity in Teacher Education (KITE) study (Davison *et al*. 2005) and a recent study of new teacher educators (Murray 2006b) both identify that, even in the early stages of HE work, there are already many ways in which these new staff have different constructions of their emerging identities as teacher educators and researchers. These differences exist even when new teacher educators enter the same universities from broadly similar professional backgrounds in school teaching to work on the same teacher education courses. Both studies show new teacher educators positioning themselves in a variety of ways within the field, by drawing on differing discourses and practices of teacher education. These include: technical-rational ways of understanding teaching and learning as acts of transmission and acquisition, and of pre-service provision as 'practical training'; seeing teacher education as involving 'deep learning' and significant identity change; embedding personal practice in models of reflective professionalism; centring craft and experiential knowledge in teacher education; and enacting practices of caring professionalism. In talking about their engagement with research these teacher educators also drew on differing discourses about research and its relationship to the work of teacher education. For some, research was constructed as practical enquiry, routinely undertaken by practitioners, while others saw it as a highly 'theoretical' activity, essentially divorced from practice.

Some previous studies of more experienced teacher educators (Reynolds 1995; Ducharme and Ducharme 1996; Hatton 1997; Murray 2002) suggest that either the UDEs, as the immediate settings for work, or the amount of time spent in HE are powerful determining factors in the creation of researcher identities. However, in both the KITE (Davison *et al*. 2005) and the new academics study (Murray 2006b), some of the new teacher educators' views of their research identities broke with such ideas of institutional or temporal determinism. For example, in the latter study, one new teacher educator, Emily, working in a university with no institutional tradition of involvement in conventional research activities, emphasised how important research engagement was to her and defined her identity as a 'practitioner academic in the making'. Emily's sense of identity may be seen as an example of the hybrid academic identities which Clegg (2005) identifies as emerging in the increasingly diversified HE sector. One of Clegg's interviewees uses the term 'pracademic' to describe himself; this is a term which could also be applied to Emily's identity.

Emily's sense of identity and her 'ownership' of research activity was in contrast to some other new teacher educators in the study, who worked in more research intensive institutions, but rejected any sense of themselves being or becoming 'researchers' or 'academics'. In the terms of Maguire (2000), Emily stands 'inside/outside' the ivory towers of conventional academic life, that is, she works in an HE setting but many of the structural and professional factors in her work might well have mitigated against her becoming an active researcher and an academic in the commonly agreed sense of that word. For example, Emily's sense of professionalism involved her willing participation in time-consuming and emotionally draining acts of student nurturing. Such gendered patterns of work have been identified as potentially detrimental to teacher educators' engagement in research and consequently to career progression (Maguire 1994; Acker 1996; Murray 2006a). Emily also worked in an institution where there were other constraints which might have limited her sense of identity as a researcher and academic: she had a heavy teaching timetable; the institution received no core research funding; and although there was a current initiative to promote research engagement, there was no institutional history of research in teacher education. Yet Emily had a strong sense of personal agency about becoming an active researcher and constructed for herself this emerging identity as 'practitioner–academic'. This identity had authenticity for Emily, not least because of the powerful sense of congruence between the practitioner research paradigm in which her research operated, her clearly stated professional dispositions as a 'reflective practitioner' and a 'lifelong learner' and her commitment to her teaching and students. This identity had continuity with her previous small-scale and informal practitioner inquiry when she was teaching in schools. Importantly for Emily's future research, this practitioner-academic identity also had clear value within her UDE, although its wider validity in the field of educational research might be questioned, as I explore in the final section of this chapter.

In terms of current agendas to develop research capacity in teacher education (Murray *et al.* 2008) the findings of both the KITE and the new academic study indicate that the issue of teacher educators' becoming researchers is neither straightforward nor accessible to quick 'fixes' at the institutional level. Rather the findings indicate that personal dispositions and senses of agency, informed by professional values and missions, are important in creating a sense of congruence between the development of an individual as a researcher and as a practitioner in HE. This chapter asserts that such development needs to be supported by well-focused and relevant induction. It also argues that well-scaffolded practitioner research may have a particular contribution to make to the creation of such congruence.

Creating learning scaffolds for research development

This second part of this chapter looks at a curriculum initiative in which a formal learning structure, in this case a type of module commonly found in PGC in HE programmes, was adapted to promote practitioner research and to scaffold learning about research in teacher education. A further aim of this initiative was to lay the foundations for the creation of authentic researcher identities, informed by a sense of congruence between the development of each new teacher educator as a researcher and other areas of work. In other words, the initiative aimed to develop research which had relevance for the individual and her/his practice.

As already stated, the PGC in HE is the qualification that most new academics in the UK take on entering the university. Since most of these new academics have Ph.D.s in their subject but little experience of teaching, PGC in HE programmes are primarily designed to support the processes of learning to teach. But, despite the existence of this formal qualification, the research on academic induction across disciplines (Boud 2001; Trowler and Knight 2004) shows that most induction provision and the majority of learning occurs within departments and teams rather than through formal qualifications and central university provision. In a national survey of induction provision specifically in teacher education (Murray 2005), our findings supported those previous studies. We found that most professional learning for new teacher educators clearly occurred within what we termed the 'micro-communities of practice' (often the immediate teaching team). The most valuable learning from individual perspectives often occurred through workplace activities at these micro-levels and resulted in tacit or informal knowledge (Eraut 2000). But this study and subsequent work (Boyd *et al.* 2007) also indicated the potential of well-designed formal courses, such as the PGC in HE, in articulating the informal knowledge gained through workplace learning. The value of such articulation between these formal learning structures and informal work-based learning occurs in part because, as Eraut (2000: 133) suggests, tacit knowledge is often developed, acquired and used 'unobserved' in the 'interstices of formal learning contexts'.

The module of the course in question was structured as enquiry-based learning (see extracts from formal module description in Figure 2.1). The central part of the module was taught to new academics from all disciplines by staff from the Learning and Teaching Support Unit (LTSU). Discipline specific mentors were also appointed within each department to work with the new academics in deciding on their enquiry focus, designing and implementing a research design and writing up the final report. Appointed as the mentor to a group of new teacher educators taking this generic module, the principles underpinning my adaptation of the module to ensure the integration of work-based learning with this formal learning structure were as follows:

- to ground the work in what current research indicated about academic induction, with particular reference to teacher education;
- to ensure that the enquiry focus was individual, deriving from the personal practice of each new academic and generated through the analysis of her/his informal learning in the workplace;
- to consider the biographical and professional starting points for individuals, aiming to draw on the existing skills and experience that each brought from previous careers in schools;
- to ensure that the research generated by each teacher educator had general relevance for the field of teacher education and the potential to contribute to further professional development for the individual, including furthering her/his awareness of practice as a teacher educator.

Each of these principles is now briefly discussed, with reference to the illustrative case study.

Teacher educators as practitioners: research in action

This illustrative case study focuses on a new teacher educator, given the pseudonym Kazia here, who was in her second year of teaching on a mathematics education course. She had entered the university 18 months previously, following a long and successful career in secondary school teaching. Prior to starting work at the university, she had taken a Masters degree in Educational Management, with a final dissertation focused on how coaching worked to enhance school teachers' professional development. She had also had a career-long commitment to reflecting on her practice as a teacher, but limited experience of any kind of practitioner research. When Kazia started this module, our initial discussions focused on negotiating the practice-based research study she would undertake. Later meetings, supported by reading and writing tasks, focused on developing the literature review and the research design, as well as on data analysis and presentation issues.

The concept of reflective practice has had a long history in teacher education in England (Furlong *et al.* 2000). This concept and its accompanying discourses and practices continues to influence much teacher education provision and the course on which Kazia taught made explicit the requirement that student teachers should 'reflect on' and 'evaluate' their practice. As a self-avowed reflective practitioner in schools, Kazia was intrigued by the varying pace at which her student teachers' abilities to be reflective developed during the pre-service course. Finding ways of facilitating student teachers' reflections were also an area in which she felt her own practice would benefit from development. The agreed focus for the research study therefore became the facilitation of student teachers' reflection on their practice. In her words:

In my second year as tutor in Teacher Education, I have recognised that trainee teachers have particular difficulties with evaluating lessons, a form of reflection which is encouraged on the course.

(Johal 2007: 2)

Models of mentoring (by school- and university-based staff) are common in pre-service teacher education in England. The course on which Kazia worked certainly had extensive guidance available on mentoring techniques and procedures, many of which she had already tried in encouraging her students to reflect on their teaching. Her previous interest in coaching and its potential power in generating professional development for serving teachers led her to question the effectiveness of the mentoring model and to consider whether coaching techniques could be used to develop enhanced student reflexivity. As she states:

Ultimately, I want to investigate whether there is mileage in changing the approach in our programme. I aim to learn some key lessons from the use of coaching to invoke reflectivity in three trainees. My research question is therefore: Can coaching enhance reflection in trainee teachers?

(Johal 2007: 2)

Following a series of tutorials, Kazia's work for the module was designed as a practitioner research initiative, centred around a series of three individual coaching sessions which each of the student teachers received from her, following formal lesson observations. The aims of her research included making the study into a learning experience for each of the students, as well as for Kazia herself in her tutor role. Kazia also wanted to acknowledge the importance of the students' voice and, as far as possible, to make her students co-researchers in the initiative. These were clearly ambitious aims, which resulted in her being positioned in the initiative in a number of complex and interwoven ways, including as coach, pre-service tutor, (co)researcher with her students and as a student herself on the PGC in HE module. There were also significant issues of ethics and power relations that Kazia tried to acknowledge in designing, implementing and writing up the study as practitioner research.

Data collection methods for the initiative included taping (and later transcription) of the coaching sessions, interviews with the student teachers after the coaching sessions had been completed and completion of a research diary. Supplementary data for the study included the students' lesson plans, lesson observation notes from the tutor and the students' biographical and professional profiles. The initial data was analysed using basic grounded theory techniques; the resulting new layer of data was then used to create case studies of each student and of the classrooms within which s/he was learning to teach. The study also included a literature review critiquing the place of the concepts of reflective practice, mentoring and coaching in teacher education in England.

This was a small-scale but complex study; with its multiple aims, different levels of researcher/practitioner engagement and distinctive ethical issues, it is in many ways typical of the richness and complexity of practitioner research (Campbell 2007; Saunders 2007). It also blurred the distinctions between action learning, pedagogical research and practice based research (Campbell and McNamara in this volume). In terms of its outcomes, the study indicated a number of tensions around the use of coaching as a professional development strategy in teacher education. Even taking into account the very small scale of the study, there were no clear suggestions for future practice arising from it. The research process did, however, result in rich professional learning, as Kazia herself identified. This learning can be categorised in three ways:

- learning about all stages of the research process, with designing a small-scale case study and qualitative data analysis as particular development points;
- learning about the general field of teacher education, particularly in terms of understanding the rationale for and antecedents of the centrality of discourses and modes of reflective practice;
- generating knowledge about the processes of learning and teaching on a pre-service mathematics course. In this third area, specific areas of learning identified by Kazia included: further development of her teaching strategies for facilitating student reflection; enhanced knowledge of the diversity of her students' development patterns; increased awareness of the impact of the school classroom as the micro-setting for her students' teaching; and further exploration of the tensions between the roles of tutor as expert and tutor as facilitator.

Ideas for future development resulting from the study included implementing peer coaching and coaching trios (with one student observing and two others involved in coaching) and the use of 'critical incidents' to provoke reflection (Johal 2007: 12).

The research study undertaken was certainly well-designed and well-implemented. It also resulted in written work of publishable quality, but perhaps its particular power was that it had deep professional and personal relevance for Kazia's work. In the process of undertaking the study, Kazia was engaged in developing as a researcher, as well as deepening her knowledge of teacher education. In other words, this practitioner study enabled her to start the process of establishing an authentic research identity.

This case study is presented here an example of how, drawing on practitioner research frameworks, a formal learning structure can articulate and extend the informal, work-based and often unarticulated learning taking place in teacher educators' everyday work. Here a well scaffolded and focused practitioner research study provided strong starting points for developing knowledge of research in and on teacher education. I would argue that such a model is not only validated by previous work on good practice in academic induction, but also has the potential to combine research induction with relevant learning about practice as a teacher educator. A further advantage of this type of research-focused induction activity is that it has professional relevance and congruence between the development of a beginning teacher educator as a researcher *and* as a teacher of teachers. As the earlier sections of this chapter have shown, previous studies of new teacher educators suggest that this congruence may be an important factor in developing authentic research identities. My personal commitment to this model of learning will have been apparent to the reader, but in the conclusion to this chapter, I turn to addressing some of the issues around the use of such practitioner research in inducting teacher educators into HE.

Conclusions

In a recent work, Anne Campbell (2007) has identified the ways in which practitioner research has gained increasing recognition in education as a valued way of exploring and developing research-informed practice. As she identifies, these gains have been achieved in part through the work of Furlong and Oancea (2005) and the inclusion of criteria for the Research Assessment Exercise of 2008, which attempt to evaluate the 'impact' of practice-based and applied research. Further emphases on the value of practitioner research in HE settings has been achieved through the Higher Education Academy's (HEA) promotion of pedagogical research (Jenkins and Healey 2007). Some authors (Burchell and Dyson 2005; Campbell and Norton 2007) have also illustrated how practitioner research in HE-based teacher education can be a way of building vibrant research communities, often within UDEs where levels of research activity among teacher educators have historically been low.

But the hard fact is that within many other UDEs, teacher educators as new researchers may still find themselves struggling to reconcile their practice-based approach with definitions of 'acceptable' and 'conventional' research outputs, often underpinned by scientific/positivistic conceptualisations of what constitutes quality research (Groundwater-Smith and Mockler 2006). Given these tensions, how do we ensure that engaging individual teacher educators in practitioner research does not become a form of 'research cul-de-sac', which will not necessarily enable them to participate in the conventional discourses and practices associated with educational research in universities? Does practitioner research lead teacher educators towards small-scale and often individualised research efforts which are not necessarily given appropriate recognition, even within other parts of the field of teacher education?

The introduction to this chapter outlined the situation in England in which the majority of the universities providing teacher education programmes no longer receive core funding for their research activities. This situation creates a dark cloud over the future quality of research-informed teacher education provision in England. But there is perhaps a silver lining here in that new spaces may be opening up for a communal and intra-professional reframing of what 'counts' as research for teacher educators whose busy day job is practice in teacher education (Day 1995). Part of such a reframing might be recognising that well-farmed practitioner action research in teacher education offers a powerful way of building a new type of 'research capacity' in teacher education. Such research would need to have both individual and communal relevance in its exploration of current issues from teacher educators' practice. It would also need to be generative (that is, grounded in previous research), well designed, theoretically informed and capable of generating new insights into practice. Perhaps we should also be rethinking the ways in which practitioner research is designed, implemented, 'written up' and disseminated across the field of teacher education? Any such reframing of research activities in teacher education could be part of a long-term and intra-professional challenge for teacher educators in establishing a new language of learning and scholarship (Rowland 2005) about the profound relationships between research and practice as a teacher educator in HE settings. This new language could be informed by an intra-professional rearticulation of the distinctive identities and expertise of teacher educators in England, together with a re-evaluation of the essential contributions which this group has to make to high-quality, research-informed teacher education provision.

Acknowledgements

I would like to thank an ex-colleague, 'Kazia', for her permission to draw on her work to construct the case study detailed here and for all the professional rewards I have reaped through being her mentor for the last two years. Thanks also go to all my other mentees on the same course and to Anne Campbell and Marion Jones for the insights I have gained through working with them on a recent British Education Research Council (BERA) conference paper.

References

Acker, S. (1996) 'Becoming a teacher educator: voices of women academics in Canadian faculties of education', *Teaching and Teacher Education*, 13(1): 197–201.

Bassey, M. (2004) 'Analysis of the research assessment exercise: Assessment Unit 18 (Education)', *Research Intelligence*, 16(1): 5–7.

Boud, D. (2001) 'Situating academic development in professional work: using peer learning', *International Journal of Academic Development*, 4(1): 29–39.

Boyd, P., Baker, L., Harris, K., Kynch, C. and McVittie, E. (2005) 'Working with multiple identities: supporting new teacher education tutors in higher education', paper presented to the *British Educational Research Association Conference*, Glamorgan, Wales. September 2005.

Boyd, P., Harris, K. and Murray, J. (2007) *Becoming a Teacher Educator: Guidelines for the Induction of Newly Appointed Lecturers in Initial Teacher Education*. Bristol: ESCalate/Higher Education Academy.

Burchell, H. and Dyson, J. (2005) 'Action research in higher education: exploring ways of creating and holding the space for reflection', *Educational Action Research*, 13(2):

Campbell, A. (2007) *Practitioner Research*. London: TLRP. (Available at www.tlrp.org/capacity/rm/wt/campbell, accessed 16 May 2008.)

Campbell, A. and Norton, L. (2007) *Learning, Teaching and Assessing in Higher Education: Developing Reflective Practice*. Exeter: Learning Matters.

Clegg, S. (2005) 'Academic identities under threat?', paper presented to the *British Educational Research Association Conference*, Glamorgan, Wales. September 2005.

Dadds, M. and Kynch, C. (2003) 'The impact of the RAE 3b rating on educational research in teacher education departments', *Research Intelligence*, 84: 9–14.

Davison, J., John, P. and Murray, J. (2005) Knowing how, knowing why: the professional knowledge base of teacher educators', chapter presented at the *European Conference for Educational Research Conference*, Dublin, September 2005).

Day, C. (1995) 'Qualitative research, professional development and the role of teacher educators: fitness for purpose', *British Educational Research Journal*, 21(3): 357–69.

Ducharme, E. and Agne, R. (1989) Professors of education: uneasy residents of academe' in R. Wisniewski and E. Ducharme (eds) *The Professors of Teaching*. Albany: State University of New York Press.

Ducharme, E. (1993) *The Lives of Teacher Educators*. New York: Teachers College Press.

Ducharme, E. and Ducharme, M. (1996) 'A study of teacher educators: research from the United States of America', *Journal of Education for Teaching*, 22(1): 57–70.

Economic and Social Research Council (ESRC) (2005) *Demographic Review of the UK Social Sciences*. London: ESRC.

Eraut, M. (2000) 'Non-formal learning and tacit knowledge in professional work', *British Journal of Educational Psychology*, 70(1): 113–36.

Fish, D. (ed.) (1995) *Quality Learning for Student Teachers: University Tutors' Educational Practices*. London: David Fulton Publishers.

Furlong, J. (2005) 'New Labour and teacher education', *Oxford Review of Education*, 31(2): 119–34.

Furlong, J. (2007) 'The universities and *education*', keynote speech at the *University Council for the Education of Teachers Conference*, Daventry, UK. 9 November 2007.

Furlong, J., Barton, L., Miles, S., Whiting, C. and Whitty, G. (2000) *Teacher Education in Transition*. Buckingham: Open University Press.

Furlong, J. and Oancea, A. (2005) *Assessing Quality in Applied and Practice-based Educational Research: A Framework*. Oxford: Oxford University Department of Educational Studies.

Gilroy, P. (2008) 'The research environment post 2008: some possibilities', presentation to the *Research and Development Committee of the University Council for the Education of Teachers*, Institute of Education, London, 1 May 2008.

Goodson, I. (1995) 'Education as a practical matter: some issues and concerns', *Cambridge Journal of Education*, 25(2): 137–48.

Groundwater-Smith, S. and Mockler, N. (2006) 'Research that counts: practitioner research and the academy', *Review of Australian Research in Education*, 6: 105–17. A special edition of Australian Educational Researcher: Counterpoints on the Quality and Impact of Educational Research.

Hatton, E. (1997) 'Teacher educators and the production of Bricoleurs: an ethnographic study', *Qualitative Studies in Education*, 10(2): 237–57.

Jenkins, A. and Healey, M. (2005) *Institutional Strategies to Link Teaching and Research*. York: Higher Education Academy.

Johal, K. (2007) 'Using coaching to develop reflectivity in trainee teachers', unpublished research paper, Brunel University.

Maguire, M. (1994) 'The job of educating teachers', unpublished Ph.D. thesis, Kings College, University of London, London.

Maguire, M. (2000) 'Inside/outside the ivory tower: teacher education in the English academy', *Teaching in Higher Education,* 5(2): 149–65.

Menter, I., Brisard, E. and Smith, I. (2006) *Convergence or Divergence? Initial Teacher Education in Scotland and England*. Edinburgh: Dunedin Academic Press

Murray, J. (2002) 'Between the chalkface and the ivory towers? A study of the professionalism of teacher educators working on primary Initial Teacher Education courses in the English education system', *Collected Original Resources in Education*, 26(3):

Murray, J. (2005) 'Re-addressing the priorities: new teacher educators' experiences of induction into higher education', *European Journal of Teacher Education*, 28(1): 67–85.

Murray, J. (2006a) 'Constructions of caring professionalism: a case study of teacher educators', *Gender and Education*, 18(4): 381–97.

Murray, J. (2006b) 'Learning to play academic games? New teacher educators' constructions of academic identities in higher education', refereed paper at the *British Educational Research Association Conference*, University of Warwick, 2006).

Murray, J. (2007) 'Countering insularity in teacher education. Academic work on pre-service courses in nursing, social work and teacher education', *Journal of Education for Teaching*, 33(3): 271–91.

Murray, J. (2008) 'Teacher educators' induction into higher education: work-based learning in the micro communities of teacher education', *European Journal of Teacher Education*, 31(1): 17–34.

Murray, J. and Male, T. (2005) 'Becoming a teacher educator: evidence from the field', *Teaching and Teacher Education*, 21(2): 107–15.

Murray, J., Campbell, A., Hextall, I., Hulme, M., Jones, M., Mahony, P., Menter, I., Proctor, R. and Wall, K. (2008) 'Mapping the field of teacher education research: methodology and issues in a research-capacity building initiative in teacher education in the UK', *European Educational Research Journal*, 7(4): 459–74.

Reynolds, R. (1995) 'The professional self-esteem of teacher educators', *Journal of Teacher Education*, 46(3): 216–27.

Rowland, S. (2005) *The Enquiring University Teacher*. Buckingham: Society for Research in Higher Education and Open University.

Saunders, L. (2007) *Supporting Teachers' Engagement in and with Research*. London: TLRP. (Available at www.tlrp.org/capacity/rm/wt/saunders2.html, accessed 10 May 2008.)

Sikes, P. (2006) 'Working in a "New" University: in the shadow of the Research Assessment Exercise', *Studies in Higher Education*, 31(5): 555–68.

Trowler, P. and Knight, P. (2004) 'Theorising faculty entry to new work contexts' in M. Tight (ed.) *The Routledge Reader in Higher Education*. London: Routledge Falmer.

Whitelaw, S., Hobson, A. and Mitchell, N. (2005) 'Does current practice in initial teacher preparation in England meet future needs? Secondary teacher educators' perspectives', paper presented to the *British Educational Research Association Conference*, Glamorgan, Wales, September 2005.

Chapter 9

Teacher researchers in the UK: what are their needs?

Some lessons from Scotland

Ian Menter and Moira Hulme

Introduction

This chapter critically reflects on the needs of teacher researchers at different career stages in Scotland: beginning teachers, early career teachers (0–5 years) and experienced colleagues. Drawing on a current research project, it illustrates some of the dilemmas and tensions for teacher researchers and their supporters or mentors. *Research to Support Schools of Ambition* (2006–09) is a collaborative project funded by the Scottish Government wherein university-based mentors support teacher researchers in a network of 52 secondary schools (pupils aged 11–16/18 years) throughout Scotland (Menter and Hulme 2007).

The resurgence of interest in teacher research over the last decade offers possibilities for the development of new relationships between the policy, practitioner and research communities. Collaborative enquiry has been associated with the promotion of collegial practices in schools, the democratising of research relations and the encouragement of participatory decision making (through devolved leadership) (Stenhouse 1975; Carr and Kemmis 1986; Elliot 1991, 2004; Kincheloe 1991; Cochran-Smith and Lytle 1993, 1999; Noffke 1997). Proponents of educational action research have long argued that traditional 'outsider' research contributes to the disenfranchisement of teachers and that the exclusion of practitioners from debates about the professional knowledge base of teaching leaves the profession vulnerable to external intervention. Practitioner research is frequently aligned with a commitment to move from 'communities of practice' towards 'professional learning communities' (Street and Temperley 2005; McLaughlin *et al.* 2006). Renewed interest in teacher research accompanies moves towards integrated professional development frameworks in the UK, Europe and elsewhere (Jephcote *et al.* 2007). A great deal of attention is currently focused on teachers' professional development amid moves to standardise and harmonise qualification frameworks internationally (NFER 2006). The move towards Masters-level postgraduate programmes in the UK further extends opportunities for research engagement at an early stage in teacher formation (DCSF 2008).

However, these opportunities proceed within a context of increased central regulation (Mahony and Hextall 2000; Olssen *et al.* 2004; Furlong 2005). There are a number of paradoxes in the promotion of teacher research that require further consideration, especially teacher research programmes sponsored by government agencies, sometimes in partnership with business sponsors or philanthropic foundations. Within HE, public responses to the endorsement of particular forms of sponsored teacher-led enquiry, on a national scale, have tended to be under-theorised. From a policy sociology perspective the broader context within which programmes to promote cultures of self-evaluation and systematic self-study within schools are located needs consideration. While practitioner enquiry is being actively promoted across the career phases, we consider the contextual constraints on school-based enquiry and contribute towards problematising the role of HE in supporting teachers as researchers. In particular, we highlight the need for reflexivity in considering partnership with schools. The practice-based research requires partners to consider 'technical' issues of means but also ethical and political issues regarding the parameters, purposes and ends of enquiry. The degree of self-determination achieved in the selection of research 'problems', the difference between problem solving and problem posing practices, is significant (Campbell 2003).

This chapter critically examines teacher learning and development in the context of *Schools of Ambition*. While certainly this project has had a significant impact on the professional identities of a number of teachers across Scotland, there have been major constraints on the achievement of the full potential for learning, the original aspiration. Finally, the chapter sets out suggestions about the conditions that might be required for a fuller realization of teacher empowerment through research engagement.

The policy context

In Scotland, research engagement is embedded within the professional development framework for teachers (Kirkwood and Christie 2006). There is an expectation that, from an early stage in professional formation, Scottish teachers will use 'research and other forms of valid evidence to inform choice, change and priorities in promoting educational practices and progress' (GTC/QAA 2006: 4). The *Standard for Initial Teacher Education* expects that, by the end of a programme of initial teacher education, beginning teachers will 'know how to access and apply relevant findings from educational research' and 'know how to engage appropriately in the systematic investigation of practice' (GTCS/QAA 2006: 11). The Standard for Full Registration (SFR) expects registered teachers to have 'research-based knowledge relating to learning and teaching and a critical appreciation of the contribution of research to education in general' (GTCS/QAA 2006: 11). A commitment to 'critical self-evaluation and development' is one of the core professional values and personal commitments within the *Standard for Chartered Teacher* (GTCS 2002: 1). The Chartered Teacher is required to demonstrate a capacity to 'evaluate practice and reflect critically on it' and to 'ensure that teaching is based on reading and research' (GTCS 2002: 10). The Scottish teacher is thus not positioned as 'policy cipher' or 'compliant implementer of curriculum designs and pedagogies' that have developed elsewhere. Further evidence of this Scottish distinctiveness appears in the model of teacher preparation advanced in the Scottish Teachers for a New Era programme (Livingston and Colucci-Gray 2006).

Participation in teacher research

When teachers participate in research as an elective activity, there is the potential for research engagement to open up new spaces for teacher agency. The following section draws on 34 interviews with some of the teacher researchers who are leading strands of evaluation activity within the Scottish *Schools of Ambition* (June and July 2007). These included a range of promoted and non-promoted teachers. The interviews focused on a number of core themes: participants' previous engagement with 'research'; how they became involved in school-based enquiry; the support available to them; difficulties encountered; processes that supported sharing and collaboration in and beyond the school; and the contribution of research engagement to individuals' professional development.

The teachers' accounts revealed different routes into participation according to individuals' position in the career structure. The 2001 Agreement (Scottish Executive 2001), sought to address the 'hierarchical nature of teacher culture in Scotland' (MacDonald 2004: 414) by simplifying and flattening the career structure to afford greater opportunities for non-promoted teachers. Many authorities have moved towards 'faculty' structures in secondary schools, wherein principal teachers have management and curriculum responsibility for clusters of subjects rather than a single subject department. These faculty leaders are positioned as 'learning leaders', leading local developments in curriculum and pedagogy. It is, as yet, unclear whether the reduction in the ratio of promoted posts has produced 'a more collegiate profession' (MacBride 2007, col. 3957). The involvement of many non-promoted teachers in evaluation activities was through a process of targeted recruitment rather than responding to open invitations from senior management or other colleagues. More senior colleagues were undertaking research because it 'was part of their remit', aligned with their day-to-day responsibilities. The method of recruitment influenced teachers' attitudes to enquiry. The allocation of 'projects' to people was a source of discomfort for some, who nonetheless valued the opportunity to participate and hoped to develop their 'own' research.

This concentration of research activity created a perception of personal ownership. Research is reduced to an individual responsibility to be packaged in CPD portfolios and appraised at review meetings, rather than as a 'stance' or commitment to sustainable whole school change (Cochran-Smith and Lytle 2001). Class teachers comment:

> The most important thing for me would be being able to choose what the focus of my research was within the school improvement plan. Teachers are professionals. We're all intelligent people. We can make our own decisions and we can read the school improvement plan and decide on an area.

> I was selected. I didn't put forth that I was interested in action research. I was chosen because I had career aspirations and I think that this school said, 'Well here's a project to run with. See if you can build up your profile.'

> I wish it had been put out to staff to say what are you interested in? 'Do you wish to do any sort of research?' So you could have chosen your own; so you had a burning desire. It would be much easier to do the action research if you genuinely had a real issue with it.

Teachers' responses to involvement in school enquiry depended on their interpretation of the purpose of the research activity – the perceived benefits for themselves and school – and their confidence in carrying research plans forward. Many expressed initial uncertainty about how to proceed and what was expected Participation in small-scale evaluation studies, using an action enquiry model, was 'challenging'. Some teachers, especially those whose previous 'research' experience was informed by a 'scientific' paradigm, were initially unsettled and uncomfortable with an alternative investigative approach. Equally, while all participants were experienced in producing data for routine performance monitoring, several doubted whether they possessed the necessary skills to interpret statistical data for evaluation purposes. In the early stages there was a tendency to seek cause and effect relations and an expectation that investigations would suggest ready solutions to complex practical problems. In this way, in some accounts, enquiry was translated into a form of 'answerism' (Goodson 2003). In all cases there was external pressure to evidence impact derived from the additional resource provided through *School of Ambition* status.

Initial low levels of confidence were evidenced in requests for 'exemplars' of evaluation planning sheets and a desire to conform to an over-arching generic model, rather than ground investigations within a specific set of local circumstances; although responsiveness to local needs was a key feature of each school's 'transformational plan'. The busyness of school life created a pull towards compliance with a 'preferred' model of enquiry (context free) rather than more open forms of questioning that were situated. The role of the mentor was important in promoting variety in thinking about evaluation and in considering a range of evidence, especially qualitative indicators or 'soft' measures. This was particularly important in formulating responses to the need for schools to gather baseline measures of pupil self-esteem, confidence and aspirations.

Accommodating extended roles and responsibilities within existing workloads is a key challenge in the promotion of teacher research, even within schools where there is a strong commitment to such developments (Hulme 2008). In taking on the interrelated roles of teacher and researcher/evaluator, time was cited as the main barrier to progress by all participants. In most cases teachers struggled to maintain negotiated schedules of planned activities:

> Do I do the project or do I develop a new thing for my higher class? I'm here to teach and of course my priorities will always go with that, so it's finding time to sit down and get things started.

> It is a lot of extra work and you start to feel burdened by it. I have to keep reminding myself – and it's helped me to cope with stress better, I think – no, I can't do that and I shouldn't be expected to do that. This research is here to support what I am doing, not to make what I am doing more burdensome, you know.

University-based mentors sought to encourage a scholarly engagement with existing literature, but many teachers expressed difficulty in identifying relevant sources of research evidence accessible to practitioners. The teachers could not access a range of electronic resources without registering with the university library and no school opted to do this. Moreover, a restricted level of information literacy was in some cases a limiting factor. Teachers who endeavoured to engage with the literature often lacked confidence in discriminating between sources and were unsure about the criteria for choosing from the wealth or dearth of material their searches generated. The negative experience of trying to engage with available literature strengthened a perception of doing research as extra work, an 'add-on', detached from a class teacher's core concerns. Paradoxically, for teachers, the involvement of the university mentors was associated with a loss of control, which the mentors were seeking to strengthen through engagement with wider literature. This encouragement was interpreted by some teachers as an unrealistic demand on time and peripheral to their main motivation in becoming involved.

Meeting the needs of teacher researchers

The promotion of practitioner research from the late 1990s opened up new opportunities for tutors in HE to become involved in supporting school-led research. The sponsorship of applied and practice-based research can be read from a number of perspectives (Furlong and Oancea 2006). For some this represented an incursion into areas previously the preserve of HE and 'professional' researchers. Advocates of evidence-informed practice saw possibilities to bring greater rigour to decision-making in schools (Hargreaves 1996; MacBeath 1999; Hopkins 2001;). For others, renewed interest in teachers as researchers offered possibilities to address the 'disenfranchisement' of teachers (McNamara 2002; Saunders 2004).

Political legitimation was afforded to teacher research as a means of strengthening the link between theory and practice and tackling the 'two communities' problem. MacLure (1996: 274), among others, has written of the well rehearsed 'oppositional dilemmas' between 'theory and practice: between the personal and the professional; between the organisational cultures of schools and the academy; between 'insider' and 'outsider' perspectives; between the sacred languages of science, scholarship or research; and the mundane dialects of practice and everyday experience' (Sikes and Potts 2008). Teacher researchers are not usually writing for publication nor are they necessarily participating on award bearing courses. Their essential concern is 'doing the job better'.

School-based enquiry is primarily concerned with improvements for pupils, rather than contributions to public codified knowledge. Teacher researchers' interests are typically tied to a specific context. Oral/visual presentations at face-to-face workshops and networking events are favoured as appropriate strategies for sharing good practice, rather than academic writing. Research 'quality' is likely to be assessed in terms of relevance and credibility in the context of practice by schools, before judgements of 'theoretical and methodological robustness' (Furlong and Oancea 2006). For many teacher researchers, undertaking the enquiry is as important as the findings. Teachers focus not on the contribution of research to the production of new knowledge, but the generation of practice-relevant knowledge. While wary of asserting essentialist or unitary readings of 'the' teacher and 'the' university researcher, the cultural values of the school emphasise the 'practicality ethic' of teaching (Doyle and Ponder 1977). Teacher researchers are more likely to be concerned with producing outcomes that are 'immediate, relevant and actionable' (Ebbutt et al. 2000: 329). The creation of a practitioner-centred model of collaborative enquiry does not remove these tensions, which remain resilient to the solutions of 'policy magic' (Ball 1998: 124), such as those conjured in Hargreaves' (1999) conception of the 'knowledge creating school'.

Selecting teacher educators as research mentors is appropriate for a number of reasons. Mentoring is central to the task of supporting beginning teachers and to the promotion of continuing professional learning among experienced teachers. University departments with established traditions of collaborative working within ITE and CPD networks are well placed to support practitioner research and have a relatively secure basis on which to claim a shared language and shared culture with practitioners. The requirement of 'recent and relevant experience' and the involvement of seconded 'teacher tutors' strengthens these claims. Mentors selected from within ITE are 'boundary crossers', having made the transition from enquiring teacher to teacher-researcher to teacher educator, although the changes undertaken in 'leaving teaching' and assuming a new identity in higher education should not be underestimated (MacLure 1996; Murray 2005; Murray and Male 2005).

However, critics have also suggested that the position of teacher educators in relation to both schools and universities can create difficulties as well as drivers to partnership work. Arguably the degree of familiarity and extent of acculturation may lead some within teacher education to seek to protect the traditional craft culture of schools. Strong bonds within 'communities' are not necessarily positive and there is an emerging body of work on the deleterious consequences of negative social capital.

A key tension in supporting beginning teacher researchers is the issue of the application of quality standards within a public framework of account-ability. Differing views on the nature of educational research and the place and quality of teacher research create dilemmas for mentors who position themselves outside the funder's frame of reference. In reconciling competing demands to both support and challenge teachers as they evaluate, mentors are guided by an ethical commitment towards an 'ethos of care' (Zeni 2001). In practice, the dilemma faced between the exertion of 'academic authority' and a commitment to support teachers in a demanding set of circumstances, can result in a loosening of levels of engagement. Difficulties in satisfactorily reconciling competing positions may invoke detachment: disengagement or distancing from the requirement to make a judgement that might be deemed 'harmful' (or at least discouraging) to participants. A subtle shifting of position away from quality assurer or evaluator towards the role of supporter or counsellor changes the nature of the mentoring relationship.

In standing back from confronting mentees with fundamental quality judgements, the mentor's position may slip along the reflectivity-activity continuum, resulting in mentors adopting a more pragmatic approach. Here greater attention is afforded to manageability (making it happen) rather than questions around the educational ends that might be served. This sense-making is associated with assessing the impact of specific interventions and bringing a research focus to the routine school data gathering. Support for teachers becomes practical guidance in terms of action planning and target setting. The mentor's role is reduced to one of timekeeper and task manager, organising a timeline for activities and supervising completion of interim stages. The core task is essentially one of helping busy teachers keep their investigation in their sights and focus on the next steps, a practical, task-oriented view of collaboration essentially concerned with 'doing' the investigation – supporting the teacher as much as the enquiry; providing solutions rather than posing questions. While necessary when helping novice researchers with full-time teaching commitments to manage heavy workloads, this is a shallow model excluding more critically reflective consideration of (shared) aims and values. The relationship that could be achieved in these complex circumstances is one of 'bounded collaboration . . . which does not reach deep down to the grounds, the principles or the ethics of practice' (Hargreaves 1992: 228). The extent to which 'ownership' of the research process remains with the teacher becomes questionable. The focus becomes the teacher's responsibility in completing the work. The teacher's choices are made in the context of setting targets to support the progression of the evaluation. A key element of the mentor's role is the encouragement of self-regulation within the given parameters of the project plan; in the case of *Schools of Ambition,* a plan devised by school management and ratified by Senior Advisors from the Scottish Government.

The value of the practical support offered by the mentors cannot be underestimated as teachers struggled to juggle commitments and find time for investigation. Several spoke of the difficulties involved in sharing work-in-progress in a fragmented and congested school day. Difficulties in communicating plans and in coordinating activities across the school were repeatedly expressed. While there was evidence of a willingness to engage with others in the research, this proved challenging at both an organisational and interpersonal level. It is likely that the restricted opportunities for dialogue that were available to teachers prevented the generation of new ideas and challenges that would have supported further learning. In relation to Little's (1990) four types of collegiality – story telling, help, sharing and joint work – as indicators of collegial interaction, there was little evidence that activity in the schools progressed towards the forms of mutual interdependence associated with 'joint work'. Most communication about the research among the teacher researchers was conducted 'informally' at the level of sharing stories and seeking help. A culture of 'privacy' (Nias, *et al.* 1989) and the enduring realities of teacher isolation and subject-based territoriality are well documented barriers to collaborative enquiry in secondary schools (Cochran-Smith and Lytle 1993). Teachers talked about the difficulty of engaging the interest of colleagues and questioned the relevance of their work beyond their own classrooms and curricular responsibilities. This hesitancy contributed to processes of responsibilisation; as individual owners of separate projects they each needed to see the activity through to its 'private completion'.

Conclusion

This chapter has argued that school-university research partnerships need to be contextualised. Participants bring their personal past experiences to new initiatives, including their initial teacher education. They are similarly influenced by the prevailing cultural and structural context and by previous partnership experiences. In interrogating the notion of partnership, one needs to consider the communities that such work endeavours to bridge. The concepts of community and partnership carry positive connotations as descriptors of 'positive social conditions' (King 2002: 245). While one might question the tendency to overstate the internal cohesion of each 'community', there are significant and well documented differences between the organisational cultures of schools and university departments of education – although of course the latter have also been subject to major incursions of managerialism over the past 20 to 30 years. These differences are embedded within the political project of centrally sponsored and coordinated practice-based research and are worked through by participants as they make sense of their respective roles and assumed place within this shared work.

Significant tensions were experienced in the early stages of research engagement within the *Schools of Ambition:* personal, practical, professional and ethical. Rather than the ideal of 'comfortable collaboration and critical reflection' described by Peters (2002: 240), our experience suggests that mentors working with schools are likely to have uncomfortable experiences characterised by conflict between supporting and challenging mentees. Unsurprisingly, given the considerable workloads, teachers value hints and tips rather than reflective prompts and are exasperated and dispirited if this kind of support is not forthcoming from their mentor 'experts'. This is consistent with Smedley's (2001: 196) claim that for many teacher researchers '"know how" is more important than "knowing that" or "knowing why"'. A preference for toolkits and recipes may align with the broader movement in teacher education towards the 'teacher as technician' (Zeichner and Liston 1996) – mastering techniques of delivery rather than engaging in questions of purpose and value. The model of learning through mentoring that many of the teachers aspire towards is closer to Alexander's (1990) notion of 'imitation' than a sense of 'exploration' based on curiosity. Resistance or difficulties encountered in negotiating the literature maze meant that many accounts fell back to 'describing' developments, giving an 'account of' rather than 'accounting for' preferred ways of working. This is not to deny that considerable professional learning has occurred for many of the teachers involved; rather, much of this has been more limited than might originally have been hoped.

This chapter has proceeded from the position that an understanding of teacher research needs to be located within an understanding of teaching as 'work' (Ozga 1988; Nias 1989) and accordingly affords attention to the discourses that currently frame teaching and re-articulated versions of 'teacher research'. Studies of teachers as researchers have tended to focus on the products of enquiry, rather than context (Furlong and Salisbury 2005). On the one hand, expressions of the 'new localism' in the self-managing school and the commitment within the 'new professionalism' to a 'career of learning' can be seen to suggest processes of empowerment. Devolution of responsibility has the potential to enhance the professional status of teachers and increase the local autonomy of school leaders. One of the main arguments advanced for extending opportunities for practitioner research is the potential it offers for 'professional growth' (Somekh and Saunders 2007). Initial experiences within the *Schools of Ambition*, however, have identified tensions between the aspirations of 'extended' or 'democratic professionalism' (Sachs 2003) and contemporary culture and performance management.

Finally, it is important to consider the nature of 'evidence' and the purposes of evidence collection and analysis; as well as the shifting relations of authority, licence and control between schools, universities and central government. Devolution of responsibility necessarily involves accounting procedures: the production of a quantifiable evidence base to demonstrate effectiveness at individual and institutional level. Deliberation on the criteria for self-evaluation continues to work on the school from the outside-in. These powerful constraining influences on experienced teachers cut across and undermine the commitment to critical enquiry engendered in the early stages of professional formation, which in Scotland includes the development of a highly regarded programme of teacher induction (Draper and O'Brien 2006).

Although the rhetoric of self-managing schools and teachers as researchers is seductive, devolving responsibilities does not necessarily produce more 'democratic' or 'expansive' forms of professionalism. As Smyth (1993: 1) notes, 'educational systems are about acquiring *more* power, *not giving it away*' (original emphasis). The orientation of 'fast policy' towards 'fast solutions' to the 'problems' of practice, reinforces rather than challenges the 'discourse of delivery' in schools (Fielding 2003; McIntyre 2005). From this perspective, the language of 'what works' represents a form of 'answerism' and 'political quietism' (Goodson 2003). Teacher research within sponsored programmes can become a form of 'managed empowerment' that is technique and outcomes-focused. This chapter has sought to problematise the professionalising claims of teacher research in order to better support teachers as they engage in professional enquiry. The potential for teacher research to enhance the standing of the profession depends on teachers' capacity to respond creatively in context. Any outcome will depend, in part, on the relations of partnership negotiated with HE. For such partnerships to be fully productive they are likely to grow from collaboration in the early stages of teacher preparation, through induction and early professional development and into career-long further development. Our account of the Scottish experience, where there is greater evidence of the policy context being facilitative, demonstrates what a major challenge this is. How much greater may it be where the constraining effects of the twin pressures of performativity and accountability are even?

References

Alexander, R. (1990) 'Partnership in initial teacher education: confronting the issues' in M. Booth, J. Furlong and M. Wilkin (eds), *Partnership in Teacher Education*, pp. 59–73) London: Cassell.

Ball, S.J. (1998) 'Big policies/small world: an introduction to international perspectives in education policy', *Comparative Education*, 34(2): 119–30.

Campbell, A. (2003) 'Teachers' research and professional development in England: some questions, issues and concerns', *Journal of In-Service Education*, 29(3): 375–88.

Carr, W. and Kemmis, S. (1986) *Becoming Critical: Education, Knowledge and Action Research*. Lewes: Falmer.

Cochran-Smith, M. and Lytle, S.L. (1993) *Inside Out: Teacher Research and Knowledge*. New York: Teachers College.

Cochran-Smith, M. and Lytle, S.L. (1999) 'The teacher research movement: a decade later', *Educational Researcher*, 28(7): 15–25.

Cochran-Smith, M. and Lytle, S.L. (2001) 'Beyond certainty: taking an inquiry stance on practice' in A. Lieberman and L. Miller (eds) *Teachers Caught in the Action: Professional Development that Matters*, pp. 45–60. New York: Teacher' College Press.

DCSF (2008) *Being the Best for Our Children: Releasing Talent for Teaching and Learning*. London: DCSF.

Doyle, W. and Ponder, G.A. (1977) 'The practicality ethic in teacher decision making', *Interchange*, 8(3): 1–12.

Draper, J. and O'Brien, J. (2006) *Induction: Fostering Career Development at all Stages*. Edinburgh: Dunedin Academic Press.

Ebbutt, D., Robson, R. and Worrall, N. (2000) 'Educational Research Partnership: differences and tensions at the interface between the professional cultures of practitioners in schools and researchers in higher education', *Teacher Development*, 4(3): 319–37.

Elliott, J. (1991) *Action Research for Educational Change*. Buckingham, Open University Press.

Elliott, J. (2004) 'Using research to improve practice: the notion of evidence based practice' in C. Day and J. Sachs (eds) *International Handbook on the Continuing Professional Development of Teachers*, pp. 264–90. Maidenhead: Open University Press.

Fielding, M. (2003) 'The impact of impact', *Cambridge Journal of Education*, 33(2): 289–95.

Furlong, J. (2005) 'New Labour and teacher education: the end of an era', *Oxford Review of Education*, 31(1): 119–134.

Furlong, J. and Oancea, A. (2006) 'Assessing quality in applied and practice-based research in education: a framework for discussion. Review of Australian Research in Education: counterpoints on the quality and impact of educational research', *Australian Educational Researcher*, 6 (Special Issue): 89–104.

Furlong, J. and Salisbury, J. (2005) 'Best practice research scholarships: an evaluation', *Research Papers in Education*, 20(1): 45–83.

Goodson, I.F. (2003) *Professional Knowledge, Professional Lives: Studies in Education and Change*. Maidenhead: Open University Press.

GTCS/QAA (2006) *The Standard for Initial Teacher Education*. Edinburgh: GTCS.

GTCS (2002) *Standard for Full Registration*. Edinburgh: GCTS.

Hargreaves, A. (1992) 'Cultures of teaching: a focus for change' in A. Hargreaves and M. Fullan (eds) *Understanding Teacher Development*, pp. 216–36. New York: Teachers College Press.

Hargreaves, D. (1996) Teaching as a research-based profession: possibilities and prospects', paper presented at the *Teacher Training Agency Annual Lecture*, University of Cambridge, Department of Education.

Hargreaves, D. (1999. 'The knowledge creating school', *British Journal of Educational Studies*, 47(2): 122–44.

Hopkins, D. (2001). *School Improvement for Real*. London: Routledge.

Hulme, M. (2008) Researching teachers, changing teachers: practitioner research and the modernisation of teaching', unpublished Ph.D. thesis, Keele University.

Jephcote, M., Hulme, M., Mahony, P. Menter, I. and Moran, A. (2007) 'Learning to teach in post-devolution UK', Keynote Symposium, presented at the *BERA Conference 2007*, University of London, Institute of Education, 6 September 2007

Kincheloe, J.L. (1991) *Teachers and Researchers: Qualitative Inquiry as a Path to Empowerment*. London: Falmer Press.

King, M.B. (2002) 'Professional development to promote schoolwide inquiry', *Teaching and Teacher Education*, 18: 243–57.

Kirkwood, M. and Christie, D. (2006) 'The role of teacher research in continuing professional development', *British Journal of Educational Studies*, 54(4): 429–48.

Little, J.W. (1990) 'The persistence of privacy: autonomy and initiative in teachers' professional relations', *Teachers College Record*, 91: 509–36.

Livingston, K. and Colucci-Gray, L. (2006) 'Scottish Teachers for a New Era: where should we start from, if not together?' *Education in the* North, 14: 36–7.

MacBeath, J. (1999) *Schools Must Speak for Themselves: The Case for School Self-Evaluation*. London: Routledge.

MacBride (2007) *Education Committee, Official Report*, 24 January 2007, col. 3957.

MacDonald, A. (2004) 'Collegiate or compliant? Primary teachers in post-McCrone Scotland', *British Educational Research Journal*, 30: 413–3.

McIntyre, D. (2005) 'Bridging the gap between research and practice', *Cambridge Journal of Education*, 35(3): 357–82.

McLaughlin, C., Black-Hawkins, K., Brindley, S., McIntyre, D. and Taber, K.S. (2006) *Researching Schools: Stories from a Schools-University Partnership for Educational Research*. London: Routledge.

MacLure, M. (1996) 'Telling transitions: boundary work in narratives of becoming an action researcher', *British Educational Research Journal*, 22(3): 273–86.

McNamara, O. (ed.) (2002) *Becoming an Evidence-based Practitioner: a Framework for Teacher Researchers*. London: Routledge.

Mahony, P., and Hextall, I. (2000) *Reconstructing Teaching: Standards, Performance and Accountability*. London: Routledge/Falmer.

Menter, I. and Hulme, M. (2007) 'Research to support schools of ambition', *Education in the North*, 15: 47–50.

Murray, J. (2005) 'Re-addressing the priorities: new teacher educators and induction in higher education', *European Journal of Teacher Education*, 28(1): 67–85.

Murray, J. and Male, T. (2005) 'Becoming a teacher educator: evidence from the field', *Teaching and Teacher Education*, 21(2): 125–42.

National Foundation for Educational Research (2006) *Cross Nation Research into Mutual Qualifications*. Belfast: NfER.

Nias, J. (1989) *Primary Teachers Talking: A Study of Teaching as Work*. London: Routledge.

Nias, J., Southworth, G. and Yeoman, R. (1989) *Staff Relations in the Primary School: A Study of Organisational Cultures*. London: Cassell.

Noffke, S. E. (1997) 'Professional, personal and political dimensions of action research', *Review of Research in Education*, 22: 305–43.

Olssen, M., Codd, J. and O'Neill, A.M. (2004) *Education Policy: Globalisation, Citizenship and Democracy*. London: Sage.

Ozga, J. (ed.) (1988) *Schoolwork: Approaches to the Labour Process of Teaching*. Milton Keynes: Open University Press.

Peters, J. (2002) University school collaboration: identifying faulty assumptions. *Asia Pacific Journal of Teacher Education*, 30(20): 229–42.

Sachs, J. (2003) *The Activist Teaching Profession*. Buckingham: Open University Press.

Saunders, L. (2004) Grounding the democratic imagination: developing the relationship between research and policy in education', professorial lecture. London: University of London, Institute of Education.

Scottish Executive (2001) *A Teaching Profession for the 21st Century (McCrone Agreement)*. Edinburgh: Scottish Executive.

Sikes, P. and Potts, A. (eds) (2008*) Researching Education from the Inside: Investigations from Within*. London: Routledge.

Smedley, L. (2001) 'Impediments to partnership: a literature review of school-university links', *Teachers and Teaching: Theory and Practice*, 7(2): 189–209.

Smyth, J. (ed.) (1993) *A Socially Critical View of the Self-Managing School*. London: Falmer.

Somekh, B. and Saunders, L. (2007) 'Developing knowledge through intervention: meaning and definition of "quality" in research into change', *Research Papers in Education*, 22(2): 183–97.

Stenhouse, L. (1975) *An Introduction to Curriculum Research and Development*. Oxford: Heinemann.

Street, H. and Temperley, J. (2005) *Improving Schools through Collaborative Enquiry*. London: Continuum.

Zeichner, K. and Liston, D. (1996) *Reflective Teaching: An Introduction*: Lawrence Erlbaum.

Zeni, J. (ed.) (2001) *Ethical Issues in Practitioner Research*. New York: Teachers College Press.

Chapter 10

The place of assessment

Creating the conditions for praxis inquiry learning

Anne Davies

Introduction

Recently we began teaching a significantly reshaped Bachelor of Education (B.Ed.) programme at Victoria University, based on three essential and interconnected features: authentic practice, praxis inquiry learning and the validation of practice and learning (School of Education 2005: 15). The course reflects our deep commitment to teacher education, which puts learning, communities and social action at the centre of practice (Kruger and Cherednichenko 2005/2006).

After two years of teaching the course, it is time to reflect on its quality. This chapter reports my inquiry into the place of assessment within a praxis inquiry conception of teacher education. I begin by describing the three-part conception that underpins our course and then focus on the second year to show how the conception has shaped practice. I then take a magnifying glass to our assessment practices, seeking a deeper understanding about our practice and questions that might take us into the future.

Authentic practice through Project Partnerships

To bring the goal of authentic practice to life we have designed our initial teacher education so that pre-service teachers' experiences in school-university partnerships are the starting point for learning. We argue that:

> the authenticity of Project Partnerships, the designation given to school-university partnerships at Victoria University, results from their commitment to the learning of all of the participants in teacher education: school students, pre-service teachers, their mentor teachers and teacher educators.
> (School of Education 2005: 14–15)

In addition to the trade time block placements, our year-long partnership also includes weekly engagement and a 'negotiated, needs-based applied curriculum project (ACP) designed to support school student learning'. These strong school-university partnerships enable pre-service teachers to express responsibility for school students and their learning while working with mentor teachers on a curriculum initiative.

In every semester, Project Partnerships are structurally linked to the B.Ed. programme through two units of study. One involves Praxis Inquiry and the other a focus on an aspect of Curriculum, Pedagogy and Assessment. In addition to being linked to Project Partnerships, these subjects are mutually linked so that the Praxis Inquiry shapes the inquiry process while the Curriculum, Pedagogy and Assessment unit of study provides discipline content.

Practice into theory using a Praxis Inquiry Protocol

As a second essential feature, we have turned the traditional theory-into-practice conception of teacher education on its head, and adopted a practice-into-theory (or praxis) conception, believing that to start from a practitioner's experiences not only 'imparts a democratic basis to learning about teaching . . . (but) it also challenges the practitioner to take responsibility for generating personal theoretical perspectives on which to build morally sustainable and effective practice' (School of Education 2007).

In order to shape praxis inquiry, we use a Praxis Inquiry Protocol (Kruger and Cherednichenko 2005/06: 8), which acts as a bridge between the partnership setting and the university coursework (School of Education 2005: 16). The protocol encourages pre-service teachers to work through four phases of inquiry by describing, explaining, (personally) theorising and changing their practice in Partnerships. Arguably, participation in authentic practice 'stimulates pre-service teachers to seek answers to personally and collectively significant questions and challenges about the relationships, curriculum and pedagogical practices experienced in the partnership settings' (School of Education 2005: 14–15).

The protocol invites pre-service teachers to begin their inquiry by engaging with *initiating questions*: What do I wonder about? What are my impressions and emotional responses? What looks to be the everyday routine? What is out of the ordinary? It then encourages them to ask different kinds of questions: *ontological questions* (about experience, understanding and commitment); *epistemological questions* (about knowledge and its application) and *technical questions* (about effective strategy and technique).

In using this Protocol to shape an inquiry process, we therefore 'encourage pre-service teachers to answer their questions . . . (and) deepen their understanding of young people and their learning, social and education theory and currently accepted curriculum and pedagogical strategies' (School of Education 2005: 15–16).

Validation of practice and understanding

The third structural dimension is an expectation that pre-service teachers will have an opportunity to validate their practice and understanding through the assessment process. Indicating the significance of the connection between the praxis inquiry units of study and the curriculum, pedagogy and assessment units, they are asked to 'account for their practice and understanding by presenting a Professional Exposition' (School of Education 2005: 16). This forms part of the assessment for both the Praxis Inquiry and the Curriculum units of study and is conceived in three ways: for pre-service teachers to report their contribution to the learning of school students; to demonstrate their own learning; and as an opportunity to validate their developing understanding and practice. The exposition seeks to incorporate all reporting associated with the pre-service teacher's activities and progress in Project Partnerships. In addition to the Professional Exposition, each unit of study has additional assessment task/s appropriate to the content.

The second year

In the second year of the B.Ed., two units run simultaneously: Making the Conditions for Learning (the Praxis Inquiry unit) and Science, Environment and Society (the Curriculum Pedagogy and Assessment unit). Across the two units are five assessment tasks designed to shape inquiry and give opportunity for pre-service teachers to present their developing practice and understanding:

- a Professional Exposition (50 per cent for each unit);
- a Praxis Inquiry Log (20 per cent for Making the Conditions for Learning);
- an Evaluation of Pedagogies (30 per cent for Making the Conditions for Learning);
- a micro-teaching activity (30 per cent for Science, Environment and Society);
- an Inquiry into an Issue (20 per cent for *Science, Environment and Society*).

There are also two ungraded requirements for satisfactory completion: an initial plan and a final report for the ACP and the Partnership mentor's report.

Through Project Partnerships, pre-service teachers are placed in an educational setting. They spend each Tuesday and three full weeks in Partnership. In addition, each tutorial group participates in focused school visits (five days over five weeks) as part of *Making the Conditions for Learning*. Working in teams in the same classroom, with the same students each week, they contribute to the classroom programme, mainly science. They focus their inquiry to consider what they and their mentors are doing to 'make the conditions for learning' and what can be learned by connecting these ideas to the teaching of *Science, Environment and Society*.

Assessment

There is a clear and explicit expectation that there will be a 'clear alignment between expected learning outcomes' what is 'taught and learnt, and the knowledge and skills assessed' (James, McInnis and Devlin 2002). It can therefore be assumed that assessment will shape what pre-service teachers will be doing and learning in our course. If there are three essential underpinning principles – authentic practice, praxis inquiry learning and the validation of practice and learning – then they need to be evident in assessment. As I have focused on assessment in the B.Ed., I have raised questions. How do we use authentic practice as a starting point for learning? What does praxis inquiry learning look like? What kind of opportunities have we created for the validation of practice and understanding?

To inform my inquiry and answer these questions, I have drawn on a range of evidence: course and unit documents; pre-service teacher evaluations and reflections; and the teaching team's documents recording planning, dialogue and reflection.

How do we use authentic practice as a starting point for preservice teachers' learning?

Wondering whether we had successfully used authentic practice as the starting point as indications, I examined the assessment tasks looking for references to Project Partnerships.

I found that three of the five assessment tasks – the Praxis Inquiry Log, the Evaluation of Pedagogies and the Professional Exposition – clearly use practice as a starting point. The Praxis Inquiry Log asks for description and reflection on experience, both in Partnership settings and university. The Evaluation of Pedagogies task asks pre-service teachers to inquire into the range of teaching strategies and pedagogical approaches practised during the focused school visits. For the Professional Exposition, pre-service teachers are asked to construct a portfolio that includes documents which are documentary evidence of practice in Project Partnerships, including: class, team and school planning documents; reflective annotations and commentaries; lesson plans with mentor feedback and personal reflections; and an ACP.

In their evaluations, pre-service teachers report that the most helpful/ stimulating aspect of their work in these two units is connected to their practice in schools: the year-long Partnership and the focused visits. While there are criticisms from some, who think that there is not enough time in the focused visits, and that they create extra work which is not always shared equally, they generally agree that the extra exposure to schools during this time is helpful and stimulating. In their reflections, the teaching team note that this five-week Partnership provides a great opportunity to scaffold the process of practical planning, delivery and reflection. From a school perspective, principals have noted that the VU model places '. . . pre-service teachers in schools for sufficient time to allow them to make a real contribution to curriculum development and teaching in the school' (Education and Training Committee 2005: 165).

The remaining two assessment tasks, Microteaching and the Inquiry into an Issue, do not require the use of Project Partnerships as a starting point, yet there is an expectation that they will consider how their learning might inform their teaching practice. They are asked to reflect on the connection between their micro-teaching and their work in Partnerships and in the Inquiry to write a statement about what has been learned and its application to teaching practice for Science, Geography or Environmental Education.

The teaching team also noted that when they encourage authentic practice as a starting point for learning about science education, many pre-service teachers argue that this is not possible. In their experience, some mentors do not teach science, and in other instances, science is taught but not during the time at the school. Thus, they feel it is hard to create an opportunity for teaching science or even collecting resources.

What does praxis inquiry learning look like?

If assessment shapes the pre-service teachers' learning, then it is also important to understand whether our assessment tasks really provide a scaffold for systematic praxis inquiry learning. I returned to the assessment tasks for a second time. By looking at the verbs used in each task, I was able to map the action that was expected of pre-service teachers. By grouping the activity according to the four phases of inquiry articulated in the Praxis Inquiry protocol (describing, explaining, (personally) theorising and changing practice), it was possible to understand the quality of engagement as four clusters of practice.

Opportunities for describing practice

I found that pre-service teachers are asked to document their practice by planning, recording experiences and collecting evidence. The recording dimension includes both the planning and the experience of practice. Planning includes preparing for a range of lessons and the ACP. Experience is recorded retrospectively. The science journal encourages a focus on content and the Praxis Inquiry Log encourages a chronological record of engagement. Mid-year reports, negotiated between mentor and pre-service teacher, add another dimension. There is also an expectation that pre-service teachers will collect the documented evidence of practice and gather resources related to the area of science, environment and society.

Opportunities for explaining practice

In the second cluster it became evident that pre-service teachers are encouraged to explain their practice by reflecting, discussing and making connections. Reflection is an integral part of evaluating teaching with an explicit focus on planning, delivery, content, pedagogy and learning. In addition, the Praxis Inquiry Log provides an opportunity to extend description into thoughtful reflection and explanation while there is an expectation that the collection of evidence and artefacts in the Professional Exposition are explained through the use of annotations and commentaries. Other activities involve seeking and responding to feedback from peers and mentors connected to tasks for *Making the Conditions for Learning*, where pre-service teachers are involved in reflecting on and explaining the efforts to create the conditions for learning and also in *Science, Environment and Society* where the discussion revolves around the micro-teaching.

The third and maybe largest area of action involves making connections. Here pre-service teachers are asked to use and refer to the State learning standards and specific progression points with a focus on Science but also with an expectation that links will be made with other learning domains and dimensions. The second aspect of making connections involves linking practice and theory by using selected readings about teaching and learning, specifically the constructivist learning model, and adopting a consistent approach to citation and referencing.

A small but articulate group of pre-service teachers note the value and relevance of focusing on multiple learning theories. One reports feeling 'fully informed about the theory of teaching', while another notes a change: 'Instead of only practice described (now I can) explain how it affects me and how I can use it in the future'. An examination of pre-service teachers' work demonstrates a growing awareness about:

- various ways of conceptualising learning (constructivism; experiential learning; behaviourist approaches; productive pedagogies);
- various ways of understanding students' individual differences (Gardner's conception of multiple intelligences; Kolb's distinction between Visual, auditory and kinesthetic learners; Hermann's brain dominance theory);
- various ways of promoting thinking (Costa's habits of mind; De Bono's Thinking Hats; the distinction between brainstorming, mind mapping and concept mapping and the usefulness of each tool);
- various aspects of the curriculum (essential learning, particularly in relation to Science, Geography and the interdisciplinary strands).

A third dimension in making connections involves engagement using conceptual and procedural scientific knowledge in the explanation of practice.

Opportunities for personally theorising practice

Each assessment task also provides opportunities to encapsulate learning, articulate beliefs and construct an account of personal learning. Written opportunities include: the Evaluation of Pedagogies; a commentary on practice in Partnership; an evaluation of the micro-teaching; and a statement about science learning. They are encouraged to articulate their personal theorising and emerging beliefs in their praxis inquiry journals and make connections back to their initial questions to identify what had been learned and how. The third aspect of practice theorised involves constructing an account as an exposition or portfolio. I first placed this action in practice described, then in practice explained and then it was the verb 'constructing' that led me to consider the activity as personal theorising. In the teaching team's experience of the presentation of portfolios, it is when the personal theories (sometimes explicit and sometimes implied) about teaching and learning underpin the construction of a portfolio it becomes possible to distinguish one from another.

Opportunities for changing practice

When it came to opportunities for changing practice, there was evidence that the assessment tasks provide opportunities to rethink, extrapolate and plan new action for improvement. The assessment tasks provide opportunities to rethink practice by identifying and discussing changes that might be made on the basis of experience, explanation, gaining new knowledge and theorising. In addition to rethinking, the Praxis Inquiry Log provides opportunity for planning action based on reflection and theorising. Possibly this dimension of praxis inquiry might also create a space for creativity, innovation and adaptation but these ideas are not specified assessment tasks. While the Praxis Inquiry Log and the Evaluation of Pedagogies incorporate a focus on changing practice, surprisingly this was not an explicit expectation in the Professional Exposition.

What kind of opportunities have we created for the validation of practice and understanding?

On returning to the accreditation documents and the assessment tasks for a third time, I realise that not only are there multiple opportunities for the validation of practice and understanding but there is also a clear expectation that learning will be made public. This inquiry revealed that the combined assessment agenda in these two units provides pre-service teachers with opportunities to present, teach and engage in dialogue. For instance, a significant aspect of the Professional Exposition is presenting in small groups. The Micro-teaching also provides an opportunity to make practice public as each member of the tutorial group works with a small group to present a lesson to peers. Finally, the inquiry and portfolio presentations and the culminating

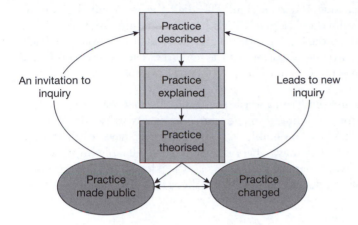

Figure 10.1 Praxis inquiry learning

conversations which follow the micro-teaching and Praxis Inquiry Log reflections provide further opportunity for making practice public through focused dialogue. When I looked at the question of validation of practice and understanding, I realised that our university classroom is the site for systematic and public validation of practice and understanding and that each of the assessment tasks provides a different kind of opportunity to be systematic about such validation.

I have come to see that validation as creating an integral and fifth dimension in the praxis inquiry process – practice made public. In this way, praxis inquiry learning explicitly incorporates practice made public and takes on both a personal and a collaborative dimension through the connected goals of improving practice and providing an invitation to new inquiry (Figure 10.1). The two assessment tasks connected with *Making the Conditions for Learning*, the Praxis Inquiry Log and the Evaluation of Pedagogies, achieve this most clearly. In combination these two assessment tasks provide a multi-faceted space for learning. Both demand a focus on practice, both providing a different kind of opportunity to describe, explain and theorise practice with an expectation in each that this process will lead to the identification of changes in practice and subsequent new inquiries. They also provide different and complementary opportunities for making practice public with the effect of inviting peers to wonder and engage in inquiries of their own. Each is explored in more detail in the following paragraphs.

Praxis Inquiry Log

Each week pre-service teachers record their experiences in Praxis Inquiry Logs. These experiences and ideas then become the focus for personal and collaborative discussion and reflection. The dialogue resulting provides an opportunity for validation of practice and understanding. In Week 5 the teaching team collects the Logs in order to give individual and group feedback, providing another layer of validation. At the semester's end, having completed the task of marking the Logs for her group, one of my colleagues emailed:

> The best logs are wonderful and the pre-service teachers have realised that the exploration has indeed made the unit/s a worthwhile learning experience. They have been able to relate what they have learnt to their practice in a very deep way. There is overall a considerable improvement since the five week mark and in some cases it is massive. There is also a general realisation that attending class makes a hell of a difference so these are pluses.

When I examined the final reflective comments in the Praxis Inquiry Logs from my group it was incredibly revealing. I cannot recall pre-service teachers articulating so clearly what they had learned. Of course some reflections were rich with observations and others sparse but there were some trends.

They note that the Praxis Inquiry Log provides a place for asking questions at different stages during the semester. They use the questions as a guide for their inquiry and learning and as a checkpoint at the semester's end to gauge success and the emergence of new questions. One pre-service teacher noted: 'I didn't intentionally answer my questions but they obviously guided me and I found answers through learning at university and practising at my partnership school'.

The structural organisational value of the Log helped pre-service teachers to: describe and reflect on experiences when still fresh; to 'remember thoughts and feelings'; and to 'really focus our minds as to what was happening in our schools and we could learn as a result'. Some feel that writing and thinking about their ideas makes them better teachers and that the log is useful for encouraging them to 'listen to others in order to write about what that person had said'.

The Praxis Inquiry Log offers opportunity to explain, evaluate, sort ideas and form personal theories. It helps them to 'recall thoughts', reflect on things at a 'whole new level' and 'sort through ideas in order to share them with others'. They noted how they used the Log to 'show the thinking' that had gone on during the semester, and then to 'work out' what ideas they liked and disliked.

Finally, they used their Praxis Inquiry Logs to think about their practice – what has 'worked well' and when there is a need to 'plan for improvement'. At a personal level they can also work out what they 'would like to learn in the future'. One pre-service teacher noted: 'It has given me a chance to reflect on my previous experiences and helped me to work and grow on these experiences.' Another explained how it had been an opportunity 'to really evaluate my lessons and learn from them before my two week block.' Another, looking back, noted how the log helped her to see how much she had learned about 'science and introducing it in my class in the future'.

Some noted how the Log really suited their learning style and the kind of person they were, with one referring to their list of dot points and observing: 'These sentences all explain the kind of person I am, so you can see exactly why I really enjoyed keeping a log book . . . it is who I am and how I learn.' Another noticed that 'by writing things down you can visually see what you need to improve . . . it's almost a motivation to improve'. Demonstrating a clear process that leads to conversations with colleagues, one noted that 'over time, after reflection and discussing with peers, I have also been able to gain the confidence to speak in front of my peers, which is something I was very frightened of at the beginning of the year.'

Not surprisingly, some pre-service teachers did not like keeping a Praxis Inquiry Log. Their reflections indicated that it was not 'productive', that the purpose was not always clear and that it was 'frustrating to answer questions with more questions'. Some found that it was 'a struggle' to keep the log up to date, with one admitting that it had been left to the last minute which meant that she 'forgot what had happened'. Several argued against having to write things down. One noted that 'it was hard to reflect on things I had learned when I prefer to mentally reflect' and another argued that keeping the Log did not 'cater for people like me who don't need to write things, who can't find the right words to put on paper . . . therefore it is an unfair assessment . . . assessment must be accessible to all.' Those who did not enjoy keeping a log indicated that they would sometimes prefer to 'talk about the answers as a whole group' or to 'write an overall reflection at the end rather than having a fixed logbook.'

Evaluation of pedagogies

Framed as an inquiry, the Evaluation of Pedagogies was designed to encourage pre-service teachers to document and evaluate their teaching experiences. Again, their work is revealing. Our team gained a clear sense of what they had been doing and what they had learned. We realised that some had developed a deep understanding about the range of pedagogies you might find in a primary classroom and awareness about the value of different pedagogies for different situations. In one semester, pre-service teacher learning was recorded in mind maps and presented to their mentors. This was not an assessment task but the work produced by the group was a great validation of their practice and their deepening understanding and the richness of their shared beliefs about what it takes to make the conditions for learning. This led me to wonder whether a mind map might be included in future assessment, especially since it provided an opportunity to model assessment as an authentic, professional engagement and also a graphic alternative to a written report.

Professional exposition

Pre-service teachers construct their Professional Expositions using evidence and reflections acquired in Partnerships. Most pre-service teachers take incredible care with their expositions, some noting that this is a 'fantastic assessment task' and 'helpful for future teaching'. An important part of the process involves annotating the artefacts in expositions but the quality of annotations is inconsistent – from excellent to none.

All pre-service teachers present their Professional Expositions to a member of the teaching team and a small group of peers in a roundtable. One noted putting 'lots of science in the portfolio . . . it was a great sharing thing as teachers should do.' Importantly, feedback indicates that pre-service teachers expect a respectful opportunity to present their portfolios and receive feedback, including a personal exchange which is on time and allows sufficient time.

While for some it has been a productive activity, it seems as though the Professional Exposition provides an unrealised opportunity. Both pre-service teachers and the teaching team have consistently raised questions about expected outcomes, criteria, content, quantity, quality and differentiation from other tasks. On the basis of this feedback, we need to clarify the value of the task, articulate clearer expectations and criteria, scaffold the process of annotation and arrange for presentations which are respectful opportunities for collaborative validation. A number of questions have emerged:

- How can practice that has been changed be built into the Professional Exposition?
- How can we be more explicit about the place of the exposition in the systematic validation of practice and learning?
- How can the emphasis be shifted to ensure the focus is on quality evidence rather than quantity? What's the difference between a scrapbook and a Professional Exposition?
- How can we build pre-service teachers skills in annotating evidence to reveal what has been experienced and learned?
- How can we be clearer about the purpose and expectations of the Exposition? What is the difference between an Exposition produced by a pre-service teacher in the second year and any one in other years of the course?
- Is it possible to use the Exposition to make a stronger connection between the praxis inquiry unit *Making the Conditions for Learning* and the curriculum/pedagogy/assessment unit *Science, Environment and Society*?

Micro-teaching and the Inquiry into an Issue

The two final assessment tasks, Micro-teaching and the Inquiry into an Issue, complement the Professional Exposition and provide additional opportunities for validation of experience and understanding associated with the Curriculum, Pedagogy and Curriculum unit *Science, Environment and Society*.

The first component of Micro-teaching involves working in a group to plan and teach a Science lesson to the group. The second component involves reflecting on and evaluating the lesson. Evaluation responses indicate that this activity is extremely popular. The opportunity to plan together and to investigate areas of science that are found interesting is appreciated and can help develop expertise in areas where confidence is lacking. The actual experience of the Micro-teaching is described as fun, engaging, practical, hands on, interesting, innovative and exciting. From their perspective, the Micro-teaching gives them good personal experience and is useful in providing ideas for Project Partnerships. The possibilities to model, share, do and see are all acknowledged.

The Inquiry into an Issue provides opportunity to inquire into and make a presentation on an issue of personal interest. The issue might be inspired by Project Partnerships, the university curriculum, passion for a particular topic, questions or a puzzle. Unfortunately, some make a pragmatic decision to select a topic where they have existing knowledge and so their inquiry is limited. However, most evaluation responses indicate that the activity is helpful and stimulating. They note that the opportunity to investigate an area of science is valuable on a personal level and builds confidence. The presentation of inquiries is a great opportunity to share what has been learned and the ideas they get from each other are interesting, helpful and useful. Amid the over-whelmingly positive observations, a few responses expressed a view that there are too many activities led by pre-service teachers that are repetitive and irrelevant.

Pre-service teachers were clear that the semester-long exposure to science had value. For one there was a shift from 'hating science to appreciating and understanding it a bit more' and another found that 'science can create fun and exciting sessions that promote questioning.' Yet another noted how the experience had led to an 'increased confidence' in her ability to understand and teach science. Indeed, many indicated the value of learning about different methods of teaching in general, and science in particular, with specific reference to the realisation that science could be 'integrated into all the subjects in the curriculum'. They also appreciated gathering and sharing useful resources. Putting a contrary point of view, one felt that 'there was no practical advice that could be taken into (the) placement'. This highlights the need for time to discuss the connections between practice in Partnerships and the university classroom experience and build a shared responsibility for generally creating interest.

The place of assessment

Embarking on this inquiry, I set myself the task of examining the place of assessment in creating the conditions for praxis inquiry learning. In the two units examined, there is a clear connection between authentic practice, praxis inquiry learning and the validation of practice and understanding; the experience in Project Partnerships is explicitly included in our university classrooms and this in turn connects to the assessment tasks. In this way assessment is embedded into the weekly programme consistent with our goal of seeing assessment *as, for* and *of* learning. In effect, the assessment tasks in these units provide a framework for a continual process of learning and improvement initiated in the Partnership experience, and supported by the Praxis Inquiry Protocol. But the notes from a recent meeting indicate that in addition to those identified in this inquiry, many questions remain. We noted over 50 on the whiteboard, including:

* How can we keep the focus on school students' learning?
* Who is being quiet and who is opening up?
* How do we keep the reality in our pedagogy?
* Are pre-service teachers still responding to what they think we want?
* If we still have set tasks, are we really doing praxis inquiry?

I want to argue that while the assessment tasks create possibilities for praxis inquiry learning, they also restrict what is possible. Smith (1993: 101–2), a cultural geographer, sees 'the politics of daily life as inherently spatial'. Drawing on his conception I have come to understand that while assessment tasks provide a partitioned geography within which learning takes place, they also contain or constrain praxis inquiry learning. If this is indeed true, then assessment is not merely a fixed framework or process but what Smith refers to as an 'active progenitor', both defining the boundaries and creating the possibilities for praxis inquiry learning.

This inquiry presents a complex assessment geography in which multiple tasks connect process and content. It highlights conditions for praxis inquiry learning, which are:

* initiated in authentic practice and realised in various settings;
* shaped by a Praxis Inquiry Protocol and evident in clusters of practice;
* validated in individual and collaborative activities that are shaped by artefacts of practice and commentaries that express understanding.

Yet the inquiry also reveals boundaries and it seems as though the questions that have emerged must take us into the future.

References

Education and Training Committee (2005) Step up, step in, step out', report on the inquiry into the suitability of pre-service training in Victoria, Parliament of Victoria.
James, R., McInnis, C. and Devlin, M. (2002) *Assessing Learning in Australian Universities*. Victoria: Centre for the Study of Higher Education and the Australian Universities Teaching Committee.

Kruger, Tony and Cherednichenko, Brenda (2005/06) 'Social justice and teacher education: re-defining the curriculum', *International Journal of Learning*, 12: 1–25.

School of Education (2005) Submission to the Victorian Institute of Teaching for the Bachelor of Education, 1. Victoria, Australia: School of Education, Victoria University.

School of Education (2007) *Unit Guide 2007: AEB2210*. Making the Conditions for Learning. Victoria, Australia: School of Education, Victoria University.

Smith, Neil (1993) 'Homeless/global: scaling places' in J. Bird, B., Curtis, T. Putnam, G. Robertson and L. Tickner, *Mapping the Futures: Local Cultures, Global Change*. London and New York: Routledge.

Chapter 11

Learning by doing

A year of qualitative research

Alexandra Miletta

Introduction

This chapter examines the educative value of designing and implementing original practitioner research projects in the classrooms of graduate students enrolled in a seminar taught and researched for the past four years. My research on how teachers' beliefs are shaped and changed by learning to do qualitative research shows how sustained inquiry can be a transformative learning experience, when guided by supportive peers. It also addresses explicit notions of developing teachers' resiliency in challenging urban school settings, particularly when teachers' autonomy is thwarted:

> Jimmy's unique relationship with asking questions, demonstrates the real impact that family and cultural teachings have on children's behaviour, feelings and learning within the classroom. Jimmy has taught me to look forward to discovering surprising answers, and allowing my questions to inspire future paths of inquiry.
>
> (Elizabeth, a second-year elementary teacher, Brooklyn)

> As difficult as this job can be, I do hope it will change for the better. I believe this will happen as teacher researchers become brave risk-takers in sharing with the community the 'whole truth' about their teaching journey. I am hoping the truth will bring about more support and resources for students, teachers, and administrators . . . so they can share their talents and essence to reboot, recharge and inspire the community.
>
> (Linda, a second-year elementary art teacher, Manhattan)

These excerpts from two of my graduate students' theses centre their insight, courage and honesty. Through my analysis of their work in my year-long practitioner research course over the last four years, I hope to convey some of what I have learned from them. I sincerely believe in the power of the tools of qualitative research to illuminate the complexities of learning in educational contexts, but accurately capturing the inspiring passion of these brave and mostly novice teachers is a formidable challenge. The odds are decidedly stacked against; urban schools lose half their teachers within the first five years (National Commission on Teaching and America's Future 2002). The familiar litany of problems in urban education is further exacerbated by the additional constraints of the No Child Left Behind legislation.

In the particular context of New York City, where I teach a graduate teacher education programme in the public university system, business-minded leaders and mayoral control of the city's schools have meant sweeping reforms in curriculum, assessment, professional development and managerial oversight. Among other consequences, these reforms have led teachers in low-performing schools to replace much of their instructional time with test preparation, not just the few weeks prior to the tests, thereby robbing students of additional learning opportunities.

Given the current highly charged political and emotional context, I have to persuade my students that learning to do qualitative research in context is not only doable but will be worthwhile, and that their hard work is not merely to satisfy Master's degree requirements.

Over a decade ago, Virginia Richardson posed questions for which there still is only limited research: 'Is the change in beliefs and conceptions that took place during a staff development program or a teacher education course a valued change? If so, why? How do we know?' (1996: 114). As a teacher educator and researcher interested in teacher beliefs, and believing in the potential of practitioner research to enact valued change, I am profoundly interested in finding answers. My research question is:

> What is the educative value for teachers of designing and implementing original qualitative teacher research projects in urban elementary classrooms? In terms of educative value, I am particularly interested in how teachers describe changes in their beliefs and attitudes, and the extent to which those changes can be conceived as beneficial to teachers, students, parents, and school communities.

In my teaching and in this research, I am guided by notions of teacher research as stance (Cochran-Smith and Lytle 1999, 2004), praxis (Brookline Teacher Research Seminar 2004) and process (Freeman 1998; Hubbard and Power 1999). By stance I mean looking at teachers learning to do qualitative research as a political response to the current climate. In praxis and process I hope they will learn to see the tools of research as useful in their teaching for furthering their professional growth, answering questions and sorting out puzzling dilemmas or seemingly insoluble problems. My sub-questions are:

How do teachers use qualitative research as a tool for inquiry, and what do they examine in their research? What impact does a year-long graduate course on qualitative teacher research have on teachers' professional growth and development?

My purpose is to convey through description and local knowledge (Donmoyer 2001) what my students learned through the process of conducting research, and the extent to which they see that learning as valuable. Using a grounded theory approach (Strauss and Corbin 1998), I first sought to identify what topics my students research explored, then what was examined as they used the tools of inquiry and finally, how they described their learning and professional growth in written reflections and conversations with me and each other.

Lily Orland-Barak (2004) has done similar research by examining what she has learned over four years of teaching an undergraduate education course in action research. She reports the results of her research in a progressive trajectory through changes made over the four years. Despite differing foci, we both note the value of small group work, share an interest in teachers' beliefs and the value of examining them in the course of their research, and accept that research is not a linear, predictable process, but an iterative cycle by 'representing how actions are informed by reflection, how one cycle of action grows out of the other and how theory grows out of the cycles' (2004: 52–53). My students are guided by the concepts of stance, praxis and process.

There is a great need for similar fine-grained research into the value of an in-depth experience in practitioner research in initial teacher education. Researchers from the Teacher Pathways Project, which is collecting data from New York City, have recently found that a 'capstone project' in graduate programmes has important effects on both teacher quality and student learning (Boyd, et al. 2007). Ken Zeichner (1999: 11) has pointed out that through research on the process of learning to teach, we have learned 'how difficult it is to change the tacit beliefs, understandings, and worldviews that students bring to teacher education programs'. Yet we know far too little about features of teacher education programs that have a notable impact on teachers' learning and in particular on their teaching beliefs and practices. Furthermore, the current constraints on teachers' autonomy and professional identity add to the urgency of the need for evidence that practitioner research is valuable.

Context and course design

The City College of New York is the oldest college in the City University of New York with a student enrolment of over 13,000, roughly a quarter of whom are graduates. Approximately half of the graduate student population is enrolled in the School of Education. The graduate course I teach, the Content Research Seminar, consists of a sequence of two consecutive semesters for a total of four credits, taken at the end of the programme in Childhood Education or Early Childhood Education. Students who were enrolled in this course in the years in which I conducted this research fall into one of three categories, known as streams.

They were either in a traditional initial certification Master's programme or in an alternative where full-time teaching replaced student teaching. Many students in this category entered the teaching profession through the alternative path provided by the New York City Teaching Fellows programme (www.nycteachingfellows.org/) and were teaching with a provisional licence while obtaining a degree and certification. Others who were certified as undergraduates were obtaining professional certification with a Master's degree and were more experienced teachers with full-time positions in public schools. The vast majority of students taught in high poverty areas of the city, and the diversity of our classes mirrored the linguistic, racial, ethnic and cultural background of their students.

Students begin with a very similar set of expectations and anxieties about what it will mean to be research engaged. Formally, my task is to assist them as they develop a line of inquiry, write a review of relevant literature and create a research design in the first half of the course. Then in the second half they enact their empirical, qualitative research projects in their own classrooms and schools, write up and present the findings and implications. They are supported in this process by a small group of their peers working on related issues. Several in-class exercises give them a chance to try out the tools of qualitative research, to look at different types of data and to categorise research articles, among other things. Informally, I am working to develop in them what Marilyn Cochran-Smith and Susan Lytle describe as the 'knowledge-*of*-practice' conception of teacher learning (1999). I try to help them learn that knowledge gained from the process of engaging in teacher research, through deliberative reflection and systematic inquiry, will inform their beliefs and practices in ways they are likely to find quite meaningful, and may help them to manage the ongoing dilemmas and uncertainties of teaching. Most students frame their research within the context of their classrooms, and include their elementary or early childhood students as subjects of their inquiries. I highly encourage this. I agree with Cynthia Ballenger who wrote, 'Teacher research, as I know it, is letting the children, whoever they are, teach you – both about themselves and about their view of the domain you are jointly studying – while you are teaching them' (1999: 9). Another reason for this focus on children is that studying one's own students and making that process visible, models for those students what it means to study something, and then act on what is being learned. As Gary Fenstermacher (1986: 48) has written:

> The goal of anyone who sets out to teach teachers is to enable these teachers to become students of their teaching. Having become students of their work, they may then, by their manner, enable those in their custody to become students themselves.

I begin the course by exploring with students their understanding of research and what it means to them. I am supported by the institutional context that has developed a conceptual framework of five features:

*   educating for and about diversity;
*   developing in-depth knowledge about the world;
*   becoming skilful and reflective practitioners;
*   nurturing leadership for learning;
*   building caring communities.

All who teach this course identify with it personally (Blumenreich and Falk 2006). Course tasks students must complete are meant to develop ongoing habits of mind that could further the personal and professional growth of my students as they advance in their teaching careers, and constitute a thorough introduction to research methodology and habits of mind.

What was examined?

The topics chosen by students were quite varied. Not surprisingly, many topics related to pedagogical concerns and issues of learning in particular areas of the curriculum, including literacy, mathematics and the arts. Also popular were topics related to issues of classroom management, diversity and parental involvement.

A second level analysis revealed that students framed their work with one of five distinct primary foci (listed in order of frequency):

*   teacher beliefs and practices;
*   students' understanding and learning;
*   parental roles and influences in classroom life;
*   culturally relevant curriculum;
*   meaningful and successful academic task structures.

There was considerable overlap. In the next section I will use some examples from students' projects to illustrate what they examined and the interrelations.

Teacher beliefs and practices

The most typical inquiry into the teacher's beliefs and practices meant a self-study, although there are also cases where other teachers were included in the research design. Melissa, who was a middle school math teacher, found she had fallen into a familiar pattern of questioning students but didn't really know if her strategies were helping or hurting. Her research question, 'How are my mathematical teaching strategies affecting the learning of my students?' led her through the ups and downs of trying to facilitate more sharing and conversation in class. She worried that formulas and procedures for calculating answers had no real meaning, and 'were just a list of letters and numbers'. Her beliefs about the need for teacher control of students' talk changed as she began to realise that even when students were sharing erroneous thinking, the discussions were creating opportunities for making math more real, as well as for making connections between prior knowledge and experience and new mathematical content. Although it was her journal that provided most evidence for her analysis, excerpts from class discussions and illustrations on the board, for example, were included as evidence of student learning.

Some of the work students did on teacher beliefs and practices was more personal and introspective. This was especially true when the emotional context of teachers' lives was plagued by the common problems of urban schools – neglected and abused children, poor facilities and resources, indifferent administrators, and violence in and out of school. In Linda's account of her art teaching, the stark details are conveyed to dramatic effect: her work and storage space, when she was not travelling from one classroom to the other, was in a putrid basement closet covered in a thick paste of dirt and infested with rats. Violent fights were an everyday occurrence, punctuated by students' threats and vulgar language:

> The pitch and tone in the school is deafening. The first few months of school you'll hear screaming at the top of everyone's lungs. 'Sit down! Shut up! Stop that!' Screaming is especially used by the new 'preppy' teachers. Well, because that's what we were taught . . . scream if you feel someone's life is in danger. Scream if you see someone bashing another person's face against a wall. Scream if someone is running after you with scissors. Scream! Scream your lungs out!

To survive, Linda had to begin by resisting the dehumanising practices she witnessed. She started to focus on careful assessment of students' work, and would ask herself at the start of a new lesson, 'What will I learn from my students today? What will they teach me?' She also began audio-taping her classes to hear if her tone was appropriate, and soon realised that 'management is a delicate balancing process'.

Needless to say, her finding that art can make a difference in students' lives, even in such a toxic school environment, is reason enough for hope. What's depressing is the decline of arts education in the high stakes testing climate in which we currently find ourselves.

Two full-time teachers who focused their research on the beliefs of colleagues in their schools had interesting findings. Rebecca was facilitating a newly implemented common planning time in a middle school in her role as a full-time staff developer. She sought to examine this experiment by asking, 'How do teachers utilize, experience and evaluate their common planning time?' Her central finding suggested considerable benefits to participants.

Although everyone had frustrations, concerns and confusions about working collaboratively, the team unanimously felt that common planning time was beneficial. Collaborative planning was a mechanism for providing both personal and professional support to teachers.

Brandon noted that in his first four years of teaching, the alarming number of curricular changes had left the teachers in his school frustrated. He chose to investigate what modifications were necessary, and how teachers' beliefs and attitudes about reform, coupled with their philosophical beliefs, affected curriculum implementation. He found that the burdens of necessary modifications, due to inadequate resources and time for professional development in his particular school, led to less adherence to the changes put in place by reformers as teachers reverted to their older practices.

> Most senior teachers . . . have spent upwards of twenty years educating children. Call me crazy but this leads me to believe that they just might know what works with children and what doesn't. If changing curriculum will negate some of their teaching practice one would have to ask, 'Is it better for teachers to teach within their beliefs of teaching and be more effective, or against it and be less effective?'

Ultimately, he found that teachers largely met change imposed in authoritarian ways without the necessary guidance and support with 'defiance and lacklustre performance'.

Students' understanding and learning

Research studies that focused on children and their learning ranged from a single child study to a focus on the whole class, or a larger group across grades. Often there was an intersection with interest in a particular teaching strategy. Naomi wondered what her second-grade students thought of an increased focus on 'accountable talk' in math, and how their criteria for satisfaction might compare with the teacher's expectations. Students were mostly positive about math partner talk and recognised its value. They were also proud of sharing and excited about an increase in participation. For some, negativity related to fear of criticism or anxiety about social repercussions. They were honest about partners who violated the classroom's 'norms of kindness'. A surprising finding was that her students' satisfaction was directly related to their sense of teaching their peers. 'Highly committed to class ideals of supporting one another, most emphasized the joy of helping others much more enthusiastically than the counterpoint of receiving that assistance.' The research also proved valuable for Naomi's own understandings of students' work in math:

> I recognised few of the landmarks of understanding and therefore was an inefficient transmitter of student ideas. Now, able to recognise the

significant components of student contributions, I am a more adept conduit of knowledge among students, and one on which students of intermediate ability depend heavily.

She also found she became more empathetic and attuned to the complex nuances of building a classroom culture that valued mutual respect and shared understandings.

Other studies that looked at students' feelings and motivation led to poignant insights on the complex nature of teacher–student relationships. In Elizabeth's study of one boy and his questioning, which revealed crucial information about Jimmy's personal life, she found new 'patience, sensitivity and understanding' in deciphering his behavior and helping him 'communicate his needs and wonderings within the classroom'.

Parental roles and influences in classroom life

In many of my students' research papers, parents' opinions and insights were gathered for triangulation purposes, but sometimes parents were the main focus of the study. Alicia wanted to understand how the personal history of three immigrant mothers shaped hopes for their children and their involvement in the children's education, and how that compared to opinions of teachers in her school regarding parental involvement. Despite personal adversity and depression at various points in their lives, the mothers all valued time spent talking with their children about school and revealed they were very supportive about their children's education, with a 'relentless hopefulness' for the future. They also noted a lack of community among parents at the school, and an environment that was not especially welcoming. The teachers expressed hope in developing stronger relationships with parents and improving their interactions with them, but only one believed parents' 'feelings and interpretations about school needed to be embraced.' Alicia warned of the dangers of forming assumptions and failing to keep the best interests of students at the heart of discussions between parents and teachers:

> As a result of the study, I realize how important it is for school members to be able to talk through the experiences that they have with parents and consider judgments that they may be forming. The dialogue between parents and teachers has to be forced and like Marie said, if it does not exist then I think we all have to make it exist. It may be unrealistic to believe that in the worst performing schools, we can reach every parent; but I have found the danger of abandoning trying and not believing that the home–school relationship can truly become a partnership.

Alicia's findings are particularly important given the additional potential obstacle to open communication when the parents' first language is not English.

Although these may seem minor findings, it is clear from my students' writing that these affirmations from parents were important to them and to their students.

Culturally relevant curriculum

Students who chose topics relating to diversity often ended up exploring culturally relevant teaching and curriculum. Dan tackled delicate issues of ethnicity and culture in his paper about teaching history. A self-described 'white male from the middle of suburban New York' he was teaching in the heart of Washington Heights, where the vast majority of seventh-grade students in his classes came from the Dominican Republic. Influenced by Vivian Paley's account in *White Teacher* (1979), Dan discovered his students were eager to talk with him about these issues. He set up an experiment by teaching a similar American history unit to two of his classes, but in one he incorporated a lot of parallel history from the Dominican Republic. Not surprisingly, those students who received a more culturally relevant instruction did better on the unit's exam, and also expressed more enthusiasm. 'I liked this unit,' wrote one student, 'because for the first time I could talk to my grandmother about what we were studying in school. I told her about the history of the United States and she told me stories about the history of the Dominican Republic that she used to learn in school'. Dan also interviewed students to understand their perspectives on ethnic and cultural differences. He learned to reframe cultural relevance, and discovered 'culture can be found in every corner of a classroom'. No longer daunted by gaps between his childhood and those of his students, Dan learned 'it is the master teacher who transforms these differences into commonalities, and uses them as tools to gain relevancy in the classroom.'

For Dan, studying culturally relevant pedagogy led to expanding definitions and influences of culture as well as its role in the life of the classroom.

Meaningful and successful academic task structures

Studies that examined specific academic tasks clearly intersected with student learning, and were often driven by a desire to find solutions to ongoing problems for which there was little to no guidance in the literature. Eric, who had concerns about an English language learner, thought that reader's theatre activities could help him to improve his student's oral fluency. He was frustrated by those who assumed that a student's lack of accomplished oral fluency meant problems with comprehension, and when his student was identified as a candidate for a pull-out programme, he was dismayed. Noticing that repeated reading methods were increasing his speed and accuracy, as well as helping him gain confidence in his reading skills, Eric introduced an eight-week Reader's Theatre routine to his whole class. Using short five-page scripts, students rehearsed in heterogeneous groups from Monday to Thursday for 40 minutes a day, and performed for the class on Friday. By taping and analysing the participation of his focal student, Eric was able to understand the pedagogical strategies he used in Reader's Theatre that were making his reading fluency and reasoning skills begin to grow and then flourish:

> I observed that he began to take notes and record them in the side margins of his script. He underscored sections of the text and drew lines that referenced back to his interpretation. In addition, he also began to record other students' observations and placed tick marks next to those that he wished to consider for his next read-through.

Above and beyond his remarkable transformation as an oral reader and performer, Eric's student 'fell in love with reading again'.

What was learned?

An important aspect of the course design is that about a month before its end, usually during spring break, I meet each student individually for an hour. These conferences often occur just as they are experiencing a mixture of emotions about their projects and are somewhat lost in the data analysis. I find that the feedback I can give in an in-depth conversation is far more meaningful than previous exchanges of drafts, or in-class consultations, but the meetings are also important for developing our relationships. I am often counselling them on the challenges they face in their schools as much as I am guiding them in the research process, and I have learned that these private conversations provide additional insights into their learning.

At the end of the course, as students finish writing up their research papers, I ask them to include a separate self-evaluation to reflect on their learning and the dynamics of their small group. Unlike course evaluations, these reflections provide specific evidence of students' learning trajectories that are honest and heartfelt accounts. Some of the most prominent themes in these self-evaluation reflections and in the individual conferences include their newfound abilities:

- to understand teaching itself as a form of inquiry;
- to see their own potential to produce local funds of knowledge;
- to appreciate new identities as teacher researchers;
- to feel empowered to defend their teaching decisions;
- to overcome the boredom and despair of endless mandatory test prep.

It is important to note that these themes are interrelated, and not every student developed these abilities to the same degree, or developed all of them. As they described their learning, it was also apparent that for some the degree to which the experience had been, and would be, robust or fragile in terms of their growth and development as teachers, would depend in large measure on the type and amount of support that they would have from others as they moved forward in their careers.

For many of them, support from their peers in the small group was an essential component of their learning. For example, Dan wrote: 'Working with a research group was invaluable, as many conversations with them were able to steer me back on track when I felt that I had lost my way.' Another student, Virginia, remarked:

> The excitement mounted as teachers realized that their wonderings were evolving into legitimate research projects, and what intrigued me most was the way in which the many diverse topics were somehow interrelated and how we were able to learn so much from each other's work . . . Now more than ever I am very interested in doing teacher research.

Some students described the conversations in their groups during class as a form of therapy that energised them and gave them new ideas. Certainly the exciting mix of teaching experience, educational and cultural backgrounds and varied school contexts made for a dynamic learning environment for everyone.

Although it is impossible to know the extent to which the year-long research experience will carry over into the rest of their teaching careers, the reflections provide some evidence of future implications. Alicia, who learned so much from her interviews with immigrant mothers and colleagues in her school wrote:

> I feel very grateful for the experience of hearing each story . . . I hope that I can be honest with other educators when I hear them make assumptions about the future of their students and the blame they often place on parents. Sometimes the enormity of the problem can break your heart. I want to continue to talk with my peers about the challenges that I face.

Another student wrote about how her inquiry into homework led her to new questions:

> As I go forward into my first year of teaching and beyond I hope that I will not only continue this path of inquiry and observation, but also go on to study in depth other issues I find of interest within the classroom.

Some students tempered their enthusiasm for doing future research: 'I learned about what teacher research actually is, and even thought for an instant about attempting to do more research someday.'

While issues of professional identity and future directions are certainly important, in terms of educative value it is also essential to examine the extent to which what is learned is worthwhile not only for the teachers, but for their students and the communities they serve. Because of my own research interests in the moral dimensions of teaching, I often probed students to consider how their findings were of personal value to participants and meaningful for them in terms of moral aspects, and to reflect on the implications of those findings. Perhaps as a result of my focus on this issue, there were many reflections with moral implications. One student who studied classroom management in an innovative kindergarten art class wrote:

> I have viewed the lack of attention and desire to complete assignments in terms of students' behavior. And like so many, tried to change misbehaviour into good behaviour by using rewards and punishments. I have looked at classroom management largely in terms of controlling behaviour as opposed to channelling behaviour. This research has served as a reminder of how my beliefs and knowledge about my students factor into the expectations I have for my students. The following questions I ask myself need to become a routine and not a consequence of misbehaviour: Did I take the time to carefully plan this lesson and make sure I have the necessary supplies? Is this lesson motivating to my students, interesting? Is this lesson challenging, but designed to allow all students to be successful? Am I modelling and scaffolding their knowledge enough? Are my expectations clear, consistent? Am I making my students feel part of the decision-making process and developing community?

Using documentation and reflecting on the evidence provided had both intellectual and moral benefits. Students described passionately their renewed commitment to 'regular and purposeful reflection' and to 'paying attention' by recording observations in journals and notebooks. Others overcame their fear of experimentation, and learned to try out new approaches. One student wrote that research enabled a closer look at herself to strengthen her weaknesses.

In summary, I feel that for the vast majority of my students, learning to do qualitative research in their classrooms provided intellectual challenges, made teaching more complex and rewarding and helped them to manage dilemmas and uncertainty. In his recent research on developing a research stance in student teachers, John Loughran found his students 'know what they need to do and how to respond to their own problems in their own practice' (2007: 233). I am not sure that my students always develop certainty about a course of action, but I do believe they gain an appreciation for the ways in which managing dilemmas is an ongoing process. Learning to document the process, posing new questions and engaging with students, colleagues and parents in finding solutions are important evidence of their professional development.

Implications

Although I am mostly enthusiastic and hopeful about the findings of this research, I also want to point out some reasons to be cautious about practitioner research, particularly in urban schools that present nearly insurmountable challenges. While I feel the findings presented here suggest that an in-depth qualitative research experience with peer support was able to help cultivate resiliency and efficacy in my graduate students, it is important to note that some had to learn about the limitations of their power and authority to effect positive change in schools. When their passion for teaching, and their idealism about helping all students, clashed with the realisation that they could not fix everything, their feelings about their research were often mixed. Other researchers have had similar findings in this regard:

> When teachers are well informed, through evidence-based practice, grounded in their own research, then they are well positioned to make the important practical and moral judgements required for schools to be both effective and socially just institutions.
>
> (Groundwater-Smith and Dadds 2004: 259)

Groundwater-Smith and Dadds go on to caution that if practitioner research uncovers dilemmas between an 'imposed, dominant government agenda and the perceived needs of the learners', teachers' sense of empowerment may be thwarted.

The harsh reality of some of my students' own limitations in effecting change within imposed power structures could lead to considerable frustration and burnout. My response was to encourage them to write about it. Donna had planned to study guided reading practices, but was forced to replace that instructional time with test preparation activities by the school administrators. Although she completed her research by meeting with students during lunchtime, she was quite bitter and titled her paper: 'How Administrative Decisions and the High Stakes on Testing Disrupted My Original Research Seeking to Identify the Strategies in Guided Reading Methods that Enable Literacy Growth in Students.' In her conclusion she wrote:

> I am a very frustrated teacher who writes my story with regret and a deep sense of loss. I feel this way because I was robbed of the very valuable opportunity to conduct classroom research, which I feel would have benefited not only my students and myself but also other teachers and educators.

Part of my task as the course instructor is to help teachers learn to recognise domains over which they have some control, hoping that as they become more experienced, both domains and ways of wielding this control would increase.

Regardless of the significant disappointment some faced, the process of learning to do research helped them become more thoughtful and informed, even more publicly engaged in their often isolated work as they developed better partnerships with parents, colleagues and the community.

I think it is inevitable, given the current political climate, that those educators working in challenging educational settings will have to learn to cope with a suspended tension between hopefulness and despair. In a longitudinal study of teachers' work, lives and effectiveness in the UK (the 'VITAE' study), researchers found that resiliency was tied to teaching as a calling. 'Underlying resilient teachers' endeavours to exert control over difficult situations, is their strength and determination to fulfil their original call to teach and to manage and thrive professionally' (Day, *et al.* 2007: 213). One important, crucial piece of managing to thrive despite adversity entails keeping a focus on the intellectual work of teaching. Learning to do research has the potential to help teachers do that. Sonia Nieto formed an inquiry group of teachers that led to their important book, *What Keeps Teachers Going?* They found that one characteristic of eight was 'teaching as intellectual work', and they argue that 'inquiry needs to be a vital part of teachers' work . . . our shared view is that teachers are above all intellectual workers' (Nieto, Felix and Gelzinis 2002: 8). I heartily concur, and I fear that one of the devastating legacies of high stakes testing is nothing short of a brutal act of sabotage on teachers' intellect and ability to make autonomous informed decisions about what is in their students' best interests.

Margaret has the honour of being my oldest graduate student to date, and she said in her final reflection that she hoped to find the necessary 'spunk and courage' to continue and to expand the experiment chronicled in her research. 'I am proud of my work; I have a lot more to do', she wrote. Whether it was due to her experience as a young activist in the 1960s, or just her insightfulness, Margaret was very articulate about managing to thrive despite the political context, which was leading many citizens to 'abandon our commitment to original thought'.

Since I began with my students' words, I'd like to end with Margaret's conclusion to her brilliant paper, which highlights the seed of hopefulness that can be found in every student, young or old:

> As I write these words of admonition and grief, I am heartened, because I recall the image of Nico, and I can hear what it is he has to say to his friend. I see Nico sitting in the middle of the floor, hard at work over his new hurling machine. I hear him tell Andrew who is trying to find just the 'right rock' for them to hurl, 'You need to keep working on a certain project, until you know if it's a complete success, or a complete failure.'

References

Ballenger, C. (1999) *Teaching other People's Children: Literacy and Learning in a Bilingual Classroom*. New York: Teachers College Press.

Blumenreich, M. and Falk, B. (2006) 'Trying on a new pair of shoes: urban teacher-learners conduct research and construct knowledge in their own classrooms', *Teaching and Teacher Education*, 22: 864–73.

Boyd, D., Grossman, P., Lankford, H., Loeb, S. and Wyckoff, J. (2007) 'Do features of preparation make a difference? The relationship of program features to student achievement', paper presented at the *American Educational Research Association Annual Meeting*.

Brookline Teacher Research Seminar (2004) *Regarding Children's Words: Teacher Research on Language and Literacy*. New York: Teachers College Press.

Cochran-Smith, M. and Lytle, S.L. (1999) 'Relationships of knowledge and practice: teacher learning in communities' in A. Iran-Nejad and P.D. Pearson (eds) *Review of Research in Education*, Vol. 24, pp. 249–306. Washington DC: American Educational Research Association.

Cochran-Smith, M. and Lytle, S.L. (2004) 'Practitioner inquiry, knowledge, and university culture' in J. Loughran, M.L. Hamilton, V. LaBoskey and T. Russell (eds) *International Handbook of Research of Self-Study of Teaching and Teacher Education Practices*. Amsterdam: Kluwer Academic Publishers.

Day, C., Sammons, P., Stobart, G., Kington, A. and Gu, Q. (2007) *Teachers Matter: Connecting Lives, Work and Effectiveness*. Maidenhead, England: Open University Press.

Donmoyer, R. (2001) 'Paradigm talk reconsidered', in V. Richardson (ed.) *Handbook of Research on Teaching*, 4th edn, pp 174–97. Washington DC: American Educational Research Association.

Fenstermacher, G. (1986) 'Philosophy of research on teaching: three aspects' in M.C. Wittrock (ed.) *Handbook of Research on Teaching*, 3rd edn, pp. 37–49. New York: Macmillan.

Freeman, D. (1998). *Doing Teacher Research: From Inquiry to Understanding*. New York: Heinle & Heinle.

Groundwater-Smith, S. and Dadds, M. (2004) 'Critical practitioner inquiry: towards responsible professional communities of practice' in C. Day and J. Sachs (eds) *International Handbook on the Continuing Professional Development of Teachers*, pp. 238–63). Maidenhead, England: Open University Press.

Hubbard, R. and Power, B.M. (1999) *Living the Questions: A Guide for Teacher Research*. Portland, ME: Stenhouse Publishing.

Loughran, J. (2007) 'Encouraging a student teacher as researcher stance in teacher education' in J. Butcher and L. McDonald (eds) *Making a Difference: Challenges for Teachers, Teaching, and Teacher Education*, pp. 221–34. Dordrecht: Sense Publishers.

National Commission on Teaching and America's Future (2002) *Unraveling the 'Teacher Shortage' Problem: Teacher Retention is the Key*. Washington DC.

Nieto, S., Felix, S. and Gelzinis, K. (2002) 'A life of teaching: reflections from teachers in an inquiry group', *Penn GSE Perspectives on Urban Education*, 1(2): 1–30.

Orland-Barak, L. (2004) 'What have I learned from all this? Four years of teaching an action research course: Insights of a "second order"', *Educational Action Research*, 12(1): 33–57.

Paley, V. (1979) *White Teacher*. Cambridge, MA: Harvard University Press.

Richardson, V. (1996) 'The role of attitudes and beliefs in learning to teach' in J. Sikula (ed.) *Handbook of Research on Teacher Education*, 2nd edn, pp. 102–119. New York: Macmillan.

Strauss, A. and Corbin, J. (1998) *Basics of Qualitative Research: Techniques and Procedures for Developing Grounded Theory*. Thousand Oaks, CA: Sage Publications.

Zeichner, K. (1999) 'The new scholarship in teacher education', *Educational Researcher*, 28(9): 4–15.

Chapter 12

Networks of researching schools

Lessons and questions from one study

Colleen McLaughlin

Introduction

This chapter uses a study of teacher research within a large-scale programme in the UK, the Networked Learning Communities' Programme, to explore what lessons might be learned about teachers' professional learning, school development and the scale and nature of partnerships or networks, in which teacher research is a central feature. The study involved undertaking case studies of six networks across England and a full account can be found in McLaughlin *et al.* (2008). I begin by examining the reasons for the current emphasis on networks and teacher research, then look at three main questions:

- For what purposes might networks of researching schools be formed and developed?
- How were these purposes pursued in the networks studied?
- What conditions sustain and develop these different purposes?

What is the problem?

Networking between schools is increasingly recognised as the key driver of school improvement.

(McCarthy *et al.* 2004: 61)

It is the teachers who in the end will change the world of the school by understanding it.

(Stenhouse 1975: 208)

As these two quotations demonstrate, these two ideas of networking and teachers engaging in research are certainly powerful ones and they are ones that have driven a move towards initiating networks in the UK. Since the National College of Schools Leadership's Networked Learning Programme, the biggest in the world up to then, there has been a significant move by policy-makers to work through networks. The Department for Children, Schools and

Families' (DCSF) website lists the following networks: the Primary Strategy Learning Networks (DfES 2004); the Best Practice Network; the Learning and Skills Network; and the Sure Start Network, among others. Hannon (2005: 7) says that these programmes are part of a 'networking landscape, which is at best confusing', and that there are significant differences between the initiatives that belong to a 'broad family of collaboration' (Hannon 2005: 8). In the early part of the twentieth century, R.G. Collingwood (Johnson and Monk 1998) argued that there was only one useful universal question: 'What is the problem to which this phenomenon is the answer?' So what are the educational problems that have led to this emphasis on networks and teacher research?

First, the widespread emphasis on networks is a general social phenomenon. It is a phenomenon that has exploded with the increased use of information technology and the expansion of communication systems. Castells (2000) has charted 'the rise of the network society' and the constant shifts and changes that are part of networks. Church *et al.* (2002) see the network as a metaphor which involves 'threads, knots and nets' or relationships, activity and structures. The relational aspects are highly emphasised in discussions about networks, and the well-being and social capital generated by them is accentuated. Gilchrist writes (2004: 147), 'robust and diverse social networks enhance the health and happiness of individuals, and contribute to the well-being of society as a whole', so the trusting or bonding nature of networks are portrayed as powerful. This can work for good or for ill, as Sampson (2004: 159) reminds us: 'networks connect do-gooders just as they connect drug dealers. [. . .] It is important to ask *what* is being connected – networks are not inherently egalitarian or prosocial in nature.'

Second, is a set of issues to do with the nature of classroom teaching and schools. Collaboration became a response to the perceived isolation of teaching since Lortie's (1975) work. Others have written about the isolation, loneliness and individualism of teaching (Hargreaves 1993: Huberman 1993). These studies have emphasised the private nature of classrooms and teachers' resistance to scrutiny. Arguably this is an inherent characteristic of classroom teaching, not just personal preference. Salzberger-Wittenberg (1996) showed that the emotional architecture of teaching is deeply connected to fear of exposure and criticism. These characteristics were seen to be potential barriers to development in education and to learning about classroom practice. To counteract them there was an emphasis on collaboration in the 1980s and 1990s (Little 1982; Nias and Biott 1992). This 'new' collaboration then fed the closely related ideas of communities of practice and collegiality. It has been argued that educational reforms in the UK have led to radical changes and increased collegiality and collaboration, although not necessarily from the 'bottom up' (McNess *et al.* 2003: 249).

The third related idea concerns teachers' learning. Stenhouse was the first in the UK to emphasise teachers' learning through research. He argued for placing teachers' research and development centrally in curriculum development and change since teachers were the key decision makers in the classroom. He saw teacher research as a mainly individual activity with the teacher researching her classroom and then sharing this with an interested, critical, collegial community along the lines of Gramsci's (1967) critical or deliberative community. Stenhouse saw this as a local activity, 'perhaps too much research is published to the world, too little to the community. We need local cooperatives and papers as well as internal conferences and journals' (1981: 17). He saw critical discourse as a fundamental aspect of learning and also saw the focus on action as important. The privacy of the classroom would also be opened up, but that was not necessarily Stenhouse's aim. His aim was to include reflective activity and research processes in the concept of being a teacher. He saw this as having three main elements:

- the commitment to systematic questioning of one's own teaching as a basis for development;
- the commitment and skills to study one's own teaching;
- the concern to question and to test theory in practice.

(1975: 143)

Elliott (2007) and Carr and Kemmis (1986) have also argued that the values behind teachers as researchers are more emancipatory and inextricably connected to teaching as a moral activity. They assert that teacher research is a way of teachers having influence and power, and that matters of social justice for teachers and students are a significant element of the tradition of teacher research. Conducting research is also a way of critiquing policy and practice and developed a critical discourse about educational practice.

The fourth relevant aspect of the current educational scene is the push for change and accountability. The current educational policy context is one that emphasises centralisation, accountability and 'standards', measured largely in pupil outcomes and standardised tests. There are very different emphases within this trend. One rationale emphasises the power of the collaborative or the group. Jackson (2002) wrote that 'a key mantra for the [Networked Learning Communities'] initiative [. . .is] working smarter together, rather than harder alone' and he argued that networks were able to 'provide a supportive context for risk-taking and creativity'. This rationale emphasises professional collaboration, joint problem solving, the exchange of ideas and the sharing of knowledge. Fielding *et al.* (2005) emphasise the development of practice, and relational qualities and values such as reciprocity and respect. Both models have a view of networking activity in education, largely local and specific, akin to the view implicit where Liebermann (1999) describes networks as 'dignifying and giving shape to the process and content of educators' experiences, the daily-ness of their work, which is often invisible to outsiders yet binds insiders together'. Lieberman and McLaughlin (1992) have portrayed networks of teachers as 'discourse communities' and have stressed the self-determination and democracy of these groups. David Hargreaves (1999, 2003, 2004) has a different emphasis. He envisions networks as transforming the educational systems in the UK and his emphasis is on scale and innovation. He sees research as key. Black-Hawkins (2008: 71) summarises this rationale well. Hargreaves maintains that networking allows *knowledge creation* to take place in a more efficient and robust manner because groups of teachers, by 'working laterally', can draw on the combined intellectual, social and organisational capital of many schools. He criticises the more customary school-based practitioner research and enquiry conducted by individual teachers within their individual schools. Hargreaves wrote:

> [A network] is so much larger than an individual school, it can prioritise a shared topic for knowledge creation and have a much more sophisticated design, both for sharing the innovative workload, so that each school undertakes a limited and variable amount of activity, and for testing it more rigorously than is ever possible in a single . . . school or department . . . generating] a far more robust evidence base . . . in a far shorter time.
> (2003: 40)

To return to Collingwood's question, it would appear that networks of researching schools are a phenomenon that aims to: reduce teacher isolation; enhance collaboration between teachers; bring about change, possibly on a large scale, through the sharing of practice, knowledge and joint problem solving; use research to facilitate these processes; and enhance feelings of well-being among teachers. These assertions are examined now through considering case studies of six networked learning communities. I explore the aforementioned questions to see how these matters played out in practice:

1   For what purposes might networks of researching schools be formed and developed?
2   How were these purposes pursued in the networks studied?
3   What conditions sustain and develop these different purposes?

The study and its context

The study was a year long (2004/5) and we wrote case studies of six networks (McLaughlin *et al.* 2008). We also examined case studies in the literature of existing networks such as BASRC (The Bay Area Schools Reform Collaborative in the USA, the Coalition of Knowledge Creating Schools in Australia and the TTA research consortia in the UK). The networks studied were all part of the Networked Learning Communities (NLC) programme, a government funded research and development project, run under the auspices of the National College for School Leadership (NCSL). The programme ran between

2002 and 2006 and involved more than 1,500 schools (a total of 24,000 teachers) from all state sectors. Groups of schools were invited to apply to become networks, and if successful, received some funding in the first three years to support their activities. Each network was expected to include a minimum of six schools and at least one other institutional member, usually a university or local authority. The NLC group also offered additional support, including regional and national meetings and conferences, publications and other materials plus the advice of a network 'facilitator'.

In consultation with members of the NLC group, the six NLCs chosen were seen to be actively engaged in practitioner research. The focus of the case studies was on what was working well rather than how and why some networks were less successful. Our sample provided a geographical spread across England, including both urban and rural locations, and represented a range of primary and secondary schools from both mainstream and special school settings. The studies involved visiting each NLC. During visits we interviewed groups and individuals, collected documentation and observed network and group sessions, plus lessons intended to demonstrate some of the effects of practitioner research on students' learning. Finally, a questionnaire was given to a sample of staff in each of the 56 schools, with a total sample of 650 (McLaughlin *et al*. 2008).

The purposes of networks of researching schools

The following summarises the possible purposes for networks of researching schools put forward in the thinking outlined in above:

1   *Teachers' professional development*
    Networks of mutually supportive groups of teachers work across the schools and engage in joint problem solving and sharing of practice, plus the study of practice. Mutual support and the sharing of ideas are underscored in this view of professional development.

2   *School improvement*
    Research for school improvement would emphasise the connection to school policy-making and school level decision-making.

These first two aspects are seen as modest purposes and achievable. The ones that follow are far more difficult to achieve:

3   *Knowledge creation through joint research*
    Hargreaves' vision of the 'knowledge creating school' (1999) is the most well-known in the UK. He saw the following research purposes as most viable in networks:

    • testing different solutions to common problems;
    • testing the same innovation in contrasting circumstances;

- taking different aspects of a common innovation so that the sum is larger than the parts;
- randomised control trials.

4   *Sharing of good practice*
This is seen as difficult to achieve for *best practice has to be demonstrated,* not just explained, and its replication by another practitioner has to be practised through trial and error; this entails *creatively adapting* the innovation that is being transferred. The donor and the recipient in the transfer process need to spend some time together if the transfer is to be successful . . . (Hargreaves 2003: 50).

So which of these purposes were visible in the networks studied, with what concomitant concerns? Some elements were common to all the networks. All members involved valued membership of the networking activities and felt a reduced sense of isolation. This transcended the feeling of not being alone but was an opening up of practice and a professional satisfaction in engaging in dialogue about classroom concerns and pedagogical matters that valued experience and independence of thought. Two teacher quotations capture that:

> The most important thing was the sharing of information and sort of having access to other people's experiences in school similar to ours and slightly different as well . . . The sharing of ideas with like-minded people.

> This gives us a chance to actually talk about education issues whereas I would say, being honest, that in your teacher training you don't really do that much of. You were given the right ideas on how to teach things but you didn't really discuss. . .

The mutual support given included the exchange of ideas, something that many might characterise as professional development or pedagogic sharing rather than learning through systematic inquiry. A further common element was the valuing of learning through enquiry, which was very broadly conceived. Other than these common elements, there was considerable variety of purpose. A spectrum ran from learning from practitioner's own research at one end, to learning from sharing ideas or very broad professional development conversations at the other. These different purposes were explicit. Many networks were concerned primarily to promote teachers' engagement in and learning from research in their own school, themselves shaping the research agenda, rather than learning from research in other schools. The worth of these networks was in their sense of cohesion and communality, their shared values, their shared understanding of research and of how it should inform practice, and their learning from others about the process. They also appreciated the shared infrastructure, particularly the external support on research and organisation, as well as the finance, which for many of the NLCs was a major factor.

The scale of the finance provided was small in comparison to other networks, such as BASRC, but it was still significant. Networking was seen as very important, as were partnerships with external agencies including universities.

For other networks in the NLCs studied, the emphasis and value were placed on the networking aspects rather than research. It was the face-to-face exchange of ideas that they spoke enthusiastically of and activities such as 'learning walks' were very popular. The tremendous energy around such activities may well be a side effect of the independent control network members felt they had over the development agenda. Studies, such as that by McNess *et al.* (2003), have highlighted the felt loss of cohesion and professionalism from the imposed educational reforms that have the English educational policy-making. Their study showed that:

> when collaboration was genuine and 'bottom up', or democratically constructed and genuinely concerned with improving teaching, it could produce real benefits for the teachers concerned and their classes though conversely when it was 'top down', managerially imposed it was more likely to be 'contrived'. . .
>
> (McNess *et al.* 2003: 249)

School improvement was the stated, key purpose of all networks, and teacher professional development seen as the main mode. There was more limited evidence of schools connecting up to the planning and resourcing processes in the schools. In one network, Blackburn with Darwen, where the network focused on learning about maths and science through these departments and the teachers in them, there was a strong fit between the structures of the collaboration and the networked activity. The schools undertook common curriculum planning and there was planning and contact at all levels: classroom teachers, heads of department and head teachers. This appeared to be powerful in enhancing the desired improvements and in ensuring implementation. There was in the other networks evidence of individual schools using the networks for their school improvement processes but less evidence of the complementary purpose of a more coordinated approach, which is challenging and complex.

Finally, what of the purpose of knowledge creation? Again this was an espoused purpose of all the networks and the NLC programme also intended to produce research to be publicly shared. Within the individual networks there was a great value placed on producing what Gibbons *et al.* (1994) called Mode 2 Knowledge, which they claimed had evolved in recent years and which Hargreaves drew on in his thinking about the knowledge creating school in 1999. McIntyre (2008) summarised Mode 2 knowledge thus:

- Knowledge is produced in the context of its application: it is produced by people who need to solve a practical problem of their own.

- The knowledge is transdisciplinary, being produced within the distinctive evolving framework of the problem it is created to solve.
- It is undeniably a contribution to knowledge, with its own distinct theoretical structures, research methods and modes of practice, and its cumulative development.
- The diffusion of the results is initially accomplished in the process of their production. Subsequent diffusion occurs as the original practitioners move to new problem contexts.
- Knowledge production is heterogeneous in terms of the skills and experience people bring to it . . . In Mode 2, flexibility and response time are the crucial factors and because of this the types of organizations used to tackle these problems may vary greatly . . . people come together in temporary work teams and networks which dissolve when a problem is solved or redefined.
- Social accountability permeates the whole knowledge production process: working in the context of application increases the sensitivity of scientists and technologists to the broader implications of what they are doing . . . because the issue on which research is based cannot be answered in scientific and technical terms alone.
- Criteria to assess the quality of the work and the teams that carry out research in Mode 2 differ from those of more traditional, disciplinary science.

(Gibbons *et al.* 1994: 3–8)

In relation to this final issue of quality control, Gibbons and his colleagues are at pains to emphasise continuity with Mode one research and its rigorous standards, but also the importance of additional criteria such as efficiency and usefulness.

(McIntyre 2008: 36)

Several of the networks we studied were committed to this form of knowledge production and to the face-to-face dissemination. They valued the interpersonal and verbal form of dissemination and found written forms less desirable and the pace slow. This was similar to the findings on the TTA research consortium (Simons *et al.* 2003). The contribution to public knowledge was not a primary purpose of the research undertaken in the networks: local knowledge was. There was little evidence of the joint research advocated by Hargreaves (1999), such as testing different solutions to common problems and innovation, taking different aspects of a common innovation so that the sum is larger than the parts, or randomised control trials. Where teachers did undertake joint research, there was some recognition of the complexity around the quality and the sharing of practice. Simons *et al.* (2003) had talked of 'situated generalisations', by which they meant the awareness by teachers of 'the situationally-bounded nature of their findings'. The teachers in this study were cautious about their findings and reluctant to go beyond face-to-face, local dissemination. Fielding *et al.* (2005) had concluded that 'a relationships model of practice transfer may be at least as relevant as a content-driven model.' Our study supported this. The questionnaire data showed that teachers were a credible source for research and that hearing colleagues share their research motivated other teachers. Similarly, engaging *in* research had motivated teacher researchers to engage *with* research. Brown (2005: 395) found similarly in the TLRP project. She noted the importance of the personal relevance and 'the level of teachers' familiarity with the particular ideas that are the focus of the research evidence (and) how these ideas relate to the ways in which they already make sense of their own classroom work.'

Finally, in relation to the purposes of engaging in research in networks, the teachers were judicious in their claims for the work, favouring tinkering purposes rather than transformation. One teacher emphasised 'tweaking versus transforming' while talking about the importance of manageable research activities. The implications of the purposes observed are commented on more fully in the final section.

Sustaining and developing networks for different purposes

Sustaining and developing networks presents significant challenges. Lieberman and McLaughlin (1992: 675–7) identified the following 'problems' that need addressing if successful networks are to be sustained: assuring the quality of the work; applying the learning; ensuring stability; protecting against over-extension; generating ownership; moving beyond the immediate classroom to wider objectives; leadership that avoids becoming bureaucratic and inflexible; appropriate and enhancing evaluation; and sustaining primary purposes or not getting blown off course. These we found to be still very live challenges for networks and also found that there were some strategies we could recommend as meeting these tests. Three types of networks are considered: networks for teacher learning, mutual support and professional development; networks for school improvement; and networks for knowledge creation and the sharing of good practice. These purposes clearly overlap but this is a useful distinction for the purposes of exploring specific conditions and the tensions and challenges.

Networks for professional development

The suggestion that collaboration is an antidote to teacher isolation is one this study substantiates. All the teachers reported considerable personal, social and professional benefits from collaborating and this is clearly a potential growth point. The conditions that were facilitative were high levels of trust and openness within relationships that were characterised by flexibility and democracy. The nature of the relationships is imperative. Activities related to research place particular demands on collegial relationships. Achinstein (2002) highlighted the importance and dangers of conflict in staff groups, yet making the familiar strange and debating differences is crucial to fruitful enquiry. Relationships need to be able to tolerate difference, ambiguity and to have the 'capacity and disposition to dig deeply into matters of practice' (Little 2002: 918). Little has also reminded us that close relationships can be a force for conservatism as well as progress:

> Closely bound groups are instruments both for promoting change and for conserving the present. Changes, indeed, may prove substantial or trivial. Finally, collaborations may arise naturally out of the problems and circumstance that teachers experience in common, but often they appear contrived, inauthentic, grafted on, perched precariously (and often temporarily) on the margins of real work.
>
> (Little 1990: 509–10)

The scale forms of and necessary conditions for collaboration are still largely unexplored in practice and will need further investigation. Our study showed that issues of scale were very important and that present schools and classroom conditions militate against large-scale collaboration. The teachers' proper emphasis on manageability is also an important message to keep in mind. The involvement in collaborative research activity also needed to be voluntary, in accord with the findings of McNess *et al.* (2003). A focus of collaborative activity on learning about classroom practices and the curriculum enhanced the activity for teachers. The closeness of the fit to the classroom is important in maintaining the primary purposes of the network activity, its momentum and credibility. The task of maintaining this focus becomes key for leaders of networks for it is this, as Liebermann (1999: 1) reminds us, that 'binds insiders together . . .'.

Networks for school improvement

All the study's networks considered research activity to be primarily for school improvement. However, the degrees of difficulty and scale are matched to the intended purposes of networks. For example, an intention to develop teachers' use of research and understanding of research processes is more easily achieved and makes very different demands to undertaking a joint research project. Other matters that interact here are the fit between the schools and the scale. A group of mathematics teachers working regularly together as part of normal school arrangements will find it easier to engage in networked research activity than a pyramid of schools located together but not having much else in common. The task of building and drawing on research activity will be very different. We found that a clear commitment from senior managers was needed, as was the establishment of links to school planning and of resources. Pooling resources within a network helped sustain and develop the activity of research. All the networks studied needed some form of external support and this is something that applies to professional development (Cordingley *et al.* 2003: Wellcome Trust 2006). Specific support needed in research networks was the provision of research expertise in two forms: research training and providing a bridge to the worlds of ideas and existing research and scholarship.

What we did find was that most networks were more interested in school improvement through developing teachers' capacity to use research processes rather than interest in joint research. However, if school improvement is to be the prime purpose of engagement then certain matters follow. The research design that is to inform school improvement needs to be robust, as does the conduct; not really a live issue. Although there were also few examples of research being used to inform whole school planning, it was smaller scale. The issues of how the quality and impact of research are judged are contentious and important. In the NLC programme, networks were asked to provide data that showed that improvement had occurred in students' attainment scores. This led to some rather forced correlations or assertions of cause and effect! While it is understandable that school improvement should be aimed at making education better for students, it should not be measured over-simplistically. Government's involvement in promoting networks as a form of educational reform may lead to measures that will undermine the trust and risk-taking necessary for the research and development of complex educational processes.

Knowledge creating networks

The notion of knowledge creating networks is very new and no infrastructures yet exist. The gap between the vision and the reality is large. This does not make the aim unworthy and it is helpful to learn from these early initiatives for future work. The task of collaboration within a school is difficult enough, given school structures and time, particularly teacher time. The task of coordination across schools is even bigger. If school improvement is the purpose, then the conditions need establishing and discipline employed for joint planning and the interweaving with individual school goals. This requires resources.

However, the major challenge is that of dissemination. We found limited recognition of this challenge and limited activity beyond the face to face. This is not to denigrate the face-to-face mode. It suggests that the conceptions of Liebermann (1999), and others who have characterised the nature of teacher research as about creating local knowledge activity, are truer to the reality today. If the activity is to be scaled up then other outside resources and people are needed. Schools-university partnerships are a way of scaling up and sharing the work and capabilities of those who are engaged in disseminating research, but this also requires considerable shifts in the ways in which universities negotiate and are rewarded for their research. Currently the ways in which research is assessed and funded, as well as the ways in which schools measure the outcomes of their labours all militate against this and encourage little close working between schools and universities in a networked fashion. The purposes of knowledge creation or the types of knowledge creation engaged in also need to be examined closely. Knowledge creating in schools should encompass a range of purposes, including critiques of policy and studies of innovation. The current policy emphasis on the replication of current practice and the measurement of a limited range of student outcomes mean that there was little evidence of or interest in these purposes.

Conclusion

It is clear that networks of schools focused on research are a phenomenon responding to a range of forces and problems in our current educational context. They can be a force for good or ill, trivial or profound. The visions vary and it would seem that the more human scale vision is one that is currently operable. Teachers enjoy working together when they have suitable conditions and appropriate resources to do so. They welcome the opportunities to explore in authentic ways the problems and practices of their classrooms and schools. They welcome also the opportunities to share and appear to want more opportunities for research. However, the bigger vision of research activity scaled up so that schools collaborate on the agendas of research and share with each other and the outside world the knowledge and learning is not so easily achieved. Radical shifts are needed in the policy context before that can happen. There has to be a shift in cultures in schools and the allocation of resources to this as a suitable task for schools. There also needs to be an expansion of the range of research which studies, such as McNess *et al.* (2003) suggest, would be welcomed. The current instrumental focus of policy-makers is too shallow. The shifts in climate, policy and practice required would be welcomed and would build on a promising and potentially healthy trend which would enable educators to work together on the complex and profound challenges they face in making schooling for young people today meaningful and engaging.

References

Achinstein, B. (2002) 'Conflict amid community: the micropolitics of teacher collaboration', *Teachers College Record*, 104(3): 421–55.

Black-Hawkins, K. (2008) 'Networking schools' in C. McLaughlin, K. Black-Hawkins and D. McIntyre (2008) *Networking Practitioner Research*. London: Routledge.

Brown, S. (2005) 'How can Research inform ideas about good practice in teaching? The contributions of some official initiatives in the UK', *Cambridge Journal of Education*, 35(3): 385–405.

Carr, W. and Kemmis, S. (1986) *Becoming Critical: Education, Knowledge and Action Research*. London: Falmer Press.

Castells, M. (2000) *The Rise of the Network Society* (2nd edn). Oxford: Blackwell.

Church, M., Bitel, M., Armstrong, K., Fernando, P., Gould, H., Joss, S., Marawaha-Deidreich, M., De La Torre, A.-L. and Vouche, C. (2002) 'Participation, relationships and dynamic change: new thinking on evaluating the work of international networks', working paper No. 121: *London: Development Planning Unit*. London: University College.

Cordingley, P., Bell, M., Evans, D. and Firth, A. (2003) *What do Teacher Impact Data Tell Us about Collaborative CPD?* London: DfES/EPPI/CUREE.

DfES (2004) *Primary Strategy Learning Networks: An introduction*. Nottingham: DfES.

Elliott, J. (2007) 'Assessing the quality of action research', *Research Papers in Education*, 22(2): 229–46.

Fielding, M., Bragg. S., Craig, J., Cunningham, I. and Eraut, M. (2005) *Factors Influencing the Transfer of Good Practice*. London: DfES. 23.

Gibbons, M., Limoges, C., Nowotny, H., Schwartzman, S., Scott, P. and Trow, M. (1994) *The New Production of Knowledge*. London: Sage Publications.

Gilchrist, A. (2004) 'Developing the well-connected community' in H. McCarthy, P. Miller and P. Skidmore (eds) *Network Logic: Who Governs in an Interconnected World?* pp. 143–54. London: Demos.

Gramsci, A. (1967) 'The organization of education and culture' in *The Modern Prince And Other Writings*. New York: International Publishers

Hannon, V. (2005) 'Network-based reform: adaptive challenges facing the English education system', paper presented at the *Conference for the American Educational Research Association*, Montreal, April 2005.

Hargreaves, A. (1993) 'Individualism and individuality: reinterpreting the teacher culture' in J.W. Little and M.W. McLaughlin (eds) *Teachers' Work: Individuals, Colleagues and Contexts*, pp. 51–76. New York: Teacher College Press.

Hargreaves, D.H. (2003) *Working Laterally: How Innovation Networks Make an Education Epidemic*. Nottingham: DEMOS in partnership with NCSL DfES Publications.

Hargreaves, D.H. (2003) *Education Epidemic: Transforming Secondary Schools through Innovative Networks*. London: Demos.

Hargreaves, D.H. (2004) 'Networks, knowledge and innovation: reflections on teacher learning' in H. McCarthy, P. Miller and S. Skidmore (eds) *Network Logic: Who Governs in an Interconnected World?* pp. 77–88. London: Demos..

Hargreaves, D.H. (1999) 'The knowledge-creating school', *British Journal of Educational Studies*, 47(2): 122–44.

Huberman, M. (1993) 'The model of the independent artisan' in J.W. Little and M.W. McLaughlin (eds) *Teachers' Work: Individuals, Colleagues, and Contexts*. New York: Teachers College Press.

Jackson, D. (2002) Networks and networked learning: knowledge management and collaborative enquiry for school and system improvement'. Conference paper. *Standing Committee for Education and Training of Teachers (SCETT) Annual Conference*, Grantham, October 2002.

Johnson, P. and Monk, R. (1998) *R.G. Collingwood: An Introduction*. London: Thoemmes Continuum.

Lieberman, A. (1999) 'Networks', *Journal of Staff Development*, 20(3): 1.

Lieberman, A. and McLaughlin, M.W. (1992) 'Networks for Educational change: Powerful and problematic', *Phi Delta Kappan*, May, 673–7.

Little, J.W. (2002a) 'Locating learning in teachers' communities of practice: opening up the problems of analysis in records of everyday work', *Teaching and Teacher Education*, 18: 917–46.

Little, J.W. (2002b) *Professional Community and the Problem of High School Reform*. Berkeley, CA: Graduate School of Education, University of California, Berkeley.

Little, J.W. (1990) 'The persistence of privacy; autonomy and initiative in teachers' professional relations', *Teachers College Record*, 91(4): 509–36.

Little, J.W. (1982) 'Norms of collegiality and experimentation: workplace conditions of school success', *American Educational Research Journal*, 19(3): 325–403.

Lortie, D. (1975) *Schoolteacher: A Sociological Study*. Chicago: University of Chicago Press.

McCarthy, H., Miller, P. and Skidmore, P. (2004) 'Network logic' in H. McCarthy, P. Miller and P. Skidmore (eds) *Network Logic: Who Governs in an Interconnected World?* pp. 11–22. London: Demos..

McIntyre, D. (2008) 'Researching schools' in C. McLaughlin, K. Black-Hawkins and D. McIntyre (2008) *Networking Practitioner Research*. London: Routledge.

McLaughlin, C., Black-Hawkins, K. and McIntyre, D. (2008) *Networking Practitioner Research*. London: Routledge.

McNess, E., Broadfoot, P. and Osborn, M. (2003) 'Is the effective compromising the affective?' *British Educational Research Journal*, 29(2): 243–57.

Nias, J. and Biott, C. (eds) (1992) *Working and Learning Together for Change*. Buckingham: Open University Press.

Salzberger-Wittenberg, I. (1996) 'The emotional climate in the classroom' in G. Alfre and M. Fleming (eds) *Priorities in Education*. Fieldhouse Press/University of Durham: Durham.

Sampson, R.J. (2004) 'Networks and neighbourhoods: the implications of connectivity for thinking about crime in the modern city' in H. McCarthy, P. Miller and P. Skidmore (eds) *Network Logic: Who Governs In An Interconnected World?* pp. 155–67. London: Demos.

Simons, H., Kushner, S., Jones, K. and James, D. (2003) 'From evidence-based practice to practice-based evidence: the idea of situated generalisation', *Research Papers in Education*, 18(4): 347–64.

Stenhouse, L. (1975) *An Introduction to Curriculum Research and Development*. London: Heinemann.

Stenhouse, L. (1981) 'What counts as research?' *British Journal of Educational Studies*, 29(2): 103–14.

Wellcome Trust (2006) *Believers, Seekers and Sceptics: What Teachers Think About Continuing Professional Development*. London: Wellcome Trust.

Chapter 13

From lesson study to learning study

Side-by-side professional learning in the classroom

Susan Groundwater-Smith and Nicole Mockler

Introduction

This chapter explores the richness and depth of professional learning for both academics and classroom practitioners when they work alongside each other in conditions of mutual trust and respect. However, it is not sanguine regarding the challenges and difficulties. Learning to engage in professional trust is increasingly difficult as different players with different degrees of agency and differing professional agenda interact. Exposing uncertainties and challenging practice is risky business. The chapter draws upon a project undertaken in Australia which originally grew from concepts surrounding Lesson Study but which became transformed into what we term 'Learning Study' with a much broader and more liberatory agenda. Such a transformation not only requires challenges to orthodoxies surrounding the methodology, but also to the adoption of the methodology by employing authorities who see it as a means of developing and delivering 'best practice', a phrase we both eschew.

Why professional partnerships for professional learning?

Developing 'actionable knowledge' must be an aspiration for all involved in the enterprise of enhancing professional learning. Such knowledge, we argue, is best constructed when there is a fruitful and interactive partnership between those who study practice, seeing themselves as practitioners, and those who are immersed in the field seeing themselves as scholars. When we create binaries where one body engages in the research and another uses the research, where one group has power and agency and the other is positioned as functionary, where one group is seen as engaging in intellectual labour and the other practical activity, then marrying systematic inquiry and action is unlikely at best, and strongly resisted at worst. What is required is a partnership based upon mutual understanding and respect.

In a paper to the 2006 annual conference of the British Research Association, one of us reported that in the first of his 2006 Reith Lectures, on the interplay between music and society, Daniel Barenboim argued that in order to make music in concert with others we have to learn to listen to what others are playing (Groundwater-Smith 2006). His point was that in a society dominated by individualism there is a need to return to a more enduring and generous collectivism. This can only be achieved when each is prepared to listen to others. The division of labour in inquiry in education in many ways mirrors the concerns raised by one of the world's great conductors; separation is still the dominant professional mode (Elmore 2000). Universities and schools occupy parallel universes.

However, achieving authentic partnerships for professional learning is easier written about than achieved. There are misgivings on both sides, in part because it may be seen that the learning itself is one-sided. In this chapter we argue that what is necessary is a re-adjustment of the positioning of each party so that they stand side by side rather than hierarchically. Authentic partnerships mean being prepared to unveil and interrogate not only what appears to be taking place, but also those implicit theories of practice that we all hold; in whatever role we are employed.

Such authentic partnerships do not naturally occur, and neither do they develop by happenstance. Wenger (1998) conceptualises practice as intrinsic to the community within which it develops, where three key dimensions provide drivers and levers for authentic community, namely:

- joint enterprise (working together)
- mutual engagement (being together)
- shared repertoire (our histories).

Figure 13.1 below elaborates Wenger's notion of the interplay between these three dimensions:

> Our contention, then, is that the best authentic professional learning partnerships between school-based practitioners and researchers and university-based practitioners and researchers emerge when attention is paid to developing each of these three dimensions of practice in the context of their joint work. Elsewhere (Groundwater-Smith, Mitchell and Mockler 2007), we refer to trust as 'the incubator of the learning community', and while this notion initially referred to whole school communities, we contend that it is further relevant here, where professional trust provides the 'glue' that binds Wenger's three dimensions into a generative professional learning community.

Reina and Reina (1999) suggest that there are three kinds of trust in operation within the workplace:

- contract trust, related to the things we say we will do and undertake to do, both formally and informally;
- competence trust, related to the trust we have that others and ourselves will be able and competent in carrying out that which we need to do;
- communication trust, related to our interactions and communications with each other within our communities.

In our experience, working with teachers in schools to develop authentic partnerships requires a conscious pursuit on the part of both academics and teachers involved of each of these three. The robust discussion and debate that needs to take place for new professional knowledge to be created is contingent upon all parties respecting the knowledge and competences that others bring, transparency of the priorities and agendas that all parties bring, and professional trust that underwrites the risks that will be required of individuals to open their practice to the critique of colleagues and from that, jointly construct new knowledge and ways of operating. The complex relationship between trust and risk, both on a macro- or societal level and a more local or individual level is well established in sociological and organisational fields (Misztal 1996; Power 2007), and we believe that the key to unlocking the challenge of the personal

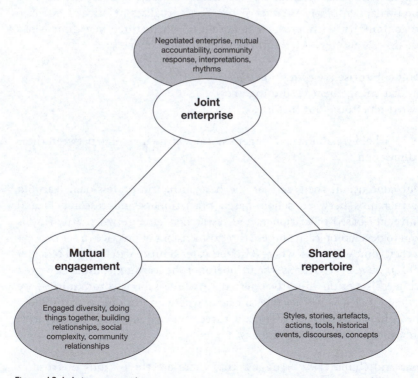

Figure 13.1 Joint enterprises

risk embedded in professional learning across boundaries such as these lies, in the proactive development of trust in these domains on the part of all. Furthermore, we argue that partnerships themselves can be developed more broadly into learning networks.

Learning networks: extending the range

In writing of learning networks we wish to return to the notion of partnerships, arguably a form of social organisation that can serve a variety of purposes. They might be fleeting liaisons of convenience with unlikely participants choosing to enhance their strength by affiliating with others momentarily or, by contrast, they may be rich and strong, established over time with social objectives directed to policies and practices designed to lead to a better society.

Partnerships of whichever ilk have individual, social, cultural and material features. While the individual voice may not be prominent, it is there nonetheless, for individuals form the agency through which the social forces are developed. Each has his or her social and professional history shaped by the norms and characteristics of the group(s) to which he or she belongs. The individual and social constantly interact dynamically. The outcomes of these interactions are produced, reproduced, contested and transformed in a cultural context that is governed by discursive practices, agreements, debates and regulations that contribute to the material conditions of the society. As Habermas (2003: 10–11) puts it:

> As historical and social beings we find ourselves always already in a linguistically structured life-world. In the forms of communication through which we reach an understanding with one another about something in the world and about ourselves, we encounter a transcending power. Language is not a kind of private property. No one possesses exclusive rights over the common medium of the communicative practices we must inter-subjectively share.

It thus follows that a significant condition for the formation of purposeful, authentic and enduring partnerships, capable of ongoing constructive learning, is the capacity for communication and connectivity. Through partnerships, networks are formed.

How then do we characterise networks and why are they an intelligent response to contemporary conditions of professional practice? Chapman and Aspin (2005: 10) have defined networks thus:

> Networks are intentional constructions, linking together in a web of common purposes. They are self-conscious and deliberately established organic entities in which all the constituent elements are equal in the weight of enmeshment that they carry and the responsibility that they bear for making contributions towards the whole.

Arguably their network integration needs to work both horizontally and vertically with multiple stakeholders. Levin (2004) has argued that much mandated reform in the public sector has not worked well. Partly this is attributable to the uni-directional nature of the intended reform with little or no consultation with those who will most bear the costs and consequences. Thus, partnerships and resulting networks as a strategy for reform have a certain appeal: the capacity to bring a number of different elements and players together into some kind of coherence. However, as Stoll (2005: 367) has noted, networked learning communities in education are a means to an end, not an end in themselves. They have a capacity to 'move ideas and good practice around the system, helping transform the whole system, not just individual schools'. Of course, this goal is only realisable in a context where cooperation transcends competition.

Do partnerships and networks have the capacity to learn? Is there evidence of growth and change? Are there collective learning outcomes? Is what is known, known collectively, albeit with different and multiple perspectives? Is there transparency, receptive capacity, reciprocity, social depth, trust, a long-term outlook, learning together and from each others, cultural compatibility, similarity of vision, a body of expertise and 'double framing'? All are seen by Keka'le and Viitala (2003: 245) as key indicators of a capacity for networks to learn. Such learning goes beyond adapting to the solutions of others, particularly those that are characterised as 'best practice' or 'what works'.

For too long policies in social services such as education, health and social care have assumed that there are indeed, fixed solutions, and that somewhere there is the elusive 'best practice' that can be created, adopted and adapted. Just as for a time there was the notion of 'one size fits all' in the clothing industry (absurd as that proposition was) there were thought to be international solutions to matters as wide ranging as literacy instruction, child care needs, housing provisions and mental health care, irrespective of contextual variations. Increasingly today there is recognition that professional knowledge formation requires input, not only from academia and government agencies but through the investigations and inquiries of those inside the professions. Many writers have recognised the need to develop professional knowledge *with* the field of practice, rather than *for* the field of practice. The prepositional change is not flippant. As Gore and Gitlin (2004: 52) claim: 'We need to work with teachers to explore the limits and possibilities of research for their work as teachers.' Furthermore, they believe that this is achieved, not only by engaging in joint research activities but also by exposing and analysing the politics of research and the power relations therein. Thus, a genuine parity of esteem within the community of practice, seeking improved learning for all, can be achieved.

For partnerships, and through them networks, to be truly educative, that is, to contribute to change for the better, several tensions need resolution: a capacity to reach intercultural understanding in a context governed by the ethics of respect and responsibility versus an expectation that everyone will think and act alike; and engagement in inquiry for professional transformation versus investigation as a vehicle for compliance. These goals are impossible where there is a hierarchy of power. Hence our concern to evolve professional learning practices that position the participants side by side.

From lesson study to learning study

To illuminate our contention that professional learning for all best occurs when participants are positioned side by side, we exemplify through a project based upon Japanese Lesson Study.

Wang-Iverson (2002) sees Lesson Study as a means of making teacher collaboration concrete by focusing on specific goals that examine not just students' work, but students' working. The process is one where teachers plan a teaching/learning episode together and observe its enactment in the classroom. They identify those moments where both understanding and misunderstanding occur and analyse contributory factors. The lesson is then re-taught with the appropriate adjustments in a new context and again analysed. The principal objective is not to manufacture 'the perfect lesson' but rather to develop greater insight into student responses. The process could be characterised as ways of seeing. It is based upon the foundation of teachers as researchers, where the classroom practitioners are engaged in systematic inquiry regarding what it is that takes place during the teaching episode, which can be characterised as a natural experiment. Academic partners play the important role of critical friend, who may indeed see things from another perspective and thus contribute to the analysis.

We argue that teaching can become professional learning when the activity is collegial and where the learning arises, principally from the students' engagement and behaviours. In their advocacy for the study of teaching and learning through the study of lessons, Fernandez and Yoshida (2004) place their emphasis upon the culture of collegiality that brings teachers together to deeply consider their practice in the context of the classroom and the diverse needs of students therein. In a similar vein, Chokshi and Fernandez (2004: 78) argue for sustained lesson study as a vehicle for helping teachers build a shared body of professional knowledge through the process of inquiry.

Rock and Wilson ((2005) see these 'research lessons' as being:

- focused on specific teacher-generated problems, goals or vision of peda-gogical practice;
- carefully planned, in collaboration;
- observed by other teachers;
- recorded for analysis and reflection;
- discussed by lesson study group members.

They argue that lesson study is based upon principles of constructivism: that knowledge is constructed through social interaction rather than individual experience; that knowledge is acquired as an adaptive experience; and that knowledge is the result of active mental processing by the individual in a social environment.

Lesson study, then, becomes a potent vehicle for teachers in collaboration with academic partners to systematically explore practice, on the basis of evidence, with an intention of improvement. Furthermore, the processes contribute to networking since often more than one school may be involved. There is a temptation in thinking about lesson study to assign to it, as a major purpose, curriculum development. As Fernandez *et al.* (2003: 174) pointed out in relation to the introduction of lesson study in a US context, the teachers' instinct was to focus on the lessons per se, rather than upon the lessons as an opportunity to research learning. Such a focus necessarily leads to somewhat narrower discussions about the design of the curriculum rather than upon actual pedagogy. Indeed, as Chockshi and Fernandez (2004: 522) argue, for some advocates lesson study is about producing a library of tried-and-tested lessons for others to use. Whereas they see the process as primarily intellectual fuelling critical group thinking about pedagogy more generally.

Employing lesson study as a means for investigating pedagogical practices would seem to be a powerful opportunity to not only improve student learning but also teacher and academic professional learning, including learning to be researchers of practice.

Much of the current discussion regarding lesson study in contexts other than Japan, where it originated, is located in various parts of the United States where there has not been a strong tradition of teachers as researchers (Rock and Wilson 2005). Indeed, Fernandez (2002: 401) has seen the lack of research skills as a 'roadblock to powerful lesson study practice'. However, this is not the case in Australia's many initiatives in relation to action learning and action research (Groundwater-Smith and Mockler 2006). Whether through such programmes as *Innovative Links between Schools and Universities for Teacher Professional Development* or the current spate of initiatives under the *Australian Government Quality Teaching Program*, many Australian teachers have become skilled at designing data collection methodologies that allow them to inquire into and reflect upon their practices. In our publication *Learning to Listen: Listening to Learn* (Groundwater-Smith and Mockler 2003), we outline a number of different strategies to assist the teacher researcher.

Arguably, when teachers become the researchers of practice then questions that are of authentic concern to them will emerge: Who is more or less engaged and why? What kinds of explanations appear to be most helpful for which learners? How do group dynamics contribute to or inhibit the learning processes? In what ways are students' questions addressed? Who gets to ask which kinds of questions in the classroom? The study of the lesson becomes a study of the learning. Furthermore, by undertaking lesson study within the context of a networked learning community, possibly different questions may arise because not all who participate are familiar with the learning environment and bring further eyes.

Each step of the lesson study process is a step in research design. Fernandez (2002) outlines the lesson study steps as set out below:

- *Selecting a lesson study goal* – This is analogous to identifying the research question, which itself must be researchable in terms of the skills and capacities of the team.
- *Working on study lessons* – This equates with planning the research and the field based stage where observations and data are collected.
- *Writing a lesson study report* – This is the stage where the inquiry is made public and available for scrutiny and critique.

In company with a number of other writers on Lesson Study, Watanabe and Wang-Iverson (2002) recommend that projects engage the services of a 'knowledgeable other'. Clearly the role can be satisfied by a number of people: content coaches, peer coaches and staff development officers. However, we would argue that because the process has an emphasis upon the collection and interpretation of data, the role (as below) of 'knowledgeable other' is best conceived as an academic partner with wide experience in working in practice-based settings such as schools.

- Draw up and collate what is already known about Lesson Study and its origins so that practitioners see themselves working within a tradition rather than inventing a process alone.
- Develop strategies for the collection and interpretation of data.
- Act as a critical friend in Lesson Study discussions.
- Draft a final report that meets the requirements of the funding body.
- Assist practitioners in writing papers for professional associations.

Moreover, the academic partner, working alongside classroom practitioners can also act to unsettle some aspects of taken-for-granted practice through new and different questions. However, we would again emphasise that this is not a one-way process; the academic partner has much to learn also. We illustrate through a particular project, Deeds not Words.

Economics and Business Educators: Deeds not Words

A major teacher professional learning initiative in Australia has been The Australian Government Quality Teaching Program. It is based upon the principles of action learning and funds a variety of small-scale projects, administered by professional associations, school systems and networks. In the case of Deeds not Words, the funding was administered by a professional association,

Economics and Business Educators. In essence, the project involved four secondary schools in Metropolitan Sydney, two in the government sector and two who were classified as independent faith schools. Four teachers from each were involved and taught economics, business and commerce to senior students. Thus a small networked community was formed, including the four schools and the academic partner.

Following a series of discussions, a number of difficult-to-teach concepts in the study of economics and business in the senior school were identified, among them the development of contracts, managing industrial relations and establishing small businesses. The specific example below relates to the teaching of contracts.

The main purpose of the lesson was to introduce students to the concept of contracts, the criteria for an effective and enforceable contract and the distinction between a contract and a verbal agreement. The lesson had been collaboratively planned by the class teachers. The tools that were used by the network to inform their professional learning were observation, student feedback, post-lesson discussion and reflection.

Observation

In each instance, two teachers and the academic partner observed three identified students. This meant that nine students in each class were observed representing almost half of the students present. The selection of students was random but the class teacher provided brief information on each. Each observer kept a time log and notes upon the given student's behaviour and indications of engagement. General notes were kept regarding key questions asked by the teacher, examples of ways in which the teacher connected the lesson's content to the students' experiences and critical moments such as digressions or time management.

Student feedback

Students were given opportunities to complete a minute paper responding to the key questions:

- What went well for you this lesson?
- What were the main points that you learned during the lesson?
- What puzzled or confused you?
- What would you like to change about this lesson?

Post-lesson discussion

The post-lesson discussion served two purposes: to discuss more broadly the perceptions of the observers and the teacher and to make decisions regarding ways in which the lesson might be improved.

Reflections

In all cases it was observed that students were able to provide examples of contractual arrangements in the home, in sport and recreation contexts and in school. Mostly the students were seriously engaged. They were alert to both the teacher's and each others' responses.

Reflecting upon their experiences, participants noted a clear atmosphere of social support. Students' responses were respected and all classrooms manifested a quietly humorous relationship between teachers and class members. Connectedness was emphasised as students provided examples of contracts in their everyday lives; similarly each teacher also drew upon their own real-life situations.

Problematic knowledge applied, particularly to sorting out the distinction between a verbal agreement, a contract and matters of duress. Throughout the lesson, the appropriate language was employed, clarified and discussed. During the post-lesson discussion, it was clear that there were cultural differences between the groups. As one participant put it: 'Students in School A expect to be directed; Students in School C allow themselves to be directed; Students in School B want to direct.'

She also observed that students in School A were more 'street smart' than their counterparts.

Following these reflections there was further discussion regarding the nature of necessary changes, including the need for more explicit instruction and greater opportunity for self direction. While there was some variation in individual teachers' approaches to the task of applying knowledge of contracts to the various scenarios, these were more attributable to the teachers' individual styles, time and resources than to a lesson structuring.

It became apparent that not only were the participating teachers learning with and from each other, but also the academic partner had an opportunity to learn about practice in different contents. For example, at each lesson's conclusion the discussion vacillated between the lesson structure itself and the responses of individual students. As one participant said: 'It has made me realise how difficult it is to have a finger on the pulse of every student in the class.' Feedback from observers enabled the particular lesson's teacher to reflect more intensively about individual students' needs.

The process also encouraged all to learn from the students themselves. The post-lesson minute paper gave the young people a voice. They were able to note that the substance of the lesson regarding contracts was interestingly presented, well explained and the flow of the lesson was smooth and interactive, They believed that their understanding had increased and that they had learned some new terms. One student noted of the class behaviour: 'We all listened as a class.'

Students referred to the opening movie, the amount that they learned, the ability to discuss, and 'I learnt a lot and had fun,' 'It was very interesting and

I learnt a lot about contracts which I didn't know before.' The lesson covered a lot of ground: 'The class went well and we got through a lot.'

They believed that the lesson was intrinsically interesting, interactive and facilitated collaborative work. 'My partner and I finished the assigned task smoothly and quickly.' 'There was a lot of communication, I liked working in groups.' They believed that there was sufficient time for them to engage with the content! 'What worked was that everything was explained to us and we were given time to do everything.' One also referred to the introduction to the appropriate technical language, 'I liked writing the contract. The language we had to write in was different and I enjoyed it. I managed to write a contract using the proper language and was more organised.'

While a number of students in all settings reported that 'nothing' puzzled or confused them, some did observe the difficulties they had with the range of different contracts, their complexity and sheer volume of information. 'The amount of information was a bit overwhelming.'

The great majority of students indicated no desire for change. Several wished the presentation to be a little more exciting and fun with more variability, 'More activities or games, more internet.'

Clearly there was much professional learning through teachers' observing and analysing each other's practice. Similarly the academic partner could engage fully in the ways in which the pedagogy was enacted and contribute to discussion.

Engaging in lesson study is about more than re-telling the story of 'what went on'. The discussion and critique of practice, within a culture of trust, and a willingness on the part of all individuals to take professional risks in sharing skills and limitations, holds potential for the breaking down of taken-for-granted assumptions, challenging long-held beliefs and seeing professional practice through new eyes. In a recent article on lesson study as a professional development tool, Devlin-Scherer *et al.* (2007: 120) point to the professional growth which can emanate from this kind of collaboration, emphasising the joint planning and construction of lessons which enable teams to take joint responsibility for the successes and challenges that emanate, rather than the 'presenting' teacher's taking full responsibility and bearing the brunt of colleagues' critique. For the teachers and academic partner involved, the process of engaging in lesson study opened doors to new ways of professional collaboration and new forms of partnership within a network that takes participants beyond their own well-known contexts.

Conclusion

This case study has sought to demonstrate the rich possibilities of learning about student learning by observing and discussing the planning, implementation and evaluation of a given sequence of lessons. It also has permitted discussion of the ways in which teachers and academic partners may also engage in mutually constituted professional learning as members of a network.

Networked learning communities foreground the complexity of teachers' professional work. Barbara Comber, in her keynote address to the AATE/ALEA National Conference 2005, noted that teachers are simultaneously engaged in and orchestrating different kinds of work, notably: interpretive work, pedagogical work, discursive work, relational work and institutional work. This study has captured all of these. Interestingly, observers in the context of lesson study are placed in a very particular position; other than the class teacher they do not know the learners well and must be astute and acute in their observations, such that the evidence may be used later when the interpretation takes place. In effect, the visitors to the classroom cannot fail but to see the learners 'in new ways'; their observations will act as an important catalyst for the subsequent discussion. Effectively, the professional participants needed to find intellectual common ground, in a constant process of developing new action scripts to apply to varying and dynamic contexts. The pedagogical documentation that occurred was critical, not merely watching and reflecting, but writing and considering.

The professional learning emanating from this and other lesson study projects for both teachers and academics is necessarily highly contextualised. This is not a methodology for building a bank of 'best practice' techniques for implementation in extraneous contexts, but rather a methodology for bringing participants to greater understanding of their students, their own practice and the lifelong teaching and learning process. If, to borrow from D'Souza, we believe professional learning to be a journey rather than a destination (and the authors of this chapter do!), we see lesson study to be a valuable tool in the journey for its capacity to open classroom doors, draw teachers and academics into new ways of working together, and foster critical professional discourse, surely an essential part of true professional learning and collaboration.

References

Chapman, D. and Aspin, D. (2005) 'Why networks and why now?' in D. Aspin, J. Chapman, D. Crandall, A. Datnow, B. Levin *et al. International Perspectives on Networked Learning*, pp. 10–14. Nottingham: National College of School Leadership.

Chokshi, S. and Fernandez, C. (2004) 'Challenges to importing Japanese Lesson Study: concerns, misconceptions and nuances', *Phi Delta Kappan*, 85(7): 520–25.

Comber, B. (2005) 'Literacies with currency: teachers work to make a difference', keynote address presented to the AATE/ALEA National Conference. Gold Coast, Queensland, 1–4 July.

Devlin-Scherer, R., Mitchel, L.Z. and Mueller, M. (2007) 'Lesson study in a professional development school', *Journal of Education for Teaching*, 33(1): 119–20.

Elmore, R. (2000) *Building a New Structure for School Leadership*. Washington, DC: Albert Shanker Institute.

Fernandez, C. (2002) 'Learning from Japanese approaches to professional development. The case of lesson study', *Journal of Teacher Education*, 53(5): 393–405.

Fernandez, C., Cannon, J. and Chokshi, S. (2003) 'A US-Japan lesson study collaboration reveals critical lenses for examining practice', *Teaching and Teacher Education*, 19: 171–85.

Fernandez, C. and Yoshida, M. (2004) *Lesson Study: A Japanese Approach to Improving Mathematics Teaching and Learning*. Mahwah NJ: Lawrence Erlbaum Associates Inc.

Gore, J. and Gitlin, A. (2004) 'Re-visioning the academic-teacher divide', *Teachers and Teaching: Theory and Practice*, 10(1): 35–58.

Groundwater-Smith, S. (2006) 'The coalition of knowledge building schools: a market place for developing and sharing education practice', paper presented to the *British Educational Research Association Annual Conference*, Warwick University, September.

Groundwater-Smith, S., Mitchell, J. and Mockler, N. (2007) *Learning in the Middle Years: More than a Transition*. Melbourne: Thomson Learning.

Groundwater-Smith, S. and Mockler, N. (2003) *Learning to Listen: Listening to Learn*. Sydney: Centre for Practitioner Research, University of Sydney and MLC School.

Groundwater-Smith, S. and Mockler, N. (2006) 'Research that counts: practitioner research and the academy' in J. Blackmore, J. Wright and V. Harwood (eds) *Counterpoints on the Quality and Impact of Educational Research. Review of Australian Research in Education (RARE) 6:* 105–18.

Habermas, Jürgen (2003) *The Future of Human Nature*, trans. W. Rehg, M. Pensky and H. Beister. Cambridge: Polity Press.

Keka'le, T. and Viitala, R. (2003) 'Do networks learn?', *Journal of Workplace Learning*. 15(6): 245–7.

Levin, B. (2004) 'Inevitable tensions in managing large-scale public sector reform', paper presented at the *Advance Institute of Management (AIM) Research Conference*, University of Bath, March 2004.

Misztal, B. (1996) *Trust in Modern Societies: The Search for the Basis of Social Order*. Cambridge: Polity Press.

Power, M. (2007) *Organized Uncertainty: Designing a World of Risk Management*. Oxford: Oxford University Press.

Reina, D. and Reina, M. (1999) *Trust and Betrayal in the Workplace*. San Francisco: Berett-Koehler.

Rock, T. and Wilson, C. (2005) 'Improving teaching through Lesson Study', *Teacher Education Quarterly*, 32(1): 77–92.

Stoll, J. (2005) 'Developing professional learning communities: messages for learning networks' in D. Aspin *et al. International Perspectives on Networked Learning*, pp. 10–14. Nottingham: National College of School Leadership.

Wang-Iverson, P. (2002) 'Why lesson study?' paper presented at the *2002 Lesson Study Conference*. wang@rbs.org

Watanabe, T. and Wang-Iverson, P. (2002) 'The role of knowledgeable others', paper presented at the *Lesson Study Conference*. txw17@psu.edu

Wenger, E. (1998) *Communities of Practice: Learning, Meaning and Identity*. Cambridge: Cambridge University Press.

Chapter 14

Learning outside the classroom

A partnership with a difference

Susan Groundwater-Smith and Lynda Kelly

Introduction

This chapter connects inquiry and professional learning in the fresh context of Museum Education. It speaks to a long-standing partnership that involves schools, a university and a natural history museum in Sydney. It portrays the evolution of methods that have captured student understanding and experience to inform the museum of approaches to educational practices. Young people have acted as consultants to the museum, informing design principles in both real and virtual contexts and also ways in which they can be engaged and active agents when visitors to the museum.

The chapter portrays several instances of consultation and draws out the conditions that have made the partnership powerful. It also examines parallels with more orthodox partnerships between schools and academia. It argues for communication that understands and is respectful of the different cultural contexts within which each partner operates.

Designing for learning in the Australian Museum

A generative partnership

Before outlining the range of projects undertaken with the Australian Museum (AM), it is necessary to explain the partnership between it, the Coalition of Knowledge Building Schools (CKBS) and the Practitioner Research Special Interest Group (PRSIG) established in the Faculty of Education and Social Work at the University of Sydney.

Over the past five years the Museum and the Coalition have been in a cooperative relationship designed to enhance learning outside the classroom. A significant synergy has developed between Australasia's oldest natural science museum and a group of schools who have made a commitment to building professional knowledge regarding educational practices (Groundwater-Smith and Mockler 2003b).

The work of the Coalition is well-documented: it is a network of schools with a commitment to action research, which is systematic inquiry conducted by practitioners and transparent and available for critique, with the aim of improvement. It meets under the auspices of the PRSIG in the Faculty of Education and Social Work. The Coalition sees itself as:

- Developing and enhancing the notion of evidence based practice.
- Developing an interactive community of practice using appropriate technologies.
- Making a contribution to a broader professional knowledge base with respect to educational practice.
- Building research capability within and between schools by engaging both teachers and students in the research process.
- Sharing methodologies which are appropriate to practitioner enquiry as a mean of transforming teacher professional learning.

Currently there are 13 schools in the Coalition: 3 Independent Girls Schools, 3 Government Girls High Schools, 2 Government Boys High Schools, 3 coeducational Government High Schools and 2 Government Public Schools (catering for primary-aged students). All but three are in metropolitan Sydney in suburbs to the north, west and east of the centre. Two are in regional towns, one in a remote rural area. They embrace both wealthy and well-provisioned schools and others that face serious socio-economic challenges. In addition, the Coalition has well-developed ongoing relationships with several environmental education centres, evidence of commitment to learning outside the classroom. Most recently, the Coalition has been joined by a respite care school that takes groups of children experiencing difficult circumstances into a residential care education programme focused upon developing empathy and resilience.

Learning and research at the Australian Museum

Museums present different contexts for learning, particularly when compared with places such as schools, universities and libraries. They have been described as free-choice learning environments (Falk and Dierking 2000) and are visited by a broad range of people. Museums have always seen themselves as having some kind of educational role. The earliest museums were founded on the premise of 'education for the uneducated masses' (Bennett 1995), 'cabinets of curiosities' established to 'raise the level of public understanding . . . to elevate the spirit of its visitors . . . to refine and uplift the common taste' (Weil 1997: 257). Current discourse has identified the need for a conceptual change from museums as places of education to places of learning, responding to the needs and interests of visitors and users.

Audience research is a discipline of museum practice that provides information about visitors and non-visitors to museums and other cultural institutions, influencing the ways museums think about and meet the needs of audiences and stakeholders. The long history of audience research in the cultural sector demonstrates the interest museums have had in their visitors over time. Studies have been conducted since the late ninteenth century, with one of the first visits to the Liverpool Museum in the UK in the 1880s (Kelly 2005). Over the past 15–20 years, increasing emphasis has been placed on increasingly quality-based research into museum learning, answering complex questions and working with a range of audiences (Kelly 2007).

The AM was established in 1827 and is Australia's oldest natural history and anthropological museum. Its mission is 'Inspiring the exploration of nature and cultures'. The primary functions are to make information, collections and research available to a wide range of audiences through undertaking scientific research and managing a vast range of collections in the areas of zoology, mineralogy, palaeontology and anthropology. Also, public communication and learning through physical exhibitions, public programs, publishing, regional outreach and online delivery of services are ways in which the Museum communicates with various audiences. The Museum established a permanent audience research function in 1994, undertaking many evaluation and research projects, both with specific Museum exhibitions and programmes and broader research questions. A recent focus has been working with young people through a close relationship between Museum and Coalition.

Learning projects

Our partnership commenced in 2003. The initial study utilised a variety of innovative methodologies to examine those features of the AM that contributed to, or made more difficult, museum learning (Groundwater-Smith and Kelly 2003). Young people in several of the Coalition schools were introduced to concepts of learning beyond the classroom and subsequently photographed aspects and experiences that 'helped' or 'got in the way' of their learning. Photographs were assembled in annotated posters, subsequently analysed, with the resultant data presented to the Museum to inform future exhibition designs and pedagogical practices.

Several Coalition schools also contributed, the following year, to the trialling of self-guided tours whose purpose was to enable independent school visits. Again the emphasis was upon young people acting as consultants to the Museum.

More recently a major project was undertaken, 'Designing for Learning in the Museum' (Groundwater-Smith 2006). The project fell into two parts. The first of these was where Coalition schools were invited to send submissions to a competition 'The Museum I'd Like'; the second was to send student delegates to a two-day *Kids' College* where the young people would hear about and evaluate the current plans for the refurbished museum and would suggest ideas for development. The following observations give a sense of the nature of the contributions to them, 'What I want to get out of my time at the Museum.'

Messages were posted on large sheets by members of the various groups. The largest number referred to understanding how the Museum operates and how they might learn from its collection.

- 'A greater knowledge of how a museum works and the care they take to create the "right" history'.
- 'I want to know more about the Museum and know the Museum managers'.
- 'I want to have fun. Learn a bit about the Museum and science. See a lot of interesting things associated with science'.
- 'I'd like to learn, but in a fun way such as picture learning, not paper and pen learning and loads and loads of talk'.
- 'I want my voice to be heard. (I want) a behind the scenes look at the Museum. More fun learning than boring learning. New exhibitions. A tour of the Museum'.
- 'I would like to learn a little bit more about the exhibitions and other things by having a look round a bit more'.
- 'I want to learn about the variety of different objects here, how they work and what they do'.

For some there was a sense of privilege in having access to things not normally experienced by Museum visitors, '(I'd like) to see interesting things that you won't usually see. Looking at things that aren't things that everyone will see.' 'Things that are only a little known about but people are curious about.'

Also some students relished the prospect of obtaining some specific insights:

- 'I would like to know how exhibitions are thought of'.
- 'What I would like to get out of the Museum experience is why the objects that are on display are on display there'.
- 'I want to know how they pick and design exhibitions'.
- 'Understanding how a museum is put together and run'.
- 'How the Museum achieves its goals, completing everything with great success'.

Others saw this as both a social experience and one that would make a contribution to the Museum, 'Being out of school, enjoying my time here, getting to know other people, putting my knowledge into the Museum.' A further theme was 'What I can contribute to these two days.'

All of these messages were posted on the first day. They came from all groups. In the main the focus was upon the contribution of knowledge, thoughts and ideas, particularly with respect to young people.

- 'I can contribute by helping the Museum see what kids would like in a Museum'.
- 'Ideas, new programs for the public. Kids want to touch things, not look. The Museum should let children touch'.
- 'I can contribute the voice of a child, so the exhibitions can teach Australia's children'.
- 'My ideas (thoughts) and help them make the Museum more appealing to children'.
- 'A young person's perspective on the Museum and its representation of Australian History'.
- 'The voice of the child so that exhibitions can be for children and for adults'.

Clearly the young people involved in both phases had provided the museum with rich consultative data of considerable value in informing the designing-for-learning process. Following consultation with Museum staff, it is seen that the information is commensurate with the Museum's Vision Statement, 'To inspire an exploration of nature and cultures'. In other words, the data collected from both the *Museum I'd Like* and the *Kids' College* informed the ways in which the AM can inspire an exploration of nature and cultures such that young people will be substantively engaged in learning.

Developing an *E-College* seemed a natural progression. Learning through social media and digital resources is increasingly a core function in the learning repertoire of today's students. The *E-College* was designed to be conducted over a full day, based on feedback from the previous participants. In preparation, a booklet was prepared for each participant with their name on the cover and a digital photograph. These booklets would be used for reflections throughout the day and were the major source of data along with the observations of museum personnel working as group facilitators.

The aims of the *E-College* are set out below:

- To understand how young people aged 12–18 are using the web and new media and where they fit into their lives.
- To seek feedback about how these technologies might be used at the Museum both in the physical and virtual spaces.
- To explore e-learning, its tools and artefacts as they relate to the Australian Museum and young people as a social medium.

The critical questions to be addressed by the *E-College* were as follows:

1   What is it like to learn using computers and digital technologies?
2   How might the AM employ digital technologies to enhance engagement in learning in two specific contexts (Search and Discover and The Fossil Collection)? And more generally?

3   What should the AM do to make its website more inviting for young people?
4   What message would you like to leave with the AM as a result of the *E-College?*

While the purpose of this chapter is principally to explore the partnership between the Museum and the Coalition, it is not possible to cover all findings of this study. However, for a flavour of the student responses we report one such here.

Several students made a distinction between visiting the Museum itself and visiting its website. Patrick, who had participated in the earlier *Kids' College* and was one of two students from a remote school and whose travel had been subsidised by the Museum had this to say:

> Last time I came here we focused mainly on new technology and we were constantly saying we needed more screens, games and interactive displays, but since then I have been thinking: I can do that at home, I can watch movies, play games, etc. at home. If I come to the museum I want to be able to get information, read it and be able to learn from it. It is good to have these things (screens, etc.) but I guess, like all things, in moderation.
>
> The website needs to suit all audiences. I got the feeling that you were trying to find bright colours, games, etc. that could be good, but it is unlikely that the reason we are at a museum site in the first place is to play the games. We can do that anywhere. If we are there we are probably looking out what we want but we are not the only people that use the museum. A section on the site, for information of some kind. So it needs to be easy to read and access without being too dry.

All the projects discussed hitherto were ones initiated by the Museum and enthusiastically engaged with by the schools. In 2008, a new direction emerged, one where a school has sought government funding for a Quality Teaching Project in relation to learning in the Museum. The partnership can be seen to be emerging as a truly reciprocal one! This last project is still very much a work in progress. Designed to cover two years, it rests upon the development of integrated teaching and learning units using the Museum as a principal resource.

Further 'Colleges' are also being planned to investigate with schools student perceptions and understandings of issues around sustainability and climate change.

As we have already indicated, it is not possible to nominate all of the complex learning arising from these projects: learning for young people; learning for the partners; and learning for the profession. However, we believe that some clear lessons can be derived from the significant synergy that has developed between the Museum, the schools and the academics.

We now briefly explore other AM issues.

Spaces and experiences that enhance learning

Contemporary understandings of learning in museums have indicated that substantive engagement for young people is not merely a whim of the educational imagination, but is critical to transforming learning productivity positively (Piscitelli and Anderson 2001). Such transformative learning can be characterised as authentic, that is: that young people need to feel welcomed and supported; that the museum exhibits/exhibitions relate to their lives and highlight ways in which learning can apply to them; that they have some control over their learning and will be involved in problem solving and inquiry tasks; that they are set challenging but achievable goals; that they can question and reflect upon what they have learned; that they can exercise judgement; that their curiosity is stimulated; that they can share new knowledge with others in a multi-directional flow; that they can understand and employ the language of learning; and they can interact with the new media.

As Lemerise (1995: 403) put it, '(Young people) say loud and clear that they like being with their friends and they want to do things with them . . . Alas the museum is generally seen as a place where there is not much to do other than look and listen.' All the data collected in the collaborative studies and reported upon in this chapter points to young people's desire to be engaged in active and interactive learning. They want to be in spaces that are colourful, vital, so that all their senses are brought into play. They want to have a sense of agency where they can follow a variety of learning pathways employing a variety of media.

How tame learning sites such as museums can appear to be to young people when they themselves inhabit such an interactive and compelling digital environment with access to mobile phones, instant messaging and the worldwide web, which encourage two-way active participation. Having grown up in a technology-rich world, adolescents, commentators have argued, have dispositions much like those of native language learners: they take their culture (and language) as natural. Prensky (2001) has aptly referred to them as 'digital natives' who are in contrast to other generations who have not grown up in a digital world. Learning digital media for them is like learning a second language.

For young people, operating in a media-rich environment is 'fun'. It is not merely by chance that the word 'fun' appeared many times in the various studies.

But it is not only a form of entertainment that these young people are seeking. They are also curious about how the Museum goes about its business of collecting and preparing collections for exhibitions. The experience of hearing stories from Museum experts was for the students a highlight of their experiences when they were being consulted. A significant issue was in relation to *how* these stories might be told. Lindauer (2005) suggested that museum staff generally adhere to implicit curriculum theories that guide their practice, these being: didactic (unelaborated information dissemination); Tylerian (information developed in logical scope and sequence order); constructivist (recognising what the visitor brings to the learning); and narrative. In the case of the last of these, she argues that a narrative curriculum theory incorporates answers to who, what, where, why and how something takes place in a manner that a good story requires. Narrative is now acknowledged as a critical component when engaging learners (Kelly 2007). The illuminative story not only serves to illustrate a concept or idea, but also stimulates further questioning and inquiry.

The young people we sampled want to find information that meets their needs, but they also want to be entertained. They want access to taboos and controversies, but they want to be comforted and reassured. They want the boundaries to be pushed out, but they want to feel safe. They need, as Cameron (2003) has reported, to transcend their fears, but not to avoid them. Paradoxically, they want the museum to be a site incorporating the most modern of technologies, but also one that continues to embody the traditional. In effect the traditional becomes the exotic.

The Museum cannot assume that the young people who visit are only wanting to be superficially entertained; or are all the same. This extended consultation reveals clearly that they *are* desirous of dealing with complex and challenging concepts. They want the fun, but also the depth. They want to be provoked, not merely informed. They want to hear questions to which there may not be ready answers. They are not empty vessels waiting to be filled. They bring with them a multiplicity of experiences and insights. Participants from a remote town such as Broken Hill have very different experiences to those who have grown up in Sydney's multi-cultural inner city.

The ways in which consulting young people can inform pedagogical and organisational practices

It is becoming increasingly clear that as Burke (2008: 1) puts it:

> New approaches to pedagogy are emerging in both the educational and cultural sectors and there are important questions arising about the roles of professionals and the rights of learners to participate in the making of meaning. We know from research that children from a very early age can participate in conversations (visual and textual) about matters of design that influence their lives and new research methodologies are developing that allow this to be realised and documented.

An important element that holds these studies together is the understanding that young people can provide legitimate insights into educational enterprises designed for them, whether within or outside schools; in real time or digital space. It is generally agreed that improvement in engagement can come about when their views are systematically collected and interrogated (Falk and

Dierking 2000; Piscitelli and Anderson 2001). Paradoxically, they are rarely consulted.

It is increasingly understood that young people, in order to participate productively in social and academic life, need to be active agents in that life. Unlike the adults who surround them, today's young people have been born into a digital world; they know it, they understand it and they can navigate within it. Old models of teaching and telling are no longer sufficient. As Cornu (2004) has observed in relation to schools, knowledge is now networked and requires an understanding of a collective intelligence over and above individual enterprise. The same holds true for Museums, which have such a vital role to play in developing enjoyable and engaging learning among their visitors.

It is clear, from the above, that this study gives much credence to the salience of 'student voice', that is, the importance of listening and responding to young people. A large British project, *Consulting Pupils about Teaching and Learning*, has run over the past three years (Rudduck and McIntyre 2007). It is argued that the present climate is one where there is unprecedented support for the idea of listening to young people. Importantly, they argue that the place where this should start is the classroom itself, where teachers take seriously their students' views and find ways of meeting their concerns. They believe that consulting with young people has many positive results. Their argument holds equally true for large learning institutions, such as the AM, that take the responsibility for learning outside school classroom seriously.

Frequently, however, consultation has tended to take place after the teachers and museum educators designed and delivered the curriculum. What is remarkable about the work of the AM and the Coalition is that increasingly the voices of young people are built into the design process itself. The purpose of the *E-College* was not so much to evaluate existing products, although that did take place, but rather to imagine what digital products might look like and how they might be used.

As Valdecasas, Correia and Correas (2006: 35) note:

> Presently, many museums do not make use of opportunities to 'dialogue' with their visitors in a creative fashion, i.e. they do not foster visitor curiosity nor enhance their sense of wonder via a conceptual dialogue that allows the visitors to develop questions and work on answers to them. Some exhibitions [and we would argue websites] nowadays speak in an almost uni-directional manner to their visitors.

Brown *et al.* (2005: 2), in considering ways of adding value to online collections for diverse audiences, have argued that school students have a need to be able to develop the characteristics of experts while still being novices:

> (They, the young people) need to be able to discover, analyse and synthesise information that addresses identified topics, but their domain knowledge

and skill levels are such, like the general public, they still need a degree of scaffolding to engage their interest and provide the conceptual frameworks required to assimilate new knowledge.

These are surely important messages for schools as well.

It is worth considering a significant difference between Museums and schools in the ways in which they view and understand young people. For the Museum the young person is thought of as an 'audience'; albeit one which wishes to learn; for the school the young person is positioned as 'student'. Indeed, in schools, other than the most senior years, the young person is there as a State requirement. Schooling is compulsory and schools are places where young people are constantly subject to the surveillance of the State through testing and assessment regimes, just as their teachers are through various inspectorial devices. The custodial nature of schooling shapes much of its practices, just as the client-focused nature of the Museum requires paying careful attention to the ways in which young visitors can be enticed through its doors, both real and virtual. Arguably schools might consider becoming more seductive and enticing places where, as Erica McWilliam (2008) suggests, radical doubt can flourish and contribute to a more original and creative learning environment. After all, Museums are not intended only as places for transmitting knowledge of culture, natural history and the like; they are also places for provocation and questioning.

The ways in which such partnerships can contribute to ongoing teacher professional learning

So far we have focused upon ways in which the Museum has benefited from its partnership with members of the Coalition. Implicit is that schools also are beneficiaries in that many of the observations apply as much to learning in the classroom as in the Museum. Student engagement is recognised as contingent upon the ways in which their learning experiences are connected to their life-worlds and contemporary youth culture.

It is our contention that forming sound partnerships can provide fruitful outcomes for students and teachers. Too much attention in teacher professional learning is directed towards technicist strategies whereby courses, developed to meet government requirements, are delivered in short bursts with little real application to the classroom. It is not entirely the case that compliance with regulatory frameworks is the enemy of authentic professional learning, but certainly it is possible to see the two concepts as uncomfortable bedfellows.

Certainly, it is much easier to measure and quantify the kinds of 'spray on' (Mockler 2005), 'drive by' (Senge *et al.* 2000) or 'hit and run' (Loucks-Horsley 1999) professional development experiences that are relatively easy to control and 'deliver' to teachers. Yet questions abound about the effectiveness of such approaches. The partnership arrangements that have been spelled out in this chapter are far more encouraging in that practitioners are active agents in their own professional growth.

Loucks-Horsely *et al.* (1987) set out the conditions for effective teacher professional growth including:

- collegiality and cooperation;
- experimentation and risk taking;
- participant involvement in goal setting, implementation, evaluation and decision making;
- designs built on principles of adult learning and the change process.

Clearly, this partnership with a difference has provided those conditions for both parties.

Conclusion: why this can be counted as a successful partnership

We are mindful that this account is being celebratory. But it is difficult to deny the power of the ongoing relationship between the Museum, the Coalition and the PRSIG. For it to have endured for so long, to have been so generative of innovative practices, to be looking forward to new projects, it must surely be deemed successful. We would argue that such success lies in a number of factors:

- the relationship's having an authentic purpose;
- the relationship's having continuity;
- the benefits being reciprocal;
- partners taking collective responsibility;
- the promotion of consultation, collaboration and democratic decision making;
- an active support of innovation and change;
- opportunities to think outside the square;
- a continuing exercise of trust and respect.

In the most recent iteration of the work of the partnership, the development of an integrated, holistic curriculum in the middle years in a single sex boys' school, we asked the boys to reflect on the project as a kind of game involving more than one person. They were asked to nominate the game and their reason for selection. Among the responses one boy reasoned:

It has been like a treasure hunt. You have to find out information if you are to succeed. In the same way we have been following the clues that we have got from our teachers and the people from the museum, and in the end you get to the glory and the gold.

References

Bennett, T. (1995) *The Birth of the Museum: History, Theory, Politics*. London: Routledge.

Brown, S., Gerrard, D. and Ward, H. (2005) 'Adding value to on-line collections for different audiences' in J. Trant and D. Bearman (eds) *Museums and the Web 2005 Proceedings*, Toronto: Archives and Museum Informatics, published 31 March 2005. (Available at www.archimuse.com/mw2005/papers/brown/brown.html, accessed 5th January, 2008.)

Burke, C. (2008) 'The view of the child and young person in museum and gallery design', paper presented at *the International Conference on the Inclusive Museum*. Leiden. The Netherlands, 8–11 June.

Cameron, F. (2003) 'Transgressing fear: engaging emotions and opinion – a case for museums in the 21st century', *Open Museum Journal*, 6:

Cornu, B. (2004) 'Networking and collective intelligence for teachers and learners' in A. Brown and N. Davis (eds) *Digital Technology, Communities and Education*, pp. 40–5. London: Routledge Falmer.

Falk, J. and Dierking, L. (2000) *Learning from Museums: Visitor Experience and the Making of Meaning*. New York: Alta Mira Press.

Groundwater-Smith, S. (2006) 'Millennials in museums: consulting Australian adolescents when designing for learning', invitational address presented to the *Museum Directors' Forum,* National Museum of History, Taipei, 21–22 October 2006.

Groundwater-Smith, S. and Kelly, L. (2003) 'As we see it: improving learning in the museum', paper presented to the *British Educational Research Association Annual Conference*, Edinburgh.

Groundwater-Smith, S. and Mockler, N. (2003a) 'Holding a mirror to professional learning', paper presented to the joint *Australian Association for Research in Education/New Zealand Association for Research in Education Conference*, Auckland, New Zealand, 29 November–3 December. (All AARE Conference papers can be found at www.aare.edu.au.)

Groundwater-Smith, S. and Mockler, N. (2003b) *Learning to Listen: Listening to Learn*. Sydney: MLC School and Faculty of Education, University of Sydney. (Available at www.edfac.usyd.edu.au/profdev/learnlisten.html.)

Kelly, L. (2005) 'Evaluation, research and communities of practice: program evaluation in museums', *Archival Science*, 4(1–2): 45–69.

Kelly, L. (2007) 'Visitors and learners: adult museum visitors' learning identities', unpublished Ph.D. thesis. Sydney: University of Technology.

Lemerise, T. (1995) 'The role and place of adolescents in museums: yesterday and today', *Museum Management and Curatorship*, 14(4): 393–408.

Lindauer, M. (2005) 'From salad bars to vivid stories: four models for developing "educationally successful" exhibitions', *Museum Management and Curatorship*, 20: 41–55.

Loucks-Horsley, S. (1999) *Designing Professional Development for Teachers of Science and Mathematics*. Thousand Oaks, CA: Corwin Press.

Loucks-Horsley, S., Harding, C., Arbuckle, M., Dubea, C., Williams, M. and Murray, L. (1987) *Continuing to Learn: A Guidebook for Teacher Development*. Andover, MA: Regional Laboratory for Educational Improvement of the Northeast and Islands and National Staff Development Council.

McWilliam, E. (2008) 'Making excellent teachers' in A. Phelan and J. Sumsion (eds) *Critical Readings in Teacher Education*. Rotterdam: Sense Publishers.

Mockler, N. (2005) 'Trans/forming teachers: new professional learning and transform-ative teacher professionalism', *Journal of In-service Education*, 31(4): 733–46.

Piscitelli, B. and Anderson, D. (2001) 'Young children's perspectives of museum settings and experiences', *Museum Management and Curatorship*, 19(3): 269–82.

Prensky, M. (2001) 'Digital native, digital immigrants'. *On the Horizon*, 9(5):

Rudduck, J. and McIntyre, D. (2007) *Consulting Pupils about Teaching and Learning*. London: Routledge.

Senge, P., Cambron-McCabe, N., Lucas, T., Smith, B. and Dutton, J. (2000) *Schools That Learn*. London: Nicholas Brealey.

Valdecasas, A., Correia, V. and Correas, M. (2006) 'Museums at the crossroad: contributing to dialogue, curiosity and wonder in natural history museums', *Museum Management and Curatorship*, 21: 32–43.

Weil, S. (1997) 'The museum and the public', *Curator*, 16(3): 257–71.

Watson, S., Dodd, J. and Jones, C. (2007) *Engage, Learn, Achieve*. (Available at www.le.ac.uk/museumstudies, accessed 20 December 2007.)

Chapter 15

School leaders using inquiry and research

A podcast between Philippa Cordingley, Kris Needham and Mark Carter and discussion by Susan Groundwater-Smith and Anne Campbell

Philippa Cordingley and Kris Needham

The Centre for the Use of Research and Evidence in Education (CUREE), is a UK facility that sifts and sorts research findings for the benefit of practitioners in schools, be they classroom teachers or members of the school executive. The podcast transcript that follows is one of a series organised by the Professional Learning and Leadership Development Directorate of the New South Wales Department of Education and Training (NSW DET). Dr Kristine Needham presented this research podcast that interviews Philippa Cordingley, founder and Chief Executive of CUREE and Mark Carter, School Principal, as part of an online learning program provided by the School Leadership and Executive Learning Unit. Other podcasts in the series may be found at www.det.nsw.edu.au/proflearn.research.htm

We thank the NSW DET for the opportunity to reproduce this material that gives us an insight into the ways in which research and practice connect, especially in relation to the role of school leaders. As a transcript, the podcast employs colloquial language that requires a slightly different orientation on the part of the reader from the ways in which more academic writing is ordinarily encountered. At the conclusion to the interviews, we elaborate a number of the issues raised, particularly as they relate to the work of CUREE and its Chief Executive.

Kris: I'm Kris Needham and in this series of podcasts I will be bringing you ideas from current research into school leadership. We'll be talking about research relevant to leading NSW public schools and talking to some of the researchers themselves. We'll be showing you where you can find out more about any of the articles, websites, books or journals that we mention. We'll also share some examples of strategies for using research in your school; as well as interviewing some school leaders who are doing just that.

My guest today is Philippa Cordingley, who is founder and Chief Executive of CUREE in Coventry in the UK. CUREE has a very useful website and the

URL is www.curee.org.uk. CUREE works with other agencies including the General Teaching Council for England and I first came upon Philippa's work when I went to the research section of that site and saw something called Research of the Month.

Philippa: Research of the Month is one of our favourites because what we have been able to do in that is take large-scale really significant research and turn it inside out so that we can tell the story of the findings and not the story of the project. And the best things about it, there are two really precious things I think. One is that we can hotlink every academic research finding with teachers' and school leaders' own practical research so that you're completely connecting the experience of what this is like on Monday morning, on Tuesdays and Wednesdays in schools with the kind of quite abstract thing that often comes out of the research. And then the other thing that I think is really important to us about the research of the month is that it is probably one of the longer research summaries and resources that we make. And one of the things, the fact that there are a few more pages and a few more words lets us do is not just say that the research tells us by the ways of findings and how it affects teachers and how it affects students.

It also lets us really get into what's the underpinning rationale. Why the thing works with this group of students but not that group of students. And we felt very strongly that it is when we give teachers and school leaders the underpinning rationale that we enable them to feel powerful and confident about adapting something that has come out of research, an approach or strategy so that it meets the needs of their particular students and pupils and their particular school community. It's that adaptation process that is really important for helping teachers move beyond learning how to talk the talk of what is coming out of research to walk the walk too, because however good the research there is always an interpretation job.

Kris: If we can just turn to look particularly at the needs of school leaders that is where our focus is in our series of podcasts. It seems to me that school leaders might be interested in research for a variety of reasons but perhaps mainly in terms of leadership itself or in pedagogy in teaching and learning where they can really make a difference in the instruction that's going on in their school. Is that your experience of the ways in which school leaders use research?

Philippa: Yes it is and I think there is some research coming up shortly from Professor Robinson in New Zealand about what we know about leadership interventions that have positive impacts for pupils and students. And that review I know is going to emphasise very strongly school leaders' role in continuing professional development and including in that modelling themselves as professional learners so when school leaders do get engaged in making sure they're up to date with what is coming of the research and channelling it to the colleagues in their school, they know who are working on and developing those areas. We've got increasing evidence about that being a very, very effective way of forcing learning and using the school leadership resource and targeting it.

The school leaders we find who are most enthusiastic and confident are the ones who get themselves, and have for themselves, opportunities to do their own enquiries, whether it's an enquiry into continuing professional development, whether it's an enquiry into teaching and learning or an enquiry into leadership itself. Leadership research itself for school leaders can be very difficult because practitioner action research, to get it to be deeply rewarding, satisfying and reflective needs to have some depth to it and leadership is such a big thing. So how do you choose a focus? We've got some nice examples of that in the National Teachers Research Panel website (www.teachernet.gov.uk) where head teachers have chosen either to do some research on their own or collaboratively with colleagues and by doing their own research that's drawn them into using other people's research, then that's built their confidence into drawing more consistently on research over time and that seems to be a nice model for getting school leaders who might not start out being very interested in research involved in using it.

Kris: What kind of support do you believe teachers need from school leaders when they're using research?

Philippa: First of all, they want to know that their leaders think it's important. If they see the school leaders sharing with them exciting examples of ideas and strategies they've come across, that will really make a difference because all learners in the end learn from what we do probably rather more than what we say. So modelling learning from research and sharing with their colleagues their own reflections prompted by engaging with their evidence about their leadership and other people's evidence is terribly important. I think the next thing they need is where the school leaders would, for example, start off a staff meeting with an 'Oh look, there's an intriguing idea from research. Let's have a little discussion about it or a little one-off activity' or something, to bring that alive for colleagues just so that in all the staff meetings they think of starting out with an idea or some evidence from research. And then I think, very strong links from the research into what does the research have to say that might help you pursuing your goals for the year. And off they'll go to the website or the school librarian or school newsletter and the related learning targets for themselves and then find resources from research that will help with that. And that's an increasing model that we are finding.

But one of the things that has been really helping us with this has been the creation of networks between schools. When schools work together in networks it seems to be easier for them to find people who've got the time to think about how to build this reflective accessing research thing and get it off the ground and that whole thing works well. School networks seem to be really powerful things in helping schools feel permeable to and very confident about using and making evidence from research a practical part of their life. I know that there's been a very big study in Australia about research use. There was an article on that by Figgis *et al.* (2000) that talks about the importance of networks in research. There does seem to be that you need something to distil and communicate really briefly, as brief as possible, to bring to you the core essence of the research but then you need networks in which you can have conversations where you can prod and poke the research and that can look meaningful in your context.

Kris: I did want to ask you if there's some current school leadership research that you feel is really hot and we could be tuning into. You've mentioned Helen Timperly and Viviane Robinson's research (2001). Where is it that school leaders can place their energy to get the most leverage? And in fact I'll be talking to Viviane in a forthcoming podcast. Is there anything else that's at the front of your mind that is a really exciting or emerging area?

Philippa: There's two things I think. We published late last year a new review about what specialists contribute to professional learning. I think for school leaders many of them have a very good grip on who's a great specialist pedagogue in their school; who's really great at facilitating the learning of their students. I think what is beginning to be really interesting is how you help school leaders know who are also the people who are really good pedagogues for their colleagues. Who amongst their colleagues can be a really good coach or mentor? And so the kind of research that helps school leaders map out the resources that they've got and map out the specialist resources they need to draw on and build significant energy amongst their colleagues for as it were sort of hoovering up the learning just seems to me to make eminent sense. There is a General Teaching Council research of the month feature on school leadership. But it's not hot. It's not new. It's been out for a little while.

Kris: Thanks very much Philippa for speaking to us.

How are school leaders in NSW currently using research for school improvement? I went to Killara High School in the north of Sydney to talk to Principal, Mark Carter, about what he's found works for him. 'Mark how do you go about using material you find in journal articles and so on to stimulate professional discussion among your staff?'

Mark: I borrow a lot of stuff from people. In my travels out and beyond the school to meetings I observe what other people are reading or referring to. I will get the librarian to acquire these bits and pieces along the way and I keep and come back to them in the course of three or six months and I dip into them occasionally. I read professional journals. I read professional association literature. I just keep reading. The media indeed: a *Sydney Morning Herald* article on John Marsden gives you an insight into schooling. There are a range of sources and perspectives that trigger, then for you a desire to go and find a little bit more about a specific area. Perhaps I might revert to a formal research paper occasionally. But the sources are more diverse than that.

Kris: How do you then use material from those sources to bring that to some sort of form that the staff can access?

Mark: I endeavour to pull out cogent bits that I think are pithy or that go to the heart of what I'm interested in and where I think the school should consider a direction. And I will distribute those directly to key people in the school. I'll hand them out and say 'Have a read of this. Consider this. Have you thought about this?' And I'll use them as starters to generate a professional discussion amongst a core of people. Before that, I tried writing papers on the future of Killara High School or what it might look like and handed them out at school development days. Now perhaps 80 per cent of them weren't read. But occasionally some people have come back to me some years after and said 'I remember when you said, or when you wrote or when you put the perspective that . . .' which was a trigger for me to understand that they got something from and indeed that sparked something else. So you lay some groundwork over a number of years. It is not an instantaneous process of providing people access to the key literature. There are no silver bullets. It's taken about five years in total to develop a culture of enquiry and significant sense of cohesion or collaboration amongst a key group of people in the school.

Kris: And that's stimulated by these little extracts and sort of eclectic mix of things that you're finding?

Mark: Absolutely. And the core to it. What underlies it all? What's the cohesive bit that says what's at the heart of the article from the *Australian Council for Educational Research* journal or the bits out of *Principal Matters* or the *Sydney Morning Herald* or even a letter to the editor or an editorial? That they all focus and relate to a core philosophy that you think ought to be pursued in a tangible form in the school. So it's not about airy-fairy waffly sort of stuff. It's about establishing a culture and underpinning that with some literature, be it research papers or more broad-based literature.

Kris: Mark, do you take some material like that to a meeting? You've talked about distributing it to individuals. Would you use it as a discussion in an executive meeting?

Mark: I have done that. I certainly have produced that. Indeed on the executive agenda at present there is a permanent section called professional reading or professional discussion. Last week it was blank but that is not necessarily a bad thing on occasions. That is one forum. There are School Development Days where you can set up a process amongst colleagues where they might present papers or material that you seed, if you like, rather than presenting your own tome. I tend to distribute stuff selectively to people who I think are going to read stuff. I will do the broad sweep. There are 17 people on the executive at Killara so you are going to get 17 people if you hand something out but probably it will be read by three and that's not through any fault of theirs. It's simply the nature of the job. See, I think you've got to target your audience a little better. If you want to get the entire school in any secondary school structure you've got to get the gatekeepers and those are head teachers. So they're the people you to have persuade there is merit in this particular piece of research or this article or this particular piece of information.

Kris: Thank you, Mark.

In this podcast we have explored some aspects of the meeting place between the world of the educational researcher and the world of the school practitioner.

Philippa Cordingley drew attention to the importance of school leaders acting in a way we might call the hunters and gatherers of research, and then sharing with their staff their excitement about particular articles or websites. This is one way of generating a collegial discussion about what the research has to say that's useful for this school at this point of time.

Mark Carter's strategy for stimulating discussion by initially sharing with particular people on the staff gives us an idea of how that might look in a school. Where schools can work in networks to do what Philippa calls 'prod and poke' research or engage in their own research, the meeting place can really come alive.

Discussion

Philippa Cordingley's contribution to educational practice in schools has been enduring and substantial. We were anxious to include this podcast, not only to demonstrate how recent information and communication technology can have a significant impact upon professional thinking and behaviour but also because it connects the work of the scholar with a response from the field; in this case a school Principal. As Cordingley puts it in her interview, we hotlink every academic research finding with teachers' and school leaders' own practical research so that you're completely connecting the experience of what this is like on Monday morning or Tuesdays and Wednesdays in school with the kind of quite abstract thing that often comes out of research. In his response, Mark Carter makes tangible the ways in which he uses such work to establish an inquiring culture in his school.

Elsewhere, Cordingley (2008) spells out her understanding of the ways in which practitioners may access and transform knowledge in images and prototypes that make sense to them as a function of professional learning. Initially she laments the manner in which so much academic writing fails to uncover the layers of research and output so that it is transparent, accessible and usable for teachers in schools. However, she also sees the responsibility that must fall to the practitioner to work intellectually and consistently with research findings as a form of professional knowledge management. She advocates a number of mediating and brokering strategies that can act to illuminate and inform practice based upon well-founded and consistent research.

In a number of chapters in this book it has been argued, in agreement with Cordingley, that knowledge is not some sort of portable self-contained *thing* that may be transmitted by technically controlled conduits, but is socially constructed and located in socio-historical space; in particular the spaces and cultures of schools. The process of meaning-making, both of and from information, is central; but can also be unsettling. Green and Hannon (2006) have suggested that there are four key components to learning: finding information and knowledge, doing something with it, sharing it with an audience and reflecting on it. But as Lawrence Stenhouse (1979) in a pre-digital world reminded us, information and knowledge are two different things; 'Information is not knowledge until the factor of error in it is appropriately estimated' (Stenhouse 1979). However, estimating error is not easily undertaken alone – it is something that requires social interaction as ideas are explored and arguments developed and justified. So that when Mark Carter, the school principal interviewed in the podcast, speaks of targeting specific conduits for the dissemination of research, he is hinting at the beginning of such a conversation.

In recent years there has been much discussion regarding the impact of educational research on practice. Too often what counts in the academy is of little relevance to schools, while what counts in schools is not sufficiently recognised and rewarded in the academy (Groundwater-Smith and Mockler 2006). Philippa Cordingley's ongoing systematic reviews of research presented through the EPPI Centre located in the Social Science Research Unit, at London's Institute of Education and consistently made available to the profession, have been a significant breakthrough in the deadlock between academic and school-based practices. In our view, the development of podcasts such as the one reported here also represents new ways of presenting and discussing educational research.

References

Cordingley, P. (2008) 'Research and evidence-informed practice: focusing on practice and practitioners', *Cambridge Journal of Education*, 38(1): 37–52.

Figgis, J., Zubrick, A., Butorac, A. and Alderson, A. (2000) 'Backtracking practice and policies to research' in Department of Education, Training and Youth Affairs, *The Impact of Educational Research*, pp. 279–373. Canberra, Commonwealth of Australia.

Green, H. and Hannon, C. (2006) *Their Space. Education for a Digital Foundation*. London: DEMOS Foundation.

Groundwater-Smith, S. and Mockler, N. (2006) 'Research that counts, practitioner research and the academy' in J. Blackmore, J. Wright and V. Harwood (eds) *Counterpoints on the Quality and Impact of Educational Research*, pp 105–18. Review of Australian Research in Education, RARE 6.

Stenhouse, L. (1979) 'Research as a basis for teaching', Inaugural Lecture University of East Anglia' in L. Stenhouse (1983) *Authority, Education and Emancipation*. London: Heinemann Educational Books.

Timperley, H. and Robinson, V.M.J. (2001) 'Achieving school improvement through challenging and changing', *Teachers' Schema Journal of educational change*, 2(4): 281–300.

Chapter 16

Joining the dots

Connecting inquiry and professional learning

*Susan Groundwater-Smith and
Anne Campbell*

This chapter brings together the major themes identified in the book to connect the issues surrounding inquiry and the potential impacts upon professional learning across the continuum of pre- and in-service education and beyond. It will briefly discuss why it is that so much recent attention has been given to the agency of educational practitioners as they investigate features of their work in schools as a means of enhancing their professional learning, albeit in an environment that is often constrained. It will argue that the potential beneficiaries are not only those students and teachers who engage in this work, but also their academic partners who may assist them and also beable to deepen their own professional knowledge. This chapter will recognise that the varying contexts for practitioner inquiry are significant determining factors shaping both policies and practices. Moreover, at a local level, it will explore the different spaces within which professional learning can occur, how those spaces are managed and even at times colonised. This chapter will summarise the exciting and problematic ways in which professional knowledge is constructed through the work reported here: how it is constructed; for whom; and by whom. It will conclude by recommending ways in which leaders in the education profession, be they in the classroom, in school management, in bureaucracies or in academia can work together for the ongoing improvement of practice to the benefit of the millions of students in our schools.

Developing professional agency

Professional learning for too long has been the province of those charged with the 'professional development of teachers'. The practice supposes that there is a body of knowledge and a contingent of those who 'know' that can be visited upon teachers in order to develop them into more effective practitioners. It is a process whereby an agenda is pressed upon teachers, rather than one in which they themselves have a degree of agency. In Chapter 13, concerning lesson study, Groundwater-Smith and Mockler argue for the capacity to generate 'actionable knowledge' as an aspiration for all involved in the enterprise. When we create binaries where one body engages in the design of professional development and another is developed, where one group has power and agency and the other is positioned as merely a functionary; where one group is seen as engaging in intellectual labour and the other practical activity, then contributing to authentic professional learning is unlikely at best, and strongly resisted at worst.

These notions are extended in a practical direction by Shirley Grundy, in her argument for the acceptance of practitioner research as a means for addressing teacher professional learning and ultimately, school improvement, contending that action research is of necessity a collaborative enterprise, one which may or may not involve an external or academic 'significant other' (Grundy 1995: 6). Her conclusions invest agency in teachers, suggesting that her underlying epistemology is one which sees teachers as active creators of professional knowledge for and about teaching. Her earlier typology of action research modes (Grundy 1982), drawing a distinction between technical, practical and emancipatory models of action research and arguing for the development of action research which liberates teachers from 'the dictates of compulsions of tradition, precedent, habit, coercion as well as from self-deception' (Grundy 1982: 358), would also indicate this.

Professional agency lies at the heart of the various forms of practitioner inquiry discussed. Not all writers use an identical terminology. Some write of action research, others of practitioner inquiry. Indeed, in their mapping of the field in the second chapter, Campbell and McNamara suggest that there is a 'plethora of terms' that are employed, but lament that the emphasis has been upon developing technical-rational solutions to the challenges presented in classrooms, rather than addressing the broader matters of curriculum and assessment reform and even beyond that to having a concern to develop a more transformative approach to large social issues associated with access and equity. Freebody (2003: 7) believes that the core of action research is 'professional self-improvement through focused collaboration . . . (with proponents) typically having been involved in concerns for social justice'. All the same, writers such as Carr and Kemmis (2005: 50), who were early advocates for action research to deeply inform professional learning, believe that 'the assumption that teachers should exercise autonomous professional judgement has been profoundly undermined'. A number of chapters examine why this might be so.

Who learns and how?

Partly the issue of teacher agency rests upon the nature of the relationship between teachers as practitioner researchers and those who may support them. Contributors have drawn attention to the ways in which the benefits may be mutual and reciprocal. For example, Lingard and Renshaw in Chapter 3, write of education as a research informed and research informing profession and make the case for practitioners to have a 'researchly disposition' that will contribute to their 'feel for the game of teaching'. McLaughlin's Chapter 12 also sees support coming from networks of schools who maintain close and profitable ties where the isolation of the individual practitioner is broken down. She refers to how research can be scaled up in networks and collaborations to meet some of criticisms aimed at practitioner research.

Groundwater-Smith (2007) in her British Educational Research Association keynote address to the annual conference, posed the question put by Bertoldt Brecht, drawing upon Lenin, *'Wie und was soll man lernen?'* (How and what should we learn?). In the address, she made the argument that the rich learning that can be the result of sustained inquiry is where all participants are beneficiaries. This view is echoed by Ponte in Chapter 6, where she argues for experienced teachers, in concert with their academic colleagues, having a capacity to raise moral dilemmas from real life and complex contexts and doing so in a new and emergent research culture that departs from the traditions and constraints that are imposed when there are distinct divisions of labour and status. Boundary crossing has been a concern of both Hulme and Cracknell in Chapter 5, and Broadhead in Chapter 4 where she considers not only the spaces both physical and metaphorical occupied by researchers in various guises, but also how those spaces are utilised by teachers and the learners themselves.

Professional learning, for all writers, results from professional engagement that includes not only undertaking enquiries, but also maintaining a stance that permits critical reflection. 'These are the precepts, but from whence do the ideas come?' This brings us to the matter of context, for it is clear that engaging in professional learning that is an outcome of inquiry is a practice that occurs *in situ*. While Australia, or England, or Scotland, or the United States or the Netherlands may have much in common, each has its own particularities. Indeed, even within a micro-context such as a specific city, there will be variations and complexity.

Varying contexts for practitioner inquiry

There are several ways in which context can be considered in relation to practitioner inquiry and the contribution that such inquiry makes to teacher professional learning. It may be that the context is in terms of the level of experience; undertaking inquiry as a process in initial teacher education is very different to that when operating with teachers who are deeply immersed in their practice. This is not to say that an initial teacher education course that focuses upon teacher inquiry is not possible or indeed desirable. As Kemmis and Smith (2008: 281–3) have noted in their case study of 'Beth' it was the repeated opportunities to 'interrogate her lived experiences, collectively reflect upon and critique her experiences and develop personal theories with her peers and receive support (from her academic mentors) that allowed her to re-frame her personal stance' and that all of this stood her in good stead when she commenced her teaching career. In Chapter 7, Livingstone reports upon an approach currently being taken in Scotland that involves an array of practitioners ranging from the student teacher to the school leader, as does Menter and Hume's discussion of Scotland's *Schools of Ambition* in Chapter 9. All the same, while these practitioners may work effectively alongside each other, it will be important to bear in mind the length and depth of experience that they have.

Moreover, the geographical context may have an impact. Teachers working in remote locations may have fewer opportunities to work alongside those 'significant others' of whom Grundy writes (1995: 6). While not reported upon in this book, it has certainly been noted in Australia, with its vast distances and its major cities clinging to the coast, that those who operate in isolated circumstances experience great difficulty in sustaining inquiry, when there may be a dearth of critical friends with whom the inquiring teacher may consult. As Massey (2005: 75) has argued, 'space inflects our understanding of the world'. Context is not merely a *background* to what is undertaken in the name of action research; it is a complex amalgam of social and material conditions *within* which action research takes place. The very word 'background' implies a stage set, a cardboard construct that suggests a time and place, but which is itself static, a mere simulacrum. When speaking of context, it is essential to see it as a construct that is far more dynamic and problematic. In effect, it is what Schatzki (2002) refers to as *The Site of the Social*.

Of course the policy context also varies greatly. Seemingly, teacher educators in England work under very different constraints determined by the policy setting of the day, than say their counterparts in various parts of the United States or parts of Europe such as the Netherlands, or even elsewhere in the UK itself. Murray, in commenting on current practices in England (Chapter 8) in terms of the academic induction for new teacher educators that might focus upon them engaging in forms of practitioner inquiry, argues:

> Given these tensions (regarding recognition and quality) then, how do we ensure that engaging individual teacher educators in practitioner research does not become a form of 'research cul-de-sac' which will not necessarily enable them to participate in the conventional discourses and practices associated with educational research in universities? Or does practitioner research lead teacher educators towards small-scale and often individualised research efforts which are not necessarily given appropriate recognition, even within other parts of the field of teacher education?

Contexts can also be local and particular. The study reported by Groundwater-Smith and Kelly discusses the ways in which an institution such as the AM can engage in inquiry that is educative in nature with members of the CKBS, a hybrid collective of schools in NSW. All the same, while the practice settings may vary and while some may be colonised for instrumental purposes, there is still much to learn from these variations in terms of the construction of professional knowledge.

Professional knowledge construction and the contribution that it might make

Throughout this book it has been asserted that knowledge is not some sort of portable self-contained *thing* that may be transmitted by technically controlled conduits, but is socially constructed and located in socio-historical space. The process of meaning-making both of and from information is central; but it is also unsettling. Part of the role of the academic in conversation with the field, through forms of inquiry, is to disturb cherished ideas and beliefs. The work of Victoria University in Australia, as reported by Davies in Chapter 10, is an example of ways in which such beliefs and understanding may be disturbed, leading to new conceptualisations for undergraduate students. Miletta, in Chapter 11, discusses the ways in which early career teachers in a graduate programme in New York daily face challenging circumstances but derive important support and benefit from working in small groups, with academic guidance. Her analysis indicated that their projects investigated five important areas, these being: teacher beliefs and practices; students' understandings and learning; parental roles and influences in classroom life; culturally relevant curriculum; and meaningful and successful academic task structures. By working closely and collaboratively they were able to develop substantial knowledge and understandings of these critical aspects of teachers' professional work.

It has often been argued that the kind of findings generated exclusively in the academy are generally not highly valued by practitioners who have more to gain by sustained dialogue with their colleagues engaged in an investigation of practice. What is an important and exciting development in the cases discussed in this book is that an authentic, generative relationship can be nurtured when the academy and the teaching profession work together, each respecting the other. The brief chapter reporting a podcast made by Philippa Cordingley in cooperation with Kris Needham (Chapter 15) is an example of the ways in which school leaders such as Mark Carter can effectively use a range of research resources. In our own commentary at the end of the chapter we conclude:

> Elsewhere, Cordingley (2008) spells out her understandings of the ways in which practitioners may access and transform knowledge in images and prototypes that make sense to them as a function of professional learning. Initially she laments the manner in which so much academic writing fails to uncover the layers of research and output such that it is transparent, accessible and usable for teachers in schools.

Usable investigations: working together with a common purpose

In making the following concluding claims for developing 'usable' investigations, we are mindful of the pitfalls associated with tick-box lists of best practice. It can be readily claimed that the chapters of which this book is composed have clearly demonstrated that there is no one 'best way' that can be captured in some kind of ring-binder or compact disk and sent out to schools, willy nilly. Thus our first desirable feature is the recognition of diversity, an investigation that is of use to those professionals who conducted it in the field, often in concert with academic partners, needs to respond to that particular landscape. This is a point that we made earlier in this chapter. Diversity recognises that there will not only be differences in contexts and the problems that they present, but also in the experience and philosophical positions of those undertaking the investigation. What matters is that diversity is recognised and honoured. An early career teacher from a language background other than English in a Scottish school will have a different orientation to one who is experienced and been raised in the European tradition in a rural school in the Netherlands. What we desire they should share is a passion for taking a moral and ethical stance.

Along with diversity, we wish to honour debate. Too often dissemination of practitioner inquiry is constructed as a means of celebration rather than genuine interrogation of results. This is partly due to the increasing domestication of practitioner research as an implementation tool; a phenomenon referenced in a number of chapters. 'Actionable knowledge', as discussed at the beginning of this chapter, means knowledge that can confront the difficult issues some of which may abrade one against the other. How, for example, does a group of teachers deal with matters of gender equity that may rub up against issues associated with recognising the needs of ethnic minorities with a different position on gender? There are no silver bullets. Instead the opening up of the debate allows some movement beyond that of compliance to one policy or another. We believe that taking a multi-vocal stance will allow such debate to occur. Not one voice, but many. However, this should not be taken as advocacy for some kind of relativism, but rather that the processes of inquiry provide conditions for those varying positions to be aired and engaged with. It is through creative dialogue that there will be authentic professional learning for all – academics and school based practitioners alike.

We are mindful of the seduction of the ephemeral and the transient. Seemingly, hardly a week goes by when one person or another, one agency or another, one commercial publisher or another does not offer a ready-made solution to the intransigent problems and challenges of the classroom. The work reported in this book is designed to act as a counter to overly simple solutions packaged in short courses often underwritten by commercial enterprises. Such solutions are often marketed as ones that reduce risk and anxiety. Someone else has done the work and found the answers. We believe that authentic inquiry will mean risk taking and, at times mistake-making. What is critical is that we learn from those mistakes – being persistent, analytic, looking forward and working backwards. All this requires courage and resilience.

Joining the dots, as editors of this book, has been a challenging and exciting enterprise. The work reported here has cut across many of the normal professional development practices that seem to emphasise an ambition that all should be harmonious and without conflict and suggests instead that there is a place for respectful and healthy dissent.

References

Carr, W. and Kemmis, S. (2005) 'Staying critical', *Education Action Research*, 13(3): 347–57.

Cordingley, P. (2008) 'Research and evidence-informed practice: focusing on practice and practitioners', *Cambridge Journal of Education*, 38(1): 37–52.

Freebody, P. (2003) *Qualitative Research in Action, Interaction and Practice*. California: Sage Publications.

Grundy, S. (1982) 'Three modes of action research', *Curriculum Perspectives*, 2(3): 23–34.

Grundy, S. (1995) *Action Research as Professional Development*. Murdoch, WA: Innovative Links Project.

Groundwater-Smith, S. (2007) 'Practitioner researchers: what can we learn from them?', address delivered to the *British Educational Research Association Annual Conference*, London: London Institute, September.

Kemmis, S. and Smith, T. (2008) 'Conclusions and challenges' in S. Kemmis and T. Smith (eds) *Enabling Praxis: Challenges for Education*, pp. 263–86. Rotterdam: Sense Publishers,.

Massey, D. (2005) *For Space*. London: Sage.

Schatzki, T. (2002) *The Site of the Social: A philosophical Account of the Constitution of Social Life and Change*. University Park Pennsylvania, PA: University of Pennsylvania Press.

Index